OUR HUMAN
ODYSSEY

Becoming Female and Male

OUR HUMAN ODYSSEY

Becoming Female and Male

Ramón Piñón, Jr.

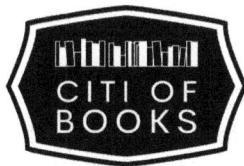

CITI OF
BOOKS

CITIOFBOOKS, INC.
3736 Eubank NE Suite A1
Albuquerque, NM 871113579
www.citiofbooks.com
Hotline: 1 (877) 3892759
Fax: 1 (505) 9307244

Ordering Information:

Quantity sales. Special discounts are available on quantity purchases by corporations, associations, and others. For details, contact the publisher at the address above.

Printed in the United States of America.

ISBN13:   Softcover   979-8-89391-018-6
             eBook   979-8-89391-019-3

Library of Congress Control Number: 2024905272

Dedication

For Kathleen and all our children

Acknowledgments

I greatly appreciate Hillel Black's editorial advice and suggestions in bringing my manuscript into ts final form.

Kathleen, my wife and partner of almost 60 years, deserves special thanks for getting me started on this project and for believing it was worthwhile.

I also thank my brother Michael Piñon, Pharm. D, for his comments, suggestions and critique of the various drafts of the manuscript.

Our Human Odyssey: Becoming Female and Male

Credits for cover image and chapter opener images

Chap 1

Scanning electron micrographs of the external genitalia of two human embryos before the sex of the embryo can be determined, 52 – 58 days after fertilization. (A) Genital tubercle, deep urethral groove, and urogenital folds, (B) Frontal view of the developing genital tubercle, urogenital folds, and the urethral groove with the external opening of the urogenital sinus. (J. E. Jirásek, 1983. *Atlas of Human Prenatal Morphogenesis*, Figs. 138 and 140. Martinus Nijhoff Publishers © Springer Science + Business Media, with kind permission from Springer Science + Business Media)

Chap 2

Diagram depicting the expulsion of the oocyte (ovulation) into the uterine tube. The fimbriae of the uterine tube are thought to "sweep" over the ovary at the site of rupture perhaps to ensure that the expelled oocyte (egg) will land in the uterine tube. With permission from University Science Books

Chap 3

Scanning electron micrograph of human sperm about to be released from the Sertoli cells into the epididymis. (A. F. Holstein and E. C. Roosen-Runge, 1981. *Atlas of Human Spermatogenesis*. Grosse Verlag, Berlin, Germany. With kind permission from A. F. Holstein)

Chap 4

Henri Matisse, *Dance, 1938* (© 2014 Succession of H. Matisse, Artists Rights Society (ARS), New York, NY)

Chap 5

Colleen Patricia Williams Seanson's End: Menopause, 2006, © 2011 Colleen Patricia Williams. The loss of leaves from the tree provides a striking metaphor for the loss of eggs from the ovary. With kind permission from Colleen Patricia Williams.

Chap 6

The initiation of fertilization. Movement of the sperm through the layer of cells surrounding the egg, and penetration into the egg itself. With permission from University Science Books.

Chap 7

Birth posture observed by United States Army surgeon in the mid-nineteenth century of a young Sioux woman who retired to the bank of a stream at the onset of labor. She sat cross-legged, thighs widely separated, arms folded, and head bowed, especially during labor pains, until birth occurred 40 minutes later. (G. J. Englemann, 1977. *Labor among Primitive Peoples*. AMS Press, New York, NY. Reprint of 1882 edition, published by J. H. Chambers, St. Louis)

Chap 8

Henny Tjon, untitled, gift of the artist

Chap 9

Colleen Patricia Williams, *Cracks in My Façade: Rupture, 2006*, © 2011 Colleen Patricia Williams. 12" x 14", encaustic on panel. An indelible scar marks those living with the aftermath of birth defects. With kind permission from Colleen Patricia Williams.

Chap 10

A flyer written in three languages – English, Hebrew, and Italian – distributed by the Margaret Sanger Clinic in Brooklyn, NY circa 1916, the first birth control clinic in the United States, inviting mothers to come to the clinic to obtain birth control information. Sophia Smith Collection, Smith College. With permission from the Sophia Smith Collection, Smith College.

Chap 11

Diagram depicting the standard method of assisted reproduction - in vitro fertilization (IVF) and embryo transfer (ET) With permission of University Science Books.

Dear Reader

When you set sail for Ithaca,
Wish for the road to be long,
Full of adventure, full of knowledge
C. Cavafy, Ithaca, 1911

Happy he who could understand the causes of things
Virgil, Georgics: Book 2

I started teaching Human Reproduction at the University of California, San Diego (UCSD) in 1973. Teaching, reading, and thinking about the many aspects of this subject led to my textbook *Biology of Human Reproduction* which was published in 2002. For me, learning about the complexity of our reproductive system has been a journey of self-discovery. My discussions over the years with students in my classes often focused on questions and issues in their lives and their parents' lives that arose from the topics in the course. These conversations gave me the impression that there would be a wider audience for the topics I covered in my course. I set out to convert my textbook into a book that would be more accessible to a non-expert, a lay reader. That effort led to two books: **Our Human Odyssey** *Becoming Female and Male*, which reviews key events and basic concepts that I think are essential in understanding our beginnings and its perils., and a companion volume **Friction and Fantasy:** *Opening Pandora's Jar,* which explores the complexities of our sexual universe.

I take it for granted that most people have an interest in learning more about how we begin. My intent was to offer something that would be different than what was available in super market magazines. Some of the concepts I cover may seem very technical and difficult to understand. I have included them because I believe it deepens our understanding of life's processes and mysteries. I think that as we enter the second decade of the 21st century these concepts should be part of our knowledge base.

As indicated in the Table of Contents, I organized my discussion into four main parts – **A** Trajectories of our Reproductive Life, **B** Glimpses of our Pre-natal and Early Post-natal life, **C** Our Perilous Beginnings, and **D** Fertility: Two Sides of One Coin. Part **A** (chapters 1 to 5) covers the different developmental stages of our reproductive system – fetal development of the genital tissues, the post-pubertal reproductive functions of females and males, the pubertal transition, and finally our reproductive twilight. Part **B** (chapters 6- 8) focuses on fertilization and implantation, birth and lactation, and exciting new studies relating the origins of chronic adult diseases to our pre-birth environment in the womb. Part **C** (chapter 9) covers pregnancy loss, birth defects, including disorders of sexual development, and finally Part **D** (chapters 10 – 11) reviews birth control methods, the causes of infertility and the new growth industry - assisted reproduction.

I have ordered the chapters in a way that seems logical to me. The early chapters define terms and concepts that will be used in later ones. I have tried to make each chapter as self-contained as possible, so that referral to other chapters is kept to a minimum. In each I provide a historical perspective to give you an idea of how our knowledge developed, and mention the individuals, circumstances, and controversies that have shaped our understanding and added to our knowledge. You may find it rough going at times. I have tried to simplify my presentation by omitting many details and keeping technical jargon to a minimum, but some effort will still be required. I am certain that you will find the effort rewarding, and I hope that my book provides you with the foundation that will form the basis for your own continuing education.

I have also included three appendices that provide additional information and details that may be helpful. **Appendix 1** reviews a few basic concepts of genes, sex chromosomes, and mutations that can give you a more in-depth understanding of the topics in Part **C**. **Appendix 2** provides additional details of the 'hardware' and 'software' of our reproductive system. It can supplement the material in the main text. **Appendix 3** surveys Disorders of Sexual Development, the details of which are complex. I have included it because some of you may be interested in exploring this subject further. In addition, definitions of terms and concepts are collected in a Glossary. The list of citations and a bibliography for additional reading appears at the end of the book.

A final word before you begin your journey. Today we have a reasonable understanding of the fascinating and absolutely amazing aspects of our formation and development. We have also learned that none of the molecular and cellular processes on which life depends are fail safe. These means that errors in these processes occur randomly, sporadically, and for the most part there is little we can do to prevent them. Pregnancy loss and birth defects are the most visible consequences of such errors. As discussed in Chapter 9 and Appendix 3 many of these errors are due to chromosomal abnormalities and mutations. As discussed in Appendix 3 the very processes that are necessary for life are also responsible for generating mutations, most of which have a harmful effect. The saving grace is that a rare few mutations may have a beneficial effect. It is these rare gems that drive the engine of evolutionary change and diversification of life. Without a mechanism for generating mutations, life would not evolve. The continuation of life depends on the infrequent occurrence of beneficial mutations. Hence, living organisms live with the consequences of harmful mutations – essentially the sacrifice and elimination of those who inherit the harmful mutations – because of the few mutations that will permit life to continue. Every meeting of an egg and sperm involves rolling of the dice. Some win, and others lose. We are the unwitting participants in a gigantic genetic lottery.

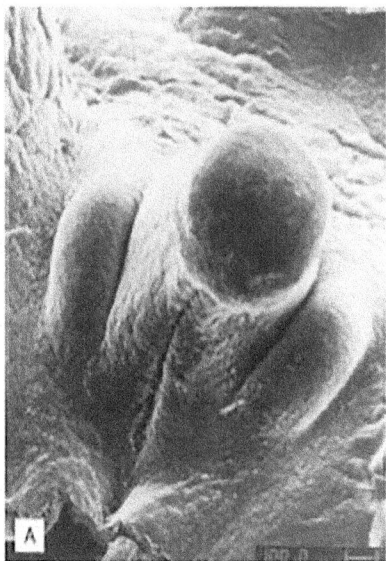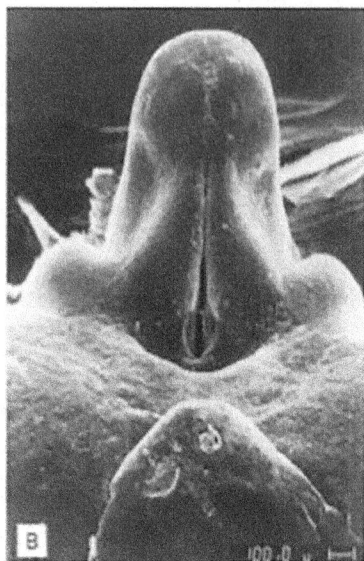

PART A

Trajectories of our reproductive life

Chapter 1

Becoming Female Or Male - Our Pre-Birth Journey

The first six weeks – the sex-less interlude

To develop as a female is to travel a highway that is straight and wide. It is the male embryo that takes the exits; should he lose the way, he will find himself back on the route to femininity (1, A. M. Leroi, Mutants On genetic variety and the human body)

We are born with our sexual anatomy fully formed. This means that sometime during our mother's pregnancy we became anatomically female or male. How we become a female or a male has been a subject of continual discussion and debate since ancient times. Creation stories from different societies tell us that the sexes were not always two as we now think of them, but were originally merged into one. An early Greek story imagined the original human race to be "androgynous" (both male, andro, and female, gyno). Anatomically, such a being is hard to picture – built like a ball, with four arms and four legs, and two sets of reproductive organs. Details are missing regarding how this being moved or how the two halves communicated with each other. Procreation was accomplished by the female half dropping eggs on the ground, and the male half spraying the eggs with sperm – much like many fish do. These primeval beings offended the gods by trying to capture Mount Olympus, the citadel of the gods, and Zeus, the father of the gods, punished them by slicing each one in half.

Plato continues with the story:

"After the division the two parts of man, each desiring his other half, came together, and throwing their arms about one another, entwined in mutual embraces, longing to grow into one, they were on the point dying from hunger and self neglect, because they did not like to do anything apart . . ." Zeus felt sorry for them and so " . . he turned the parts of generation round to the front, for this had not been always their position, and they sowed the seed no longer like grasshoppers in the ground, but in

1

one another; and after the transposition the male generated in the female in order that by the mutual embraces of man and woman they might breed, and the race might continue; or if man came to man they might be satisfied, and rest, and go their ways to the business of life." (2, Plato, Symposium)

One nice feature of this story is that it provided a ready explanation for the powerful force that drives the two sexes to seek union with a mate. The union makes them one again, as they were originally, and restores whatever is missing in each. Quite interestingly, male-male or female-female unions also found a respectable place in what we now dismiss as a quaint story.

Much more powerful in Western imagination has been the Hebrew biblical creation story, or in fact, stories, because the book of Genesis in the Hebrew Bible provides two versions for the origin of the two sexes. In Genesis 1:26-27 both sexes are created at the same time.

"And God said, Let us make man in our image, after our likeness. . . God created man in his image, in the image of God he created he him; male and female he created them."

In contrast, Genesis 2:7, 2:18, 2:21 proposes that the male was fashioned first, and the female was formed later from one of the male's ribs. And finally, in 2:23 *"That is why a man leaves his father and mother and clings to his wife, and the two of them become one body."*

A definitive interpretation of the first story has not been achieved despite over two thousand years of scholarly commentary, but presumably the two sexes emerge from a unitary image in the mind of God. The second seems to say that both were originally one, or at least complimentary, and that is why they desire to cling to each other. However, the male is given supremacy, and the female is the derived sex. In both stories, however, only two possibilities exist – male or female. Significantly, no ambiguity, as appears in the Greek story, is permitted. We can infer that the writers of Genesis struggled mightily with the question of the origin of the two sexes, and they were unable to agree on one vision. By presenting the two, were they hedging their bets? Significantly, in neither story is the female given primacy.

We can tell a different story now, and it is much more profound and compelling than the old creations stories. The deeper we get into the story the more perplexing and interesting it becomes, and the more it draws us in.

Consider what's involved. At fertilization, when the sperm fuses with the egg, the chromosomal sex of the conceptus is set, that is, it is either XX (female) or XY (male). Eggs carry an X chromosome, while sperm come in two forms, those that carry an X chromosome, and those that carry a Y chromosome. The X-bearing and Y-bearing sperm are produced in equal proportions. (See Appendix 1 for a discussion of the sex chromosomes, X and Y). However, the anatomical structures that distinguish the female from the male do not develop instantaneously. In fact, these tissues develop in stages over several weeks during the first half of gestation. In particular, there are two distinct processes at work – the formation of the gonads (ovaries or testes), and the formation of the internal and external genitalia. Under normal circumstances an XX embryo will develop ovaries, and female internal and external genitalia. An XY embryo will develop testes, and male internal and external genitalia.

The real mystery lies in the details. So let's begin.

The germ line – the mystery cells

The gonads, ovaries or testes, develop from two small tissue pockets adjacent to the embryonic kidney. They are known as the genital ridges, and are same in XX and XY embryos. Beginning at the end of the third week after fertilization a group of cells known as the primordial germ cells (PGCs) appear and begin to migrate into the genital ridges from outside the embryo itself. The PGCs, numbering perhaps around 50 when they begin their migration, define the germ line, that is, these are the cells that are predetermined to eventually give rise to either the eggs or the sperm. The PGCs and the genital ridges are imbued with a dual capability, that is, if the embryo is XX the genital ridges will develop into the ovaries, and PGCs will develop into the eggs. If the embryo is XY the genital ridges will develop into the testes, and the PGCs will develop eventually into sperm.

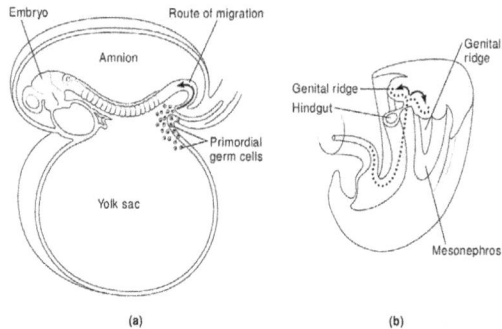

Figure 1.1

Fig.1.1 is a schematic diagram of a human embryo at the end of the third week of gestation. Fig. 1.1 (a) indicates the position of the primordial germ cells (PGCs) when they first appear along the yolk sac membrane. Fig. 1.1(b) shows the PGC route of migration along the hind gut and into the genital ridges.

For the biologists of the late 19th century when the existence of the primordial germs cells was first recognized, the PGCs were imbued with a sense of mystery. It is easy to see why. The PGCs define the source of continuity from one generation to another, hence, the name germ line. Individuals are born, die, and their bodies decompose. The germ line, however, links one generation with another. Despite their importance we know much less about the PGCs than most other cells in our body. They make a cameo appearance that lasts maybe three weeks and then they are transformed into the cells that will eventually become the egg or sperm. Many questions about their origin, biology, and migration remain unanswered, and these are some of the most interesting questions in reproductive biology today.

The founding tissues – two for the price of one

The migration of the primordial germ cells into the genital ridges takes place over a three-week period. During this interval the PGCs proliferate so that at the end of the sixth week of gestation the genital ridges contain thousands of PGCs. The genital ridges themselves have embarked on their own developmental program dictated by chromosome constitution of the embryo (XX or XY), but have not yet formed true testes nor true ovaries. The term indifferent gonad is used to describe the composite tissue consisting of the PGCs and developing genital ridges that is not yet an ovary or a testis.

The anatomical sex of a human embryo cannot be determined by simple visual inspection until about the end of the seventh week of gestation. In embryological terms this is quite late since by the sixth week after fertilization, most of the organ systems of the body have been formed. The embryonic heart, for example, has begun to beat. Hence, the reproductive tissues of the human embryo are late bloomers.

Chromosomally, the embryo is either XX or XY, but the tissues by which we normally distinguish the two sexes have not yet developed definitively. The scanning electron microscope image shown at the beginning of this chapter shows two different views of the external genitalia of a human embryo at about 52 to 58 days gestation. The external genitalia of both XX and XY embryos at this stage are indistinguishable.

The embryonic tissues that will give rise to the internal and external genitalia also make their appearance at this stage. They develop from the same precursor tissues that are present in both female and male embryos during the indifferent gonad stage. The internal genitalia develop from tiny tubes known as the Mullerian (also known as paramesonephric) and the Wolffian (also known as mesonephric) ducts that appear adjacent to the genital ridges. (see Fig. 1.2)

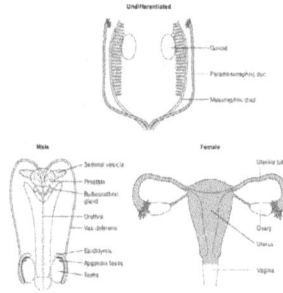

Figure 1.2

Fig. 1.2 The external genitalia in both sexes develop from three different embryonic tissues – the genital tubercle, urogenital folds, and urogenital sinus. All of these tissues, present in both XX and XY embryos at this stage, also remain expectant, awaiting the proper signal to stimulate their development in either the female or male direction. The schematic diagram in Fig. 1.3 shows the development of the external genitalia in females and males from the same progenitor tissues (the bipotential stage).

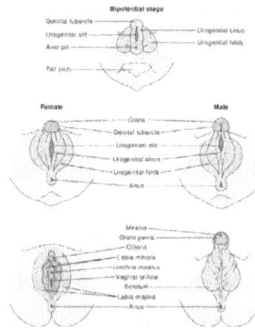

Figure 1.3

The male – jump-started by the Y

The Y chromosome makes its mark early in an XY embryo. The SRY gene, the male determining gene on the Y chromosome (see Appendix 1 for a fuller discussion of SRY and the Y chromosome), provides the trigger that begins the transformation of the indifferent gonad into a testis, and the seventh week is when we can see the result of the SRY action. SRY, the male determining gene, activates a cascade of events that changes the internal architecture of the genital ridge, the most visible of which are the formation of the seminiferous cords, and the differentiation of the PGCs into spermatogonial cells, which represent the first stage in the pathway that will form sperm. In addition, the developing testis begins two produce two really important hormones – testosterone and anti-Mullerian hormone. The transformation of the indifferent gonad into a definitive testis is completed by around the twelfth week.

Testosterone and anti-Mullerian hormone are absolutely essential for the development of the internal and external genitalia in the male. Under testosterone stimulation the Wolffian ducts differentiate into the male internal genitalia from week 9 to week 11. The Müllerian ducts, programmed to begin their development into a uterus and uterine tubes (also known as Fallopian tubes or oviducts) by week 9, must be prevented from developing in the male. And this is the job of anti-Mullerian hormone – its action leads to the degeneration of the Mullerian ducts from week 8 through week 9.

Beginning about the middle of week 9, under the action of dihydrotestosterone (DHT, for short), a hormone derived from testosterone, the genital tubercle develops into the penis, the urogenital folds form the scrotum, and the urogenital sinus develops inwardly to form the prostate gland. The formation of the external genitalia in the male is completed in about 3 weeks. Finally, the last stage in the formation of the external genitalia is the movement of the testes, which were formed adjacent to the kidneys, into the scrotum beginning around week 24. In over 95% of male infants, the testes have descended into the scrotum by birth. In others, descent will generally be completed by a few months after birth.

The female - takes her time

In an XX embryo, formed by the union of an egg with an X chromosome-bearing sperm, the transformation of the indifferent gonad into an ovary is delayed by several weeks with clearly visible changes beginning around the twelfth week and being completed by the twentieth week of gestation. It seems likely that changes in the incipient ovary begin to take place before the twelfth week but we know very little about them. Nevertheless, ovarian development does appear to be delayed compared to testicular development. This timing difference is quite likely significant, and as we shall suggest below, the delay may ensure normal male development.

During the formation of the fetal ovary there is rapid proliferation of the PGCs and their differentiation into a cell known as the oocyte, and encasement of the oocytes into a structure known as the primordial follicle. The oocyte will eventually become what is generally called the egg – the cell that is ovulated about once a month beginning at puberty. The population of primordial follicles expands rapidly and by twenty weeks of gestation the ovaries contain about 7 million of them. Then abruptly and mysteriously the expansion comes to a halt. (Fig. 1.4)

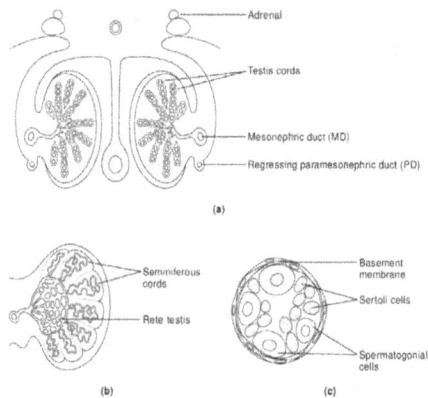

Figure 1.4

In contrast to the male, where development of the internal and external genitalia depends on two fetal testicular hormones, the development of the internal and external genitalia in the female is independent of any ovarian product, and in fact, takes place even before the definitive ovary has formed. The Müllerian ducts develop into the uterus, the uterine tubes and the upper third of the vagina. Müllerian duct differentiation begins around week 9 and is generally completed by week 12. The Wolffian ducts, which require testosterone for their continued development, self-destruct in its absence during this same interval. External genitalia development is completed by week 12. In the female the genital tubercle forms the clitoris, the urogenital folds form the labia, and the urogenital sinus develops inwardly to form the lower two-thirds of the vagina.

I have provided a brief sketch of an incredibly complex process. In summary, the tissues and organs that define our sexual anatomy develop from a set of primordial tissues that are bipotential, that is, they will develop in the male or female direction depending on whether the gene SRY is activated or not. Also take a moment to picture in your mind what is happening: the formation of the ovary or a testis is taking place in an embryo during the early stages of the pregnancy. The ovary or testis of the very young embryo is harboring the germ cells that eventually will produce the eggs or sperm after the embryo matures, is born, and reaches adulthood. The pregnant female is carrying an embryo that harbors the germ cells that will yield her grandchildren. This is true long-term planning.

Who came first, Eve or Adam?

In my alternative scenario, the female is the ancestral sex, and the male the derived sex. . . Every male must contain evolutionary traces of femaleness. (3, D. Crews, Animal Sexuality)

Don't worry if you get lost in the terminology and the timetable of all the events taking place. You won't be taking an exam on this. Perhaps what's important is to understand that the progenitor tissues for the ovaries and testes as well as the internal and external genitalia are the same in both sexes. Let's compare the female versus the male mode of development.

First, notice that there is a fundamental asymmetry in the development of the two sexes: in the male the development of the internal and external genitalia, requires a functional testis, but the development of the internal and external genitalia in the female does not require a functional ovary. The critical event in male formation is the activation of SRY, the male determining gene, which initiates the transformation of the indifferent gonad into the fetal testis, and two fetal testicular hormones in turn determine the formation of the male internal and external genitalia. In an XX embryo, that is, in the absence of SRY, the indifferent gonad becomes an ovary, but in great contrast to the testis, no ovarian hormones are required to form the female internal or external genitalia.

What does this asymmetry mean? One possible answer is that the female mode of development is in some important sense autonomous, while in contrast the male mode is not. In computer jargon, we would say that the female mode is the default pathway; the male mode is a deviation from the default program. Does this asymmetry imply as some investigators have suggested that the female is the 'ancestral sex'?

We can imagine that the activation of SRY, the testis-determining gene, derails a developmental process that seems to be pre-programmed to form an ovary. Perhaps this explains why the fetal testis develops before the fetal ovary: if it didn't, an ovary would form. In fact, some human geneticists have suggested that development of the testis is absolutely necessary to prevent the ovary from forming. The hormones of the developing testis may suppress ovarian development.

Is there an ovarian counterpart to SRY, in other words, is there an ovary-determining gene? None has been identified yet, but at least five genes necessary for the development of the ovary in mice have been identified, none of which appear to have the role that SRY has in triggering the formation of the testes. As you can see many fascinating questions about the mysteries of the embryonic origin of the female – male dichotomy remain to be answered.

Table 1 summarizes what we have learned. The sexual anatomy of both sexes develops in stages. The chromosomal sex is set at fertilization. Gonadal sex begins with the conversion of the indifferent gonad into an ovary or a testis. The internal and external genitalia development defines the phenotypic sex. At puberty the individual becomes fertile.

Table 1

Stages of Sex

Stage	Female	Male
Chromosomal sex	*XX*	*XY*
Gonadal sex	Ovary	Testis
Phenotypic sex		
Internal genitalia		
	Uterus	Epididymis

	Uterine tubes	Vas deferens
		Prostate
		Seminal vesicles
		Bulbourethral glands
External Genitalia		
	Vagina	Penis
	Labia	Scrotum
Puberty		
	Ovulation	Sperm production
	Menstruation	

The full sexual phenotype in humans develops sequentially. Chromosomal sex is set at fertilization. The gonadal sex period begins with the conversion of the indifferent gonad into an ovary or a testis. This is followed by the formation of the internal and external genitalia, which defines phenotypic sex. At puberty, the individual becomes fertile.

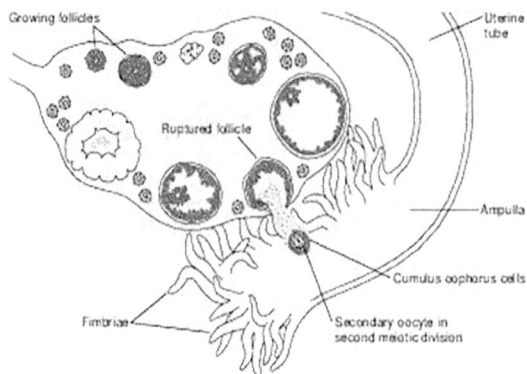

Chapter 2

The Post-Pubertal Female

Nothing is more ordinary than the egg: its likeness appears in the painted hands of kings and saints, under the paws of stone lions, bouncing across ball fields. Yet nothing is more mysterious. (1, Shelly Jackson (2002) The melancholy of anatomy)

As we saw in the previous chapter, the ovary completes its development around the middle of gestation (about 20 weeks after fertilization) and enters a quiescent state that lasts through the rest of gestation. The quiescence continues after birth, through infancy and childhood. We know relatively little about the activity of the ovary during this long period. The term 'quiescent' is a relative term (compared to the post-pubertal ovary) because the childhood ovary is not really quiet. It is preparing itself to take on its responsibilities when it transforms itself into the pubertal and post-pubertal ovary.

At puberty, the 'quiescent' ovary is reawakened from its long mini slumber, and now its real work begins (see Chapter 5 for the discussion of puberty). And work it is. The ovary is perhaps the dominant organ during the post-pubertal life of the female. Its hormonal secretions regulate the production of the egg during each menstrual cycle, prepare the uterus for pregnancy, and also influence other important aspects of a woman's life, such as her mood and sense of well-being.

So, let's begin to consider the post-pubertal ovary. It may not always be easy going, but if you persist, it is well worth the effort. At the end of this section, a short summary of the main points of our discussion is available. You may wish to begin there, and then at your leisure return to the more detailed discussion.

The reproductive tissues of the female

Fig. 2.1 is a schematic diagram of the internal and external genitalia of the adult female. The uterus, the uterine tubes (also known as the fallopian tubes, or oviducts), and the inner part of the vagina define the internal genitalia. The innermost layer of the uterus is the endometrium, which is built up and sloughed off every menstrual cycle. The labia, major and minor, clitoris, and the lower part of the vagina represent the external genitalia. The adult ovary is oval shaped, about 2.5 – 5 cm (1 – 2 inches) long, 1.5 – 3.0 cm wide, and 0.6 – 1.5 cm thick, and is connected to the pelvic wall by ligaments.

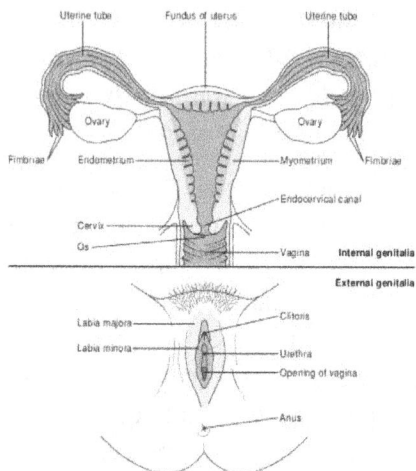

Figure 2.1

The discovery of the ovary

If it tastes like an egg

The ovary was a mysterious organ for probably thousands of years. It is, after all, a small, rather inconspicuous, internal organ, certainly not as strikingly visible as the testis, and connecting it to reproductive functions was not at all obvious. We cannot date its discovery; rather our understanding of ovarian function has grown slowly over the centuries. We do know, for example, that the spaying of sows and female camels to limit their fertility was well established by Aristotle's time (384-322 BCE). Despite this empirical knowledge, the relationship of the ovary to the egg remained unknown.

Finally, in the 17th century, the Dutch anatomist, Regnier de Graaf, proposed that the human ovary was the equivalent of the chicken ovary, which he knew produced the chicken egg. de Graaf may have argued like

Gertrude Stein 400 years later that 'an egg is an egg is an egg'. The important difference is that the woman's egg is microscopic – not visible to the naked eye – and it doesn't have a hard shell around it. Otherwise the chicken and human egg are very similar. They both produce many of the same types of proteins –the yolk and albumen – that give the chicken's egg its flavor – a flavor that those of us who like our eggs sunny-side up appreciate.

He proposed a simple way to test his idea: if the human ovary produces eggs, then it should taste like an egg. He then took the extraordinary step of removing the ovaries from a cadaver, cooking them, and eating them. He was very clear about his findings: ***"That albumen is actually contained in the ova of women will be beautifully demonstrated if they are boiled, for the liquor contained in the ova of the testicles (here he means ovaries) acquires upon cooking the same colour, the same taste and consistence as the albumen contained in the eggs of birds." (2, Regnier de Graaf On the human reproductive organs)***

So, thanks to this crazy Dutchmen, the role of the ovary as the producer of the egg was somewhat tenuously established. The egg itself, however, was not identified until 1827. The human egg was just too small to be visualized by the crude microscopes available before then.

Ovarian hormones

By the end of the 19th century, the egg-producing capability of the ovary was established beyond doubt. Some twenty years later we began to understand that the ovary was also the source of active substances – later called hormones – that had very important effects on the female body. Scattered reports had appeared previously in the clinical literature that clearly suggested that the ovary had major effects on female physiology. One particularly interesting observation regarding ovarian function appeared quite early, but as it sometimes happens in science, it went unnoticed and its significance unappreciated. This was the report of the results of an operation – removal of the ovaries - carried out by the English surgeon, W. Pott in1775:

A healthy young woman about 23 was taken into St. Bartholomew's hospital on account of two small swellings, one in each groin, which for some months had been so painful, that she could not do her work as a servant. The woman was in full health, large breasted, stout, and menstruated regularly, had no obstruction to the discharge per anum, nor any complaint but what arose from the uneasiness these tumours gave her, when she stooped or moved so as to press them. (3, W. Pott, Chirurgical Observations)

Pott removed the ovaries, and commented about the woman's recovery:

She has enjoyed good health ever since, but is become thinner and more apparently muscular; her breasts, which were large, are gone; nor has she ever menstruated since the operation, which is now some years. (3, W. Pott, Chirurgical Observations)

The significance of this observation – the association of the ovaries with the female body shape, breast maintenance, and menstruation - was not followed up until more than a century later, when it was shown that the ovary was the primary source of two critically important hormones, estrogen and progesterone. Progesterone, for example, was isolated and characterized in 1934, and in 1936, in an epic study, estrogen was isolated from four tons of sows' ovaries. By the end of the 1930s the twin functions of the ovary -- producer of the egg and of its two hormones -- were clearly recognized.

Let's turn to the egg-producing function of the ovary now.

The life history of the egg

The ovulatory cycle

The dual role of the ovary – producer of the egg and preparation of the uterus for pregnancy - imposes a cyclical quality to the reproductive physiology of the woman. The cyclical nature of ovarian function manifests itself most obviously as the menstrual cycle, the more or less monthly bleeding from the uterus that marks the beginning of puberty in the female and continues until the time of menopause. The menstrual cycle is itself a reflection of the ovulatory cycle, which is not as easily visible as the menstrual cycle, but is just as real.

By convention the length of the normal cycle is taken as 28 days, although the length can vary from about 24 to 35 days, not only among different women, but also in the same woman. The first half of the cycle is known as the follicular phase, and the second as the luteal phase. Ovulation, or the release of the egg from the ovary, divides the two phases of the ovulatory cycle. By convention, the follicular phase begins on the first day of menstrual flow. Except for extreme variations in length, it is very difficult to tell when the length of a cycle is "abnormal" and a source of concern. The length of the luteal phase is generally relatively constant at 13±1 days, while the follicular phase tends to be more variable.

The first role of the ovary – to produce or ovulate the egg – is carried out during the follicular phase. The second role, which we can define more precisely as the preparation of the outer lining of the uterus, the endometrium, is carried out during both the follicular and luteal phases.

A tale of suspended animation

The human egg is the rarest cell in the body. Simply consider the following. Whereas all other tissues in the body consist of millions of cells, the egg stands out because it is one of a kind, existing for a very short time in a kind of solitary grandeur. As you will see below, the destiny of most eggs is to commit a genetically programmed suicide. Only very few ever manage to escape this self-destruction, and the ones that do are the ones that led to you and me. The life history of the egg is one of the most interesting in all of remarkable life histories in human reproduction.

The development and formation of the female gamete -- the egg -- is known as oogenesis. In humans, oogenesis is a prolonged and rather mysterious affair, beginning during embryonic life, and continuing throughout the reproductive life of the female. Recall from Chapter 1 that the progenitor cells for eggs or sperm are the primordial germ cells (PGCs). The PGCs make their appearance about the end of the third week after fertilization and they move into the genital ridges the site at which the ovary will form. Probably around 500 cells form the starting PGC population. The PGCs proliferate and around week 12 differentiate successively into cell types known as primary oocytes. Proliferation and differentiation continues until about week 20 at which time the ovaries contain about 7 million primary oocytes. Then, rather abruptly the primary oocytes stop their development, and enter a quiescent, or resting stage. The primary oocytes can remain in this resting stage for many years. We know very little about what is happening in the primary oocytes during this period. The primary oocyte is technically not yet the egg, that is, it is not yet the cell that will be fertilized.

The 7 million or so primary oocytes that are formed by around week 20 in gestation represent the full stock of oocytes from which the egg will be chosen. Recall also that the oocyte does not exist as an independent cell but as part of a larger structure, known as the follicle. The primary oocyte when first formed is encased in the primordial follicle – a structure consisting of the primary oocyte surrounded by a single layer of cells.

Hence, when we say that the fetal ovary at around 20 weeks of gestation contains 7 million oocytes, we mean 7 million primordial follicles since all oocytes are found in follicles. This stock forms the reservoir from which potential eggs will be selected many years later. For many years we believed that this stock was made only once and was not replenished. However, a few recent, although controversial, experiments have suggested that, at least in mice, this old view may not be completely valid. We will have to wait sometime before we have a more definitive answer.

The follicle – the perilous journey

Atresia – death by the millions

What we do know is that beginning at about week 20 the destruction of the primordial follicles – a process known as atresia – begins. Amazingly, most of the follicles are lost even before birth. At birth, for example, perhaps 1 million of the original 7 million follicles are left, and by the time of puberty, only around 40,000 may be left. Menopause represents that time when the ovaries have been depleted of follicles. Hence, the rate at which follicles are lost from the initial reservoir determines the age at which menopause will occur. Atretic loss does not take place willy-nilly, but is in fact a genetically programmed form of cell suicide. We are beginning to understand that different circumstances can affect the rate of atretic loss. There is good evidence now, for example, that chronic smoking increases the rate at which follicles are destroyed, leading therefore to an earlier menopause.

Follicles not lost to atresia remain quiescent. With the onset of puberty an important change takes place in the dynamics of the ovary: on a periodic basis sets of follicles from the resting pool are stimulated to begin growing and maturing. Atretic loss continues, however. Hence, in the post-pubertal female three processes are taking place in her ovaries – many follicles remain quiescent, some are lost to atresia, and some begin to grow and develop. At the present time we know very little about the factors within the ovary that regulate these three distinct processes.

The quiescent follicles in the continually depleted pool of follicles can remain in that stage for a long time. For example, at puberty the primordial follicles in the reservoir have been in a quiescent state for 12 - 13 years (from birth to puberty). The primordial follicles remaining at the age of 25 have been in the resting state for 25 years, and so on.

The generation and subsequent destruction of so many follicles remains a real mystery. During the lifetime of the female very few of the primordial follicles develop to any extent, and even fewer are ovulated. Consider the following scenario as an example – let's say that the first ovulation takes place at 13 years and the last one at 50 years, and that ovulation occurs once each month. We can estimate that a maximum of about $37 \times 12 = 444$ follicles will be ovulated during the female's lifetime. Hence, out of the 7 million follicles produced, at most about 1 of every 20,000 will be ovulated. It is difficult to understand such profligacy. Indeed, we can say that the destiny of almost every follicle is to be destroyed. Ironically, ovulation enables a few of them to be rescued temporarily, and the even fewer that are fertilized are the ones that have led to you and me.

Some investigators have suggested that atretic loss may represent a type of quality control process. That is, we can imagine that the oocytes are being continually tested to select the best qualified to be ovulated and possibly fertilized. The principal question is: what distinguishes the follicles that are destroyed from the very few that eventually are ovulated? In other words, do the follicles that survive atresia possess some intrinsic advantage over those that do not? We don't know the complete answer to this question. We do know, however, that at the late stages of the development of the follicle, many otherwise "good" follicles are destroyed. We will return to this question when we consider reproductive aging and assisted reproductive techniques in later chapters.

The dominant follicle – rescued from oblivion

To get a clearer picture of the work of the ovary it may be helpful to think of it as drama in a theater stage. Some of the action may take place on the stage, easily visible, but some of the action may take place off the stage, in the invisible background. We hear what has taken place back stage from references to it by the actors

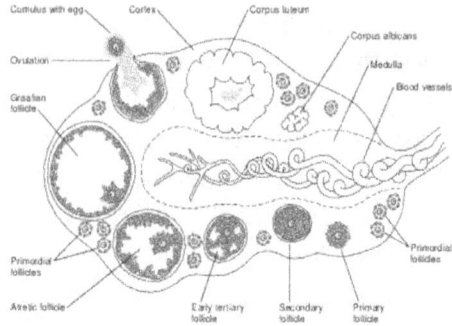

Figure 2.2

This analogy may be useful especially when trying to understand the factors and conditions that take a primordial follicle from the quiescent pool and transform it into the follicle, that is, ovulated in any given cycle. The follicle chosen to be ovulated, is known as the dominant follicle, sometimes also known as the Graafian follicle, after the crazy Dutchman who ate the cadaver's ovaries.

The ovary, as shown in Fig. 2.2, carries within it the life history of the development of the egg, from its birth as the primordial follicle. All of the subsequent stages in its development from the primordial follicle through the dominant (or Graafian) follicle, ovulation, formation of the corpus luteum, and its involution to form the corpus albicans can be seen within the adult ovary.

The dominant follicle is selected about day 4 of the follicular phase of any given cycle, and after that dominates the activity of the ovary for the next 10 days or so until ovulation. What is not easily apparent, however, is that the follicle that becomes the dominant follicle started its growth and development many months before. The precise time is not known with any certainty, but estimates suggest 9 months to perhaps more than one year. Hence, we can think of the activity in the ovary that pertains to the current cycle as the front center stage – this is the activity most easily visible. In the background, however, is the backstage activity that takes place continually over many cycles and which eventually brings the follicle to the center stage.

The dominant follicle starts out as one of many follicles recruited from the quiescent pool and stimulated to start their long journey in a competition from which only one will emerge as the winner, that is, one will be ovulated. The rest will be destroyed. During this journey of several months growth takes place continuously, but slowly. We know very little about the factors that stimulate and regulate this growth, or the mechanism that chooses the primordial follicles from the primordial reservoir to initiate such growth.

By about approximately 3 months before the beginning of the follicular phase of any given cycle the group of primordial follicles that initiated their growth about nine months before have developed into what are termed as the secondary follicles. Estimates suggest that around 300 or so secondary follicles are poised to enter the race to see who will become the dominant follicle three months later. The pituitary hormones, FSH and LH, become now the principle regulators of the growth of these relatively large follicles.

During the next 3 months most of these secondary follicles will destroyed, but a few (10 to 30) will continue to grow and reach the tertiary follicle stage. Hence, only about 10% of the group that began their growth 3 months before survive to this stage. These tertiary follicles are now clearly visible to the naked eye. Then at the beginning of every follicular phase the few surviving tertiary stage follicles (10 to 30 perhaps) are poised to enter the final stage of their growth. As before, most of these follicles are lost. However, one follicle – the dominant follicle – survives, and its growth during the next approximately 10 days is even more impressive – it can reach a diameter of 20 to 30 millimeters (about 1 inch). It is so big that it bulges out of the ovary. The growth of the follicle from its primordial stage to the dominant follicle is impressive – the diameter increases 1000-fold.

Ovulation – expulsion from Eden

Ovulation then is the last step in an extremely long process that begins when the female is still in her mother's womb. It culminates when the oocyte, the egg, contained within the dominant follicle is expelled out of the follicle and out of the ovary and into the uterine tube to await fertilization. Ovulation is the shortest stage in the life history of the follicle but certainly the most dramatic. Consider what is required. First, the follicular wall consisting of the millions of cells that encased the oocyte is ruptured; second, perhaps even more traumatic, the ovarian wall is ruptured at a particular site – known as the stigma; and finally, the oocyte has to be propelled out of the follicle and out of the ovary with sufficient force so that it will be caught by the finger-like projections of the uterine tube. Despite the dramatic nature of ovulation most women are not aware of it taking place. A small number of women report a mild abdominal ache at the time of ovulation.

Special hormonal conditions are required for ovulation, and the dominant follicle itself is responsible for ensuring the conditions are met. The crucial hormone is estrogen, produced in large quantities by the cells of the dominant follicle. The absolutely critical role of estrogen is to induce a huge surge in the secretion of pituitary hormone LH – known as the LH surge. Then, about 36 hours after the LH surge, ovulation occurs. If the dominant follicle does not produce enough estrogen, there will be no LH surge, and no ovulation will take place.

Ovulation, then, is a very special event. Many cases of infertility are due to disturbances in either the ability of the dominant follicle to produce adequate amounts of estrogen or inability of the pituitary to respond to the estrogen stimulation. It is probably the case also that even in normally fertile women, not every cycle is an ovulatory one.

In most cycles only one dominant follicle is generated per cycle. In fact, this is the rule not only for humans, but for primates as well, such as chimpanzees. This is in contrast to many other mammalian species that normally ovulate several eggs at the same time, and therefore have large litters. The reason for this difference most likely is that the human uterus will carry optimally only one fetus at a time, and the human ovulatory dynamics has been adjusted for ovulating one egg per cycle.

The corpus luteum – the productive aftermath

The expelled oocyte is caught by the fimbriae, the finger-like projections at the ends of the uterine tubes, and then moved along the interior of the uterine tube until it arrives at a special site in the tube called the ampullary region. Movement stops and the oocyte waits for sperm to come by. We don't really know how long the oocyte can remain viable, perhaps 24 to 48 hours. If the oocyte is not fertilized within the window of viability, the oocyte will begin to self-destruct and be absorbed by the uterine tube tissue.

Meanwhile, within the ovary after the expulsion of the oocyte from the dominant follicle, the remaining cells of the dominant follicle collapse upon themselves and regroup to form the structure known as the corpus luteum, a Latin term meaning "yellow body". The color of the corpus luteum is due to pigments that its cells begin to produce. In the cow, the corpus luteum is yellow; in some animal species, the corpus luteum has no pigment, while in humans the corpus luteum has an orange-yellow color.

The corpus luteum produces high levels of progesterone and estrogen, and together their role is to ensure that the uterus is prepared to receive the newly formed embryo if fertilization has occurred. In fact, corpus luteum function is required not only for implantation, but for the first two months of pregnancy as well. If the ovulated oocyte is not fertilized, the corpus luteum will begin to self-destruct about 8 days after ovulation, and estrogen and progesterone levels will begin to decrease. The luteal phase comes to an end after an additional 5 – 6 days, and the cellular remnants of the corpus luteum form an inert structure called the corpus albicans. The corpus albicans serves as a record of ovulations, because the ovulation history of the ovary can be determined by counting the number of corpi albicans. The beginning of the follicular phase of the next cycle begins with the initiation of menstruation.

A short re-cap

You may perhaps feel overwhelmed by the complexity of ovarian function. The complexity is due in part to the fact that many things are taking place simultaneously, and it is sometimes difficult to keep track of or understand the significance of what is happening. Let's review what we have learned.

- The follicular reserve and atresia. The storehouse of follicles, each of which contains the immature egg, is formed by around 20 weeks of gestation. About 7 million follicles are formed, but almost as soon as they are made a genetically programmed process of cell death, known as atresia, begins to deplete the reservoir. As a consequence, the follicular reserve is down to about 1 million at birth and numbers perhaps 40,000 at puberty. Atretic loss continues until the ovaries are empty of follicles, initiating the menopausal transition. We know relatively little about the factors that regulate atretic loss.

- Follicular recruitment. The follicle that is ovulated in any given cycle, known as the dominant follicle, starts its growth trajectory many months before. It is one of many follicles recruited from the follicular reservoir, escapes atresia and survives to be ovulated. In humans and the other higher primates, the hormonal environment that regulates follicular development generally ensures that only one follicle is ovulated at each cycle. This is why single births are the norm. However, as we will see in a later chapter, we can artificially manipulate the hormonal environment of the ovary to ovulate several eggs in one cycle.

- Ovulation. The ovulatory cycle is divided into two phases – the follicular phase beginning the first day of menstruation, and the luteal phase beginning the day of ovulation. Ovulation is the most dramatic event in the ovary during the follicular phase. It depends on a carefully controlled relationship between estrogen produced by the dominant follicle and the pituitary hormones FSH and LH, culminating in a very rapid rise in LH, known as the LH surge. Ovulation, which involves the expulsion of the mature egg from the follicle and the ovary and into the uterine tubes, generally takes place 24 – 36 hours after the day of the LH surge.

- Preparation for pregnancy. The ovary has another equally important role – preparation of the uterus for pregnancy. This is accomplished in two stages. First, during the follicular phase, estrogen from the dominant follicle stimulates the growth of the endometrium, the outer lining of the uterus, preparing the uterus for pregnancy in case the egg is fertilized. Immediately after ovulation, another major structure is formed – the corpus luteum is assembled from the remnants of the ovulated follicle. The corpus luteum secretes progesterone, which is required to transform the developed endometrium into tissue receptive for implantation. Corpus luteum function, in fact, is necessary to support the first two months of the pregnancy, before the placenta takes over that role.

The uterus - the weeping matrix

We don't remember when we were linked to our mother in what is the most intimate relationship we will ever know. The Greek word for the organ that nurtured us for the first nine months of our existence is hystera, from which is derived uterus, the term currently used in the medical literature.

Somehow the word uterus has a cold clinical sense devoid of feeling, in contrast to the Old English word womb, which evokes warmth and protectiveness, qualities that clearly are also associated with the Latin word matrix. Hystera also gave rise to hysterectomy (surgical removal of the uterus), and to hysteria, a term originally used to describe the 'fits' and convulsive behavior typically associated with women.

The association of an anxiety syndrome with the uterus is said to date from a Greco-Roman idea that the 'fits' seen in some women were caused by the uterus moving from the pelvic region into the abdomen and into the chest cavity. This view, subscribed to by male physicians, became very popular during the latter part of the 19th century. Among the many different types of therapy for the hysteria included inhaling noxious fumes meant to push the uterus back down to its proper place, or, interestingly, placing pleasant aromatic substances in the vagina, in this case, meant to draw the uterus back down. To us now, of course, this idea seems quite ridiculous, but it is worth remembering that we still tend to apply the term hysterical more to women than to men.

Menstruation

And what is semen? Clearly the active principle of the animal, the material principle being the menstrual blood. (4, Galen On the Natural Faculties)

Menstruation has probably been one of the most puzzling and mysterious of phenomena for most of the history of humankind. The mystery of the monthly shedding of blood must have made a deep impression on our ancestors because in the folklore of all pre-literate and even literate societies an ordinary biological event was given extraordinary symbolic significance. The diversity and complexity of menstrual taboos regulating the conduct of both men and women during menstruation illustrate the power of the human imagination as it struggles to give meaning to the unknown.

In the Western world speculations about the nature of menstrual blood and the purpose of the bleeding began with the Greeks. In the third century BCE Greek physicians proposed that every human being was formed from the action of sperm on the menstrual blood. The view that menstrual blood was the raw material from which an individual is formed persisted until the 17th century when the English physician W. Harvey showed that it could not be true. At the same time, however, menstrual blood was considered to have some really ghastly properties. A Spanish physician of Sevilla contended that *"On contact with this gore, crops do not generate, wine goes sour, trees lose their fruit, iron is corrupted by rust, copper is blackened. Should dogs eat any of it they go mad."* *(5, A Source Book in Medieval Science)*

The first significant clues in our understanding of menstruation came around the beginning of the 20th century with descriptions of the changes in the endometrium, the outer most layer of the uterus (looking from inside the uterus), during the cycle. The menstrual cycle consists of the periodic building up and subsequent destruction of this very specialized tissue.

In 1940 J. Markee in a remarkable series of experiments carried out first detailed descriptions of the lifecycle of the endometrium as a continuous process. He removed small pieces of the endometrium from a female Rhesus monkey and transplanted small bits of the tissue into the anterior chamber of the same animal's eye, placing the tiny grafts just behind the cornea. Markee was able to observe the changes in the small bit of endometrial tissue with a microscope. Because this area is well supplied with blood capillaries from the iris, the grafts are assured an ample blood supply. The grafts not only survive, but because of their connection to the circulatory system, they develop and self-destruct just as if they were still part of the uterus. Menstruation in the graft occurred in synchrony with that of the uterus and ceased at the same time. If the ovaries of the female were removed, the grafts immediately atrophied, demonstrating that the menstrual cycle is orchestrated by the ovulatory cycle, and hence, its periodicity is determined by the periodicity of the ovulatory cycle.

The menstrual cycle

By convention the cycle begins on the first day of menstruation, and the regeneration of the endometrium begins after the menstrual flow has ceased, generally about 4 – 5 days after it began. Estrogen produced by the dominant follicle is the driving stimulus for the growth of the endometrium. Estrogen stimulates the proliferation of the endometrial cells, and during the remainder of the follicular phase, the endometrium increases in thickness. After ovulation, progesterone, produced by the corpus luteum, is responsible for significant changes in the endometrium. The endometrial cells swell with water, and begin to secret a variety of compounds that are important in preparing an endometrium that will not only be receptive to implantation, but will have the properties to be able to support the demands of the pregnancy.

If fertilization does takes place, the 5 – 7 day old embryo begins to imbed itself in the endometrium, and as it does so it releases a hormone, called human chorionic gonadotropin (hCG), that signals to the corpus luteum to keep producing estrogen and progesterone. In effect, the embryo is signaling to the mother that she is pregnant. A clinical pregnancy begins at the time of implantation. The pregnancy kits routinely available nowadays are in fact hCG test kits. If the test is positive, the woman knows that implantation has been initiated, and that a clinical pregnancy is now established.

If no fertilization takes place involution of the corpus luteum begins and estrogen and progesterone levels fall rapidly. The endometrium can no longer be maintained. Endometrial cells begin to self-destruct, small arteries that provided the blood supply when the endometrium was being regenerated, break off. The blood flow that accompanies menses comes from the blood released from the destroyed arteries.

Ovulation is not required for menstruation. Menstruation simply marks the response of the endometrium to the changing levels of estrogen produced by the ovary. Withdrawal of this hormonal support leads to menses. Ovulation, on the other hand, requires very special conditions, particularly with respect to estrogen, conditions that may not be met in each cycle. The consequence is that a woman may have fairly regular menstrual cycles, but she may not always be ovulating in each cycle.

Why do women menstruate?

Menstruation is quite rare in the animal world. Human females are exceptional in this regard, a fact that was noted a long time ago. It must have been apparent to our ancestors that the animals with which they had the most contact did not menstruate. Why was menstruation confined to human females?

This is not a trivial question, for it forces us to try to understand a very significant aspect of human reproductive biology. Surprisingly, the full significance of menstruation remains elusive and reproductive biologists still debate its origin. To appreciate this question, it is instructive to contrast the menstrual cycle with the reproductive cycle of non-menstruating mammalian species. Such species have an estrus cycle. Estrus is the term, coined in 1901, for the recurrent periods during which the female animal is receptive to the male, commonly called 'heat'. Ovulation occurs in these species when the female signals her receptivity to the male in a variety of species-specific ways. Hence, mating is promoted at the opportune time for fertilization to occur.

Many wild animals have estrus cycles tuned to the seasons, timed so that the birth of the young occurs when food is plentiful. In domesticated species a variety of estrus cycles are found. The shortest cycle is that of the hen, which can lay an egg once a day. Cows, mares, and sows have 21-day estrus periods during most of the year, while sheep have several estrus cycles during the summer, but during the rest of the year they are anestrus, that is, sexual activity ceases completely. Dogs and cats generally have two or three estrus periods per year, while many carnivores have only one estrus period per year.

In estrus species, the endometrium is built up only if fertilization has occurred. The important consequence is that such species do not menstruate because they don't need to destroy an unneeded endometrium – they only generate one when they need one. In humans, however, the development and destruction of the endometrium is autonomous in that it does not depend on the sexual activity of the female or whether fertilization takes place.

Estrus and menstrual species also differ significantly in one aspect of their sexual behavior. In humans and the higher primates, the female is continuously receptive to the male, and her sexual receptiveness is disassociated from ovulation. Moreover, there is no outward or public manifestation by the human female to indicate that she is approaching ovulation. Males in estrus species are acutely aware, even from a distance, when a female is in heat. Human males are clueless. This difference in sexual behavior is of enormous importance. What would you imagine human societies would be like if ovulation were not silent?

Does menstruation serve some function? Our immediate response probably would be ' yes, of course, otherwise why does it exist?' But what could be its function? Several suggestions have been made: (a) to eliminate bacteria and pathogens brought into the uterus by sperm after sexual intercourse; (b) to signal reproductive readiness in the female; (c) to remove defective embryos. Hippocrates proposed long ago a version of (a) when he argued that menstruation was a form of detoxification, a way of cleansing the female. Reproductive biologists have debated the pros and cons of each of these ideas extensively for many years, without reaching any consensus.

An alternative way of looking at menstruation proposed a few years ago is to consider that it did not evolve to meet some specific function, but that instead it is a consequence, a byproduct, of the special features of the primate or human implantation process. The human embryo implants deeply into the endometrium and even the underlying uterine tissues. Compared to other species the human embryo is highly invasive, and only a specially prepared endometrium would be able to sustain the implantation. This special endometrium cannot be generated instantly or even in two or three days. Hence, the needs of the primate embryo for protection and sustenance have led to the development of a highly elaborate and complex endometrium in anticipation of pregnancy. When no fertilization occurs, progesterone levels drop, and the endometrium breaks down, initiating menses. Human females menstruate because of the special needs of the human embryo in pregnancy. Eliminating pathogens or defective embryos may be a beneficial consequence of menstruation, but not its driving evolutionary stimulus.

Mood disturbances during the menstrual cycle

Young people for the most part have a crisis in their complaints ... and such complaints as remain in females about the commencement of menstruation, usually become chronic. (6, Hippocrates. Aphorisms The Hippocratic Writings)

Conditions or disturbances linked to the menstrual cycle have a long and complex history in medicine. Examples of symptoms that change with the menstrual cycle include mood changes, such as anxiety, tension, irritability, and depression, menstrual cycle-linked memory and learning disturbances, insomnia, disturbed eating behavior and alcohol intake, changes in concentration, and stress sensitivity. The most common pattern of symptom change is the increase in their severity during the latter stages of the luteal phase followed by amelioration of the symptoms during menses.

This is the type of pattern that is seen with the condition known as premenstrual syndrome **(PMS)**. Another type of pattern is an increase in symptoms during menses itself. Two disorders that exhibit this pattern are partial epilepsy and menstrual migraine. In the former, the frequency of seizures increases significantly during menses; in the latter, migraine attacks increase in frequency as soon as menses begins.

The origin of menstrual cycle-linked disturbances, some of which can be very debilitating, has been a subject of debate and controversy for many years. It is only recently, however, that significant clues about the nature of the precipitating factors have begun to emerge, and importantly to provide a rational basis for treatment. Let's begin with **PMS** because we probably know more about it than the other disorders.

Premenstrual syndrome **(PMS)**

Hippocrates, the "father of medicine," described a disorder referred to as 'hysteria' caused by the cyclic wandering of the uterus (low to high position in the abdominal cavity). The wandering of the uterus was linked to the lunar cycle, and was the cause of changes in women's behavior during her menstrual cycle. The wandering idea was discarded during the later Greek period, and the cause of women's behavioral changes was said to be due to sexual inactivity – the therapy proposed was marriage and sexual intercourse. During the rise of Christianity, female hysteria was seen as evidence of devil possession or ascribed to temporary insanity or moral failings.

In 1931 'female hysteria' was given a more scientific name - premenstrual syndrome (PMS) – and defined as a set of physiological and behavioral symptoms of varying degrees of severity that manifest themselves during the latter part of the luteal phase of the ovulatory cycle. Giving these symptoms a name did not bring us significantly closer to understanding them. The maddening feature of PMS is that no straightforward diagnostic test for it exists. It's not like diabetes where a simple blood test can tell us whether we have it or not. For the PMS patient the symptoms are real enough, but the variability in the number of symptoms and in their severity among women frustrated attempts for many years to agree on suitable diagnostic criteria. It also prevented the full acceptance of PMS as a clinical disorder. Until relatively recently PMS was viewed primarily as having a neurotic or psychiatric origin, rather than a physiological origin.

PMS interestingly has a rich non-medical history. For example, in the criminal literature, an association between crime and PMS has also been noted. Crimes by women apparently are committed most frequently during the premenstrual period, while fewer crimes are committed during the ovulatory or pre-ovulatory stages. A number of studies have also shown that the incidence of child battering during the premenstrual period may be relatively high. In most such cases, the women involved may be perfectly normal and maternal during other stages of the ovulatory cycle.

Since the first half of the nineteenth century, courts in France have taken the menstrual cycle into account when dealing with female offenders. For example, acquittals for shoplifting during the PMS interval took place on a more or less regular basis. Indeed, in France, PMS-induced changes have been recognized legally, so that women who commit a crime during the few days before menses can claim temporary impairment of sanity. In England, in some circumstances PMS has been considered a mitigating factor in crimes committed by women. This defense has not had much success in the United States.

Despite many disagreements in deciding what PMS is, some progress has been made in refining the diagnostic criteria, and the most recent compilation, which attempts to distinguish between the mild and severe forms of PMS, appears in the fourth edition of the Diagnostic and Statistical Manual of Mental Disorders (DSM-IV). A generally accepted set of criteria is that developed by the University of California, San Diego, and summarized as follows.

At least one of the following affective and somatic symptoms during the five days before menses in each of the last three previous cycles:

Affective (behavioral) symptoms – depression, angry outbursts, irritability, anxiety, confusion, social withdrawal

Somatic (physiological) symptoms – breast tenderness, abdominal bloating, headache, swelling of extremities

Symptoms relieved from days 4 through 13 of the menstrual cycle

Depending on the epidemiological surveys one reads 50 - 80 percent of women experience some of the symptoms of PMS. In most women the symptoms are mild and do not interfere significantly with their daily activities. In 3-8% of women, however, PMS symptoms are much more severe and debilitating, and the women require medical attention. This circumstance has led to the delineation of a separate disorder within the PMS category, and named premenstrual dysphoric disorder (PMDD). The PMDD criteria are much stricter than for simple PMS, requiring in particular a minimum number of symptoms and severe functional impairment. The implication is that PMDD differs qualitatively from PMS, that is, that it is distinct from PMS, and not simply an extreme version of PMS. There is no general agreement on this point, however.

The array of treatments or therapies that have been tried and promoted for relief from the PMS symptoms is long and wide. For women in whom the symptoms are mild and do not require medical attention, a variety of self-management techniques have been tried and include vitamin and trace element supplementation, exercise, yoga, a large number of herbal remedies, and even hypnosis. The efficacy of these treatments is extremely variable, and it is not uncommon for different treatments to be tried in combination.

The PMDD patient, on the other hand, does not respond to this gamut of self-management methods, and requires medical intervention. Extreme measures have included removal of the ovaries, an operation recommended especially for menstrual-related epileptic seizures, and which became popular in the nineteenth century. Despite the high mortality associated with the operation its practice continued into the twentieth century. It was performed with some frequency in the 1950s, and still resorted to on occasion today.

What's the cause of PMS?

PMS disappears in post-menopausal women. PMS also disappears after removal of the ovaries and suppression of ovarian function. These observations clearly indicate that an ovarian product is necessary to precipitate PMS symptoms. The obvious question: what is the product, and how does it elicit the different PMS symptoms?

Although we don't have a comprehensive answer to this question yet, one model proposes that PMS is provoked by a group of compounds known as GABA-steroids, which are compounds derived from progesterone produced during luteal phase by the corpus luteum. The GABA system in the brain is a neurotransmitter - receptor network that has long been known to regulate mood and behavior. Drugs that have significant effects on mood and behavior such as barbiturates, benzodiazepines, and alcohol exert their effects through the GABA system.

One of the major GABA-steroids, known as allopregnanolone, has been shown in both animal and human studies to elicit the same effects as these drugs. Hence, we can think of PMS mood disturbances as arising from GABA system responses to the cyclical production of progesterone metabolites. This model accounts for the luteal phase dependency of PMS symptoms, and helps us understand why post-menopausal women do not suffer from PMS, and why certain therapies for PMS have been successful.

What accounts for the extreme variability in the PMS symptoms? We can imagine that the mild forms of PMS may be considered normal responses of the GABA system to the cyclically produced GABA-steroids. In other words, variations in mood, behavior, and other symptoms can be considered perfectly normal and expected. The more severe manifestations of PMS, on the other hand, may reflect cyclically triggered abnormal

GABA system responses to the GABA-steroids. PMDD patients, for example, may have genetically altered components in their GABA response network, and it is this alteration that leads to the extreme changes in symptoms that are typical for this group of women.

The GABA response network is not the only one responsible for the PMS symptoms. At least one other brain neurotransmitter system is involved – the serotonin system. This is suggested by the success of SSRI (selective serotonin reuptake inhibitors) therapy for some of the severe forms of PMS. SSRIs are anti-depressants, the best known of which is fluoxetine (Prozac). Fluoxetine was first tried on PMDD patients because the disorder shares many of the features of a number of mood and anxiety disorders – such as depression - many of which are due to disturbances in the serotonin hormone system. Today, SSRI therapy is probably the pharmacological treatment of choice for PMDD patients. The serotonin and GABA systems probably do not act independently of each other. For example, SSRI-treated PMDD patients exhibit a decreased sensitivity to the GABA-steroid allopregnanolone in the luteal phase, indicating that the two hormonal networks may be functionally related.

Still, other aspects of this complex response system remain unclear. For example, not all PMDD women respond to SSRIs. Second, the relief experienced often diminishes after a few months. Does this suggest that other as yet unknown neurotransmitter systems are also involved? We don't really know, but our ignorance about this and other questions indicates that we are only seeing the tip of what may be an immense PMS and PMDD iceberg. Nevertheless, the therapeutic successes with SSRIs, even if limited, are welcome news for many PMDD sufferers. Perhaps even more importantly the focus on an abnormal neurotransmitter systems to ovarian cycling may be best approach for understanding and treating the severe forms of PMS. There is good reason to be optimistic about the future.

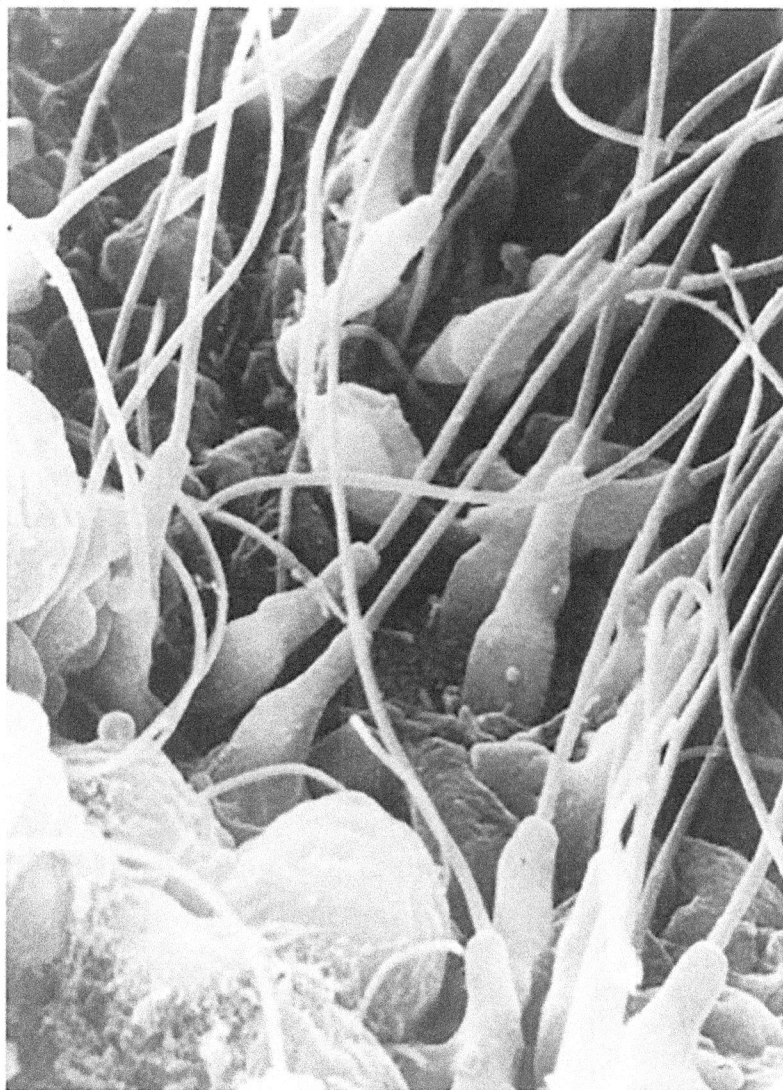

Chapter 3

The Post-Pubertal Male

Human spermatozoa stand apart from the gametes of virtually all other mammals in the paucity of their phenotype, the inadequacy of their function (1, R. J. Aitken and J. A. M. Graves The future of sex)

Why are the testis and ovary so different in form and function? In reply you might say: "Well, it's obvious – the ovary produces only a few large eggs, while the testis produces a huge number of very small sperm. And the structure of each gonad is designed to this end."

So let's focus on testicular function, particularly that of the adult or post-pubertal testis. The testis, like the ovary, passes through stages – the fetal, the postnatal and pre-pubertal, the post-pubertal, and there may even be a 'twilight' period at an advanced age. Recall from Chapter 1 that the fetal testis has its own very specific and necessary job. We know less about the function of the post-natal or pre-pubertal testis, but we probably should assume that its role is not negligible. We don't really know whether a 'twilight' period really exists as a distinct physiological stage, but we will consider that question later in Chapter 6.

The mythology of the 'witness'

Men have always been attached to their testes, both literally and symbolically. And for countless generations they have also been aware of the importance of the testes. The testes, unlike the ovaries, never had to be discovered. They have always been there, palpable, and the subject of experimentation and speculation throughout most of human civilization. Removal of the testes, castration, does not ordinarily lead to death, and this was probably recognized very early in our history. For example, archaeologists tell us that evidence of the castration of animals date to about 7000 BCE, around the period when animals were first domesticated. The routine castration in cattle in order to produce tender meat is an ancient practice.

The effects of testes removal on reproductive function in both animals and men must have been recognized very early. In animals castration rendered the animals sterile, and permitted their control. Handling a bull is difficult and dangerous, while handling a castrated male, a steer, is much easier. Human castration is also an ancient practice. Castration was the punishment for adultery in the Babylonian Code of Hamurabi (ca. 2000 BCE.) and in Egyptian law of the 20th Dynasty (1200 - 1085 BCE.). In Assyria (ca. 1500 BCE.) castration was prescribed for sexual offenses. This suggests that the effect of castration on the male sexual drive and erectile function was already known.

Castration for social purposes, especially of pre-pubertal boys, to produce eunuchs to guard the women in harems, is thought to have originated in the Middle East, but was adopted by most of the high cultures of China, India, and Europe. In Europe, the castration of young boys to maintain a supply of male soprano singers was continued until the late nineteenth century, although the practice had been condemned by the Roman Church in 325 CE. Many primitive societies also practiced castration, in numerous cases for ritualistic purposes. The Caribs of Brazil were reported by their European conquerors to castrate their prisoners of war in order to increase their weight and the tenderness of their flesh before they were killed for a ritual feast.

It is quite likely that differences between castrates and non-castrates is the source of much of the mythology about the testes, specifically the association of the testes and its secretions with physical strength, courage, strength of character, and sexual vigor. In many languages "to have balls" is a way saying that a man (or sometimes even a woman) is courageous or strong in character. The association of the organ with these virtues may explain the use of word "testis" for the organ itself. "Testis" comes from the Latin for 'witness' or 'spectator', and the words 'testify' and 'testament' also has the same root. Possibly because the testes were evidence of virility, and only adult males could be witnesses in Roman law (boys, eunuchs, and women could not be witnesses), the act of testifying of swearing an oath required placing the hands on the testes.

This practice was common in many other societies in ancient times. References to this practice are found in numerous instances in the Hebrew Bible. A good example comes from the Book of Genesis where the 'thigh' was a euphemism for testes: ***"And Abraham said unto his eldest servant of his house, that ruled over all that he had. Put, I pray thee, thy hand under my thigh: And I will make thee swear by the Lord, the God of heaven, and*** *the God of earth." (Genesis 24:2-3)*

Especially poignant is the psychological distress experienced by men who have one or both testes removed for medical reasons, an operation referred to as an orchidectomy (from the Greek word for testis, orchid). This operation is typically performed for testicular cancer or prostate cancer. Physiologically an orchidectomy is of minor importance. However, most men experience this as a tremendous assault on their sense of masculinity, a response that reveals a deeply ingrained psychological and cultural belief that the testis is a critical sign, the 'witness' of male identity. Younger men, in particular, may request a testicular prosthesis as a way of restoring their body image. The traumatic effect of such an operation may be diminished by prior discussion and counseling regarding the myths and cultural values about the testes.

The association of the testes with sexual potency is quite ancient. Extracts of testes in ancient India (ca. 1400 BCE) were used to restore sexual potency, and during Greek and Roman times preparations made from goat or wolf testes were commonly used as aphrodisiacs. However, it was not until the nineteenth century that systematic experiments with testes and testicular extracts began to be carried out. The landmark experiment came in 1849 when the Danish investigator transplanted testes from roosters into castrated cocks and the animals recovered their masculine characteristics.

The first studies on humans came in 1889 when Brown-Séquard, a 72 years old French physiologist, injected himself with extracts of dog testes and claimed to have recovered his potency. In his famous lecture, he mentioned (with an obvious meaning to all the members of the audience) that he had "paid a visit" to his wife that morning. The reported effects were eventually shown to be invalid, and Brown-Séquard was forced to admit that his long-sought remedy for the loss of potency was "wishful thinking".

In the early twentieth century two other therapies for lost potency were introduced. One was the Steinach operation (named after a Viennese surgeon) that involved the occlusion of the vas deferens, equivalent to a unilateral vasectomy. This procedure was promoted as a way to improve blood flow to the testis, and therefore testicular function. Even more extreme was the Voronoff procedure, which involved transplanting testes from monkeys or from executed criminals. The effects in both types of procedures were short-lived or nonexistent. Nevertheless, variants of these practices continued, and private clinics in Europe, promising a return of youthfulness and an increase of sexual activity, prospered during the 1920s and 1930s, and even after the World War II. In Vienna, over 100 well-known men, including Sigmund Freud and W. B. Yeats, underwent the Steinach operation, and many others volunteered for the Voronoff testicular grafting protocol. There were reports in the 1950s that Pope Pius XII underwent such treatments. After the practice disappeared in Europe, it continued in other countries. As late as the 1970s, a clinic in Tijuana, Mexico, across the border from San Diego, California, was still attracting patients.

"Vanity of vanities" you might say, simply a sad example of the length to which men will go to recover their lost youth. But the effort to rejuvenate aging men continues, and its modern version is known as "testosterone replacement therapy" (TRT). In this case the testosterone is delivered topically in the form of a patch.

The post-pubertal testis

The male genitalia – internal and external

In the male, the external genitalia are the penis and scrotum, the scrotum being the sac that holds the testes (the testes are called the testicles in most non-medical publications; testes, is the plural form, the singular being testis). Several tissues – the epididymis, vas deferens, prostate, seminal vesicles, and bulbourethral glands – form the internal genitalia (Fig.3.1).

The testis contains two compartments, which we can simply refer to as the inner and outer compartments. The inner compartment contains the seminiferous tubules, an extremely long, network of folded tubular structures (total length perhaps 100 meters (over 100 yards) long in the adult), within which the sperm are produced, in prodigious numbers, between 100 to 200 million per day. Sperm are produced all along the length of the seminiferous tubules. After they are made they move out of the site at which they are generated, and transported down the length of the seminiferous tubules.

Eventually they reach the epididymis, the duct into which all of the seminiferous tubules empty. The epididymis serves in part as a holding tank for sperm. In ejaculation, the sperm are expelled out of the epididymis into the vas deferens and eventually pass into the penile urethra that provides the exit route to the outside. Along the way they are bathed in secretions from the seminal vesicles, the prostate, and the bulbourethral glands. The fluid secreted by these three tissues is known as seminal fluid. The term semen refers to the suspension of the sperm in the seminal fluid. In sexual intercourse the ejaculated sperm are deposited at the vaginal-cervical boundary. A few of them will pass through the cervix, into the uterus, and eventually into and down the length of the uterine tubes in search of the egg.

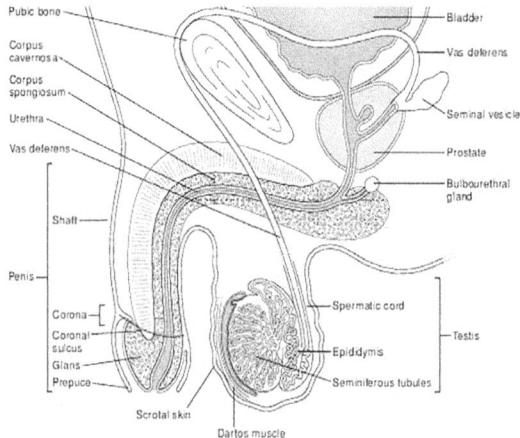

Figure 3.1

The sperm factory

Sperm production, or spermatogenesis, begins at puberty in response to hormonal signals ultimately originating in the hypothalamus (see Chapter 4 and Appendix 2). Spermatogenesis differs from cogenesis, egg production, in a number of ways. One fundamental difference is that whereas in females the stock of oocytes capable of being fertilized is produced only once (see Chapter 1 and 2), in males sperm are produced continually once spermatogenesis begins, that is, the production of fully developed sperm cells. The progenitor cells for spermatogenesis are known as spermatogonial cells. Recall from Chapter 1 that these cells were produced during week 7 through week 12 of fetal life. After they are produced they enter a dormant stage that extends all during the rest of gestation, infancy and childhood. At puberty they are triggered to initiate a process that once started appears to continue until late in the male's life. Hence, in contrast to oogenesis, spermatogenesis is a continually renewable process.

The continuous production of spermatozoa requires a continuous generation of cells, known as spermatogonial stem cells, able to embark on the spermatogenesis pathway. Without the stem cell population, sperm production would stop as soon as the supply of stem cells ran out. Hence, the first step in spermatogenesis is a special cell division that ensures that a stem cell population is regenerated.

Spermatogenesis takes place within the seminiferous tubules (Fig. 3.1), which also contain another type of cell, the Sertoli cell. The Sertoli cells are absolutely essential for sperm production, but we know relatively little about their precise function. The image for this chapter is a scanning electron microscope image of human sperm being released from the Sertoli cells and beginning their journey through the seminiferous tubules.

We do know, however, that the number of Sertoli cells determines the adult sperm count and the testis size. Sertoli cells are formed early in gestation, but the adult number of Sertoli cells is set during the first six to nine months after birth. Although spermatogenesis does not begin until much later the Sertoli cells are quite active during the first few months after birth, and this activity appears to be essential for normal spermatogenesis. This means that sperm production in the adult is determined by events that take place before birth and during the early post-natal period. There are good indications that infertility in some males may eventually be traced to disturbances in testicular development during fetal and the early post-natal life.

In humans, spermatogenesis is a prolonged process, taking about 3 months to go from a spermatogonial stem cell to a fully developed sperm cell, known as a spermatozoon. Nevertheless, sperm production reaches astronomical proportions, or about 80,000 spermatozoa per minute, or about 110 million spermatozoa per day. This is an average figure, with actual values ranging from a low of 20 million to a high of 270 million or greater per day. Many conditions have been reported to affect the rate of sperm production – overall health, age, illness, temperature, climate, altitude, and stress. For example, men in prison have been reported to have higher sperm counts than men who are engaged in high stress jobs. It is not clear the men in prison are under less stress than other men.

Sexing sperm

The desire to predetermine the sex of offspring may be as old as human society. In many, perhaps most human groups, males have tended to be more desired than females. Historically, this desire may have been even more important in animal husbandry, where the breeding of horses or cattle of the appropriate sex would have significant economic benefits. To select the sex of offspring we would need a method to separate the X-bearing from the Y-bearing sperm.

Nature, however, has gone to extraordinary lengths to minimize differences between X-bearing and Y-bearing sperm. Nevertheless, during the last 15 – 20 years Nature's roadblocks, as it were, have been slowly dismantled. A number of laboratories specializing in animal husbandry have developed high-tech protocols that are reasonably efficient in separating X-bearing from Y-bearing sperm from cattle and horses. Recall that in males sperm carrying and X chromosome and sperm carrying a Y chromosome are produced in equal proportions. The sperm fractions enriched for X-bearing or Y-bearing sperm are collected and used in artificial insemination protocols to generate the pregnancies of a predetermined sex with 90% efficiency. The fertilizing potential of the sexed spermatozoa is lower than normal spermatozoa, but the incidence of birth defects in progeny is no higher than in normal fertilizations. Although equipment costs are high and the procedures complex, the sexing of spermatozoa in cattle and horse production is used routinely in many countries.

These separation procedures have been applied to human sperm in only limited circumstances, especially for the prevention of genetic disorders due to mutations in genes on the X chromosome (see Appendix 1 for the importance of mutations on the X chromosome). A typical case may involve a couple in which the wife may be a carrier for an X-linked disorder. Since she transmits one of her X-chromosomes to her sons, half of her sons will receive the X chromosome carrying the defective gene. Because males have only one X chromosome, the sons receiving the defective X-linked gene will develop the disorder. Such a couple may, therefore, desire to have only daughters, and may want to try one of these sperm sexing protocols. However, the sperm sexing procedures used in animal sperm do not work with as high efficiency with human sperm. Nevertheless, these protocols have been used successfully in some cases in enabling such couples to avoid having sons. The cost and complexity of these methods limit their general availability, however.

Even if the costs would come down and the efficiencies were improved, is pre-ordering the sex of your baby advisable? We can easily imagine that one outcome would be a change in the sex ratio of offspring. Nature has arranged things so that the sex ratio is essentially 50:50. Any significant change in the ratio will mean that some 20 to 30 years later, there will be a shortage of mating partners for one or the other sex. Hence, extension of desires of individual families could have serious consequences for the society. China, for example, has recently become acutely aware of the consequences of its one child policy. Since males are still favored over females, one important consequence of the one child rule is that many female fetuses are being aborted. The reality of the situation is made clear by the fact that China has begun offering financial incentives for couples to have girls.

The scrotum puzzle

One of the enduring puzzles of the anatomy of the human male is the scrotum. The scrotum is the external sac that houses the testes. Recall from Chapter 1 that migration of the testes from their initial abdominal position near the kidneys into the scrotum (referred to as testicular descent) occurs during the latter stages of fetal life or early in the post-natal period. Over 90 percent of male infants at the time of birth have descended testes. In the remainder, descent generally takes place within 2 or 3 months after birth. Failure of the testes to descend is known as cryptorchidism, meaning hidden testes. Cryptorchid males are infertile, and are at high risk of developing testicular cancer. For this reason, if the testes have not descended by themselves after a few months after birth, they are brought into the scrotum surgically.

It wasn't clear until 1924 why cryptorchidism led to infertility - it was the high temperature. Wrapping the scrotum of a fertile ram, for example, with woolen socks so that the temperature of the testes is the same as that of the body leads to a cessation of spermatogenesis. Placing the testis of a guinea pig together with its blood supply back into the abdominal cavity resulted rapid cessation of spermatogenesis. If the testes were left too long in the abdominal cavity the damage was irreversible, and spermatogenesis could not be restored when the testis was brought back into the scrotum. In humans the scrotum is $2 - 3C$ lower than body temperature, a very small temperature difference but apparently enough to permit spermatogenesis to proceed.

In fact, at least some human societies have been aware of the connection between fertility and testes temperature for a long time. An early form of birth control was the Roman custom of taking very hot baths, a practice apparently that is still followed, for the same reasons, in some parts of Japan. A more controlled experiment showed that 15-minute exposures to 100 - 104F in a hot spa every day leads to over 80 percent decrease in sperm production in a two-week period. Wearing tight pants or spending too much time seated has been shown to result in lower sperm counts.

The puzzle about the scrotum is that only a few mammalian species have them. Humans and our primate cousins have them, as well as dogs, cows, horses, and rats, but elephants, pigs, and some marine mammals don't. If we argue that the scrotum is necessary to maintain the testes at a lower temperature, then what about the non-scrotal species? The answer came from experiments in two non-scrotal species, whales and dolphins in the 1980s. We now know that non-scrotal species have a network of veins and arteries around each testis, known as a plexus, which functions as a heat exchanger, that is, cooling the testes so that spermatogenesis can take place. It turns out that scrotal species also have a plexus that works to cool the testes.

Hence, since it doesn't appear as if the real purpose of the scrotum is to keep the testes cooler, what might be its significance? One interesting proposal is that species that lead a very active life – running, jumping, or bounding, for example, have scrotal testes, while species that have quiet life, have internal testes. Sea lions and walruses, which have scrotal testes, lead vigorous lives in defending territory and fighting for mates. "Earless" seal species, which do not have scrotal testes, do not fight for their mates and do not defend their territories.

But what's the connection between scrotal testes and an active life? One possibility is that scrotal testes prevent the expulsion of sperm from physical activity that generates abdominal pressure. The bladder has a sphincter, effectively a one-way valve, which prevents the urine from leaking out continually. The male reproductive tract does not have a sphincter, and leakage of sperm from vigorous physical activity is minimized by having the testes outside of the body.

There is still another interesting observation about the scrotum. In most men, the right testis is larger than the left, and higher up in the scrotum. We don't know the explanation for this difference, but the Greeks sculptors were aware of this asymmetry because they correctly placed the right testis higher, but very often, and incorrectly the left testis was placed higher than the right.

The ejaculate – semen quality

The fertilizing ability of an ejaculate is assessed by several parameters. The table below lists the most common ones. The sperm count, measured as number of sperm per milliliter (ml) (1 ounce equals about 30 milliliters), is one of the most important measures of fertilization potential. The sperm count for normal fertility varies from 20 million per ml (in about 5% of men) to 250 million per ml (in about 5% of men), with the majority of men having counts of 60 to 160 million per ml. Although sperm counts are quite variable, the likelihood of conceiving does not increase with the sperm count, and remains fairly constant as long as the sperm count is over 20 million per ml. A male is said to be subfertile if the sperm count is between 1 and 20 million per ml, and infertile if his sperm count is below 1 million per ml. Despite these definitions there are documented cases of fertility of males whose sperm count was 100,000 per ml. However, the couples in these examples tried to get pregnant for up to 12 years. These cases suggest that although the probability of conception per intercourse decreases as the sperm count decreases below 20 million/ml, over a long period of trials, a conception is possible.

Table 3.1	Normal Parameters for Evaluating Semen Quality			
Semen Parameters		Normal	Marginal	Abnormal
Sperm count (106/ml)		20-250	10-20	< 10
Sperm motility (%)		>50	40-50	< 40
Normal sperm morphology (%)		>50	40-50	< 40
Volume (ml)		2-5	1-2	< 1

Sperm motility, in particular, the ability of sperm in a culture dish to alternate between two types of movements – more or less in one direction and switching suddenly into moving in circles (hyperactivated motility) is required for normal male fertility. For normal fertility the fraction of sperm exhibiting this type of motility should be greater than 50%. The fertilizing potential of the ejaculate decreases significantly if the fraction of non-motile sperm approaches 50%. The fraction of non-motile sperm may also be affected by the duration of sexual abstinence, that is, the length of time the sperm spend in the epididymis (see Appendix 1) before being ejaculated. For this reason, the European Society of Human Reproduction and Embryology (ESHRE) recommends an abstinence time of 3-4 days for semen analysis in cases of infertility examinations.

Sperm morphology is another important determinant of fertilizing potential. Different types of abnormalities are seen even in normal ejaculates. Abnormalities commonly seen in normal ejaculates include sperm with abnormally large or small heads, sperm with short tails, or sperm with two heads and/or two tails. Even more complicated morphologies are seen in ejaculates of men with teratospermia, ones characterized by a high frequency of morphologically abnormal sperm. Compared to other species, humans tend to have a large fraction of the abnormal sperm. In a species such as a bull, for example, 5 percent or less abnormal sperm is considered normal; higher values would disqualify a bull for stud purposes. In humans, a species not selected for high fertility, the fraction of abnormal sperm can be quite variable, and the quantitative relationship between the fraction of abnormal sperm and functional deficiency is not clear. Probably a value of greater than 50 percent abnormal sperm would be considered to compromise the sperm quality.

The volume and composition of the ejaculate are also important parameters in determining overall fertility. Ejaculate volumes of 2 to 5 ml are considered normal for humans, and volumes less than 2 ml or greater than 5 ml are associated with subfertility. It is interesting to note that ejaculate volumes, as well as the number of sperm per ejaculate, vary significantly among mammalian species. Humans do not appear to enjoy any unusual status in this regard. The highest recorded ejaculate volumes (500 ml) have been observed in the wild boar, a remarkable circumstance given its relatively small size. This may explain why the boar was such a powerful totem in many societies familiar with the species.

Most of the ejaculate volume consists of seminal fluid contributed primarily by the seminal vesicles and the prostate, while the testes and the bulbourethral glands contribute less than 10 percent of the ejaculate volume. Each of these four tissues contributes characteristic compounds. For example, the seminal vesicle marker is fructose, a sugar that provides the energy reservoir for the sperm in the ejaculate. Hence, absence of a particular component in the ejaculate is indicative of abnormality in the tissue that provides that component.

The plight of sperm – are men in trouble?

Investigations of the adverse influence of 'xenobiotics' – molecules that are foreign to biological systems – on male reproduction have turned up more evidence, of various kinds, that all is not well in the man's world (2, R. J. Aitken, P. Koopman, and S.E.M. Lewis (2004) Seeds of concern)

Several recent studies have suggested that the sperm count in some countries has been decreasing since World War II. In a comprehensive summary of 61 studies involving a total of 14,947 European men, the sperm count between 1938 and 1990 was found to have decreased from 113 million per ml to 66 million per ml. These and other studies suggest that the decline in sperm counts is greater in Europe and Australia (3% per year), than in the U. S. (1.5% per year), or non-Western societies where little or no decline has been observed (the conclusion from non-Western societies is more problematic because sperm count data is much more limited).

An additional finding from the European studies is that the decline in semen quality (sperm count and motility) is determined by the date of birth, with men being born before 1959 having higher motile sperm counts. One of the perplexing observations from more recent studies is that the decrease in sperm count is not geographically or regionally uniform. Denmark, for example, appears to have suffered a greater decline than other European countries. Indeed, the first indications of significant changes in the sperm count came from studies carried out in Denmark in the 1970s. In one study 25% of 19-year-old Danish men had sperm counts in the subfertile range (less than 20 million per ml).

On the other hand, the sperm count in Finland, with a climate and level of socioeconomic development similar to that of Denmark, appears not to have undergone any change. The average sperm count of Finnish men appears to be higher than Danish men. In the U. S. fertile men in one agricultural area of Missouri were found to have sperm counts 40% lower than the average in three urban areas. All of these studies have generated considerable controversy and have been criticized on many grounds, and some investigators question the reliability of the date and conclusions.

However, what adds credibility to the decrease in sperm count in the minds of many investigators is its correlation with an array of pathological changes collectively grouped under the umbrella known as testicular dysgenesis syndrome (TDS). The main characteristics of TDS are poor semen quality, testicular cancer, cryptorchidism (failure of the testes to descend into the scrotum), and malformations of the external genitalia, such as hypospadias (failure of the urethral folds to fuse properly during the development of the penis, resulting in the external opening of the urethra being on the underside of the penis, rather than at the tip). The worldwide increase in the incidence of TDS may reflect a global deterioration of male reproductive health.

The incidence of testicular cancer, for example, which in contrast to other cancers, is a cancer of young men, has doubled in all the industrialized countries during the period 1970 to 2000. That the decline in sperm count and rise in testicular cancer may be causally related is suggested by the fact that Danish men not only have the lowest sperm counts in Europe, but they also have the highest incidences of testicular cancer and hypospadias. In contrast, the incidence of testicular cancer in Finland is nearly three-fold lower, sperm counts are the highest in the world, and genital malformations are rare.

Taken at face value, these different studies indicate that a decline in male reproductive health may be taking place in some, but not all regions of the world. There is no general agreement about the nature of the factors that might account for the differences. The Danish investigators whose studies first brought this complex question to scientific attention have suggested that the decline could be due to exposure during pregnancy to a variety of chemicals that have been shown to behave as estrogen agonists or as androgen antagonists. The supposition is that such compounds may interfere with normal male sexual development during the fetal period when the internal and external genitalia develop. Denmark, which industrialized much before Finland, would have experienced a higher and longer exposure to such putative endocrine-interfering substances than Finland.

However, other geographical regions that industrialized early do not appear to have experienced similar decreases in sperm count. Another recent suggestion is that maternal smoking may interfere with normal male development. Maternal smoking has been suggested as a possible way to account for the differences between Denmark and Finland. The smoking rates among Finnish women have been significantly lower than in other countries at least until the late 1980s. There is some evidence from studies with animals to suggest that maternal smoking can affect the fertility of both male and female offspring. No clear-cut data for humans are yet available.

In summary, it seems reasonable to infer that toxic environmental compounds may be responsible for the increase in TDS. The authors of an authoritative review published in 2012 on the status of male reproductive health end their discussion as follows:

In our minds there is little doubt that a large part of the male reproductive health problems that are apparent in men from Western countries are caused by environmental exposures acting prenatally or postnatally on testicular development and function. A clear connection between the diseases and specific toxicants has not been established in humans, most likely because the effects appear after exposure to multiple chemicals and life-style factors. Further research is needed to detect and isolate these underlying factors. In humans, semen quality may be the most sensitive marker of such exposures, and we suggest that standardized surveillance studies of semen quality are continued or initiated to monitor the combined effects of various preventive actions. (3, Loa Nordkap et al Regional differences and temporal trends in male reproductive health disorder: semen quality may be a sensitive marker of environmental exposure)

Sex hormones of the male

The androgens – testosterone and DHT

The post-pubertal testis is not only a prodigious sperm factory but an impressive testosterone factory as well. Most of the testosterone produced remains within the testes, the remaining is transported out into the general circulatory system. The testosterone levels within the testis are more than 50-fold greater than they are in the circulatory system. The presumption is that very high intra-testicular testosterone levels are required to maintain the astronomical levels of daily sperm production.

Another male hormone is dihydrotesterone (DHT). Recall from Chapter 1 the role of DHT in the development of the external genitalia in males. DHT is derived from testosterone and is much more potent than testosterone. This means that DHT can exert its effects at much lower concentrations. However, DHT is found in much lower concentrations than testosterone. The functions of testosterone and DHT are divided in a very interesting way.

Within the testis, the Sertoli cells produce DHT, whereas outside of the testis, the many tissues are responsible for DHT production. Testosterone produced by the testis, is secreted into the blood stream and therefore is available to all cells. The cells that produce DHT (DHT target tissues) are those that produce the enzyme 5-alpha reductase, which converts testosterone to DHT upon the entry of testosterone into the cell. 5-alpha reductase is found in great abundance in the penis, scrotum, and prostate, and is required for the development and growth of these tissues during puberty, as well as their maintenance afterwards.

Table 3.2	Contrasting Functions of Testosterone and Dihydrotestosterone (DHT)	
Stage	Testosterone	DHT
Fetal	Internal genitalia	External genitalia
Infancy	Musculoskeletal development	Maintenance of external genitalia
Childhood	Spermatogenesis	Growth of external genitalia
Puberty and later	Muscle mass increase	Maturation of external genitalia

	Pigmentation of penis and scrotum	Erectile function
	Vocal cord enlargement	Sexual drive (libido)
	Regulates LDL/HDL cholesterol ratio	Body, Facial, and axillary hair
	Regulates synthes is of liver enzymes	Head hair regression
		Prostate gland growth
		Acne

In the post-pubertal male testosterone is absolutely required for spermatogenesis, maintenance of the sexual drive, and for erectile function. DHT is necessary for maintenance of the external genitalia and prostate gland function. Both testosterone and DHT also have a number of important somatic functions. Testosterone, for example, is responsible for the thickening and enlargement of the vocal cords leading to the male's deeper voice. In conjunction with growth hormone, testosterone stimulates skeletal growth during the latter pubertal stages. Testosterone also regulates the synthesis of a number of liver enzymes, including several blood clotting factors, and the ratio of high-density lipoprotein (HDL) to low-density lipoprotein (LDL), which is generally lower in men than in women. This lower ratio may possibly be a factor in the higher incidence of coronary heart disease in men. Certain types of anemia are associated with low testosterone levels, indicating that testosterone may also play a role in the maintenance of hemoglobin levels.

DHT is active in the sebaceous glands of the skin. Sebum production by these cells increases significantly during the onset of puberty resulting in well-known problem of acne. Severe acne is not associated with higher testosterone levels, but instead with an increased conversion of testosterone to DHT in certain cells of the skin. Axillary (underarm) hair and hair in the low pubic area is produced by relatively low androgen levels, and hence, is found in both males and females. On the other hand, higher DHT levels are required to produce hair on the face, chest, and in the upper pubic area, and hence, this type of hair is found normally in post-pubertal males.

Estrogens in the male – a case of serendipity

Is life possible without estrogen? Recall from the previous chapter the great importance of estrogen in the reproductive life of the female. This was not a rhetorical question, but in fact one that was being asked by reproductive biologists in the early 1990s. It was known then that testosterone is not essential for life. The best example of this is androgen insensitivity syndrome (AIS) (see Chapter 10 for a discussion of this syndrome). AIS individuals carry a mutation in the androgen receptor (the androgen receptor is required for all actions of testosterone and DHT), and a consequence of this mutation is that androgen dependent functions cannot be carried out. An AIS individual is genetically male (XY) but looks anatomically like a normal female, and aside from the infertility is perfectly healthy. What was not clear at the time was whether estrogen could also be dispensed with – that is, in the sense that estrogen action was not necessary for life. Estrogen receptors were present in many different non-reproductive tissues, and it seemed plausible to imagine that estrogen action was in some sense a more fundamental than androgen action.

The answer to this question came with the serendipitous discovery in 1994 and 1995 of two very tall young men – both about 28 years old and about 6 ft 8 in. They had gone through normal puberty, were fully masculinized. A unique feature in both of them were highly demineralized bones resulting in osteoporosis, and a bone age of 15 years, the latter meaning that their long bones (legs and arms) were still growing. Clearly this was a very serious condition for both of them.

The important clue about the cause of their condition came with the finding that one of them had normal testosterone levels and significantly elevated estrogen levels. Such high estrogen levels would be expected to result in pronounced feminization of the body (for example, breast development), but none was seen. The high estrogen levels indicated some form of insensitivity to estrogen, which was quickly shown to be due to a mutation in the estrogen receptor gene. Hence, deficiency in estrogen action led to osteoporosis and lack of skeletal maturation.

The second man also had normal testosterone levels, but essentially zero estrogen levels, in his case due to a mutation in the aromatase gene (aromatase is the protein that converts testosterone to estrogen). Hence, the second man is also deficient in estrogen action, but in his case because of estrogen absence. Both men are deficient in estrogen action, and the consequence is the same.

Aromatase deficiency, in contrast to estrogen receptor deficiency, is correctable by administering estrogen. Estrogen supplementation in the aromatase mutant male led to the cessation of skeletal growth and significant increase in bone density. These two cases demonstrate clearly that estrogen is essential for the establishment of peak bone mass in growing boys and for the maintenance of bone mass in adult men.

In males, estrogen excess is manifested by the development of breast tissue, a condition known as gynecomastia. Gynecomastia is seen in about 50% of male infants during the early neonatal period, and is attributed to the high estrogen levels present during gestation. It normally disappears after a few months. Transient breast development, lasting for up to two years, is also observed in about 30 percent of normal pubertal boys, and even in post-pubertal males. Recent studies using careful examination techniques have reported that 36 percent of military recruits had palpable breast tissue, suggesting that gynecomastia may be more prevalent than previously thought.

Breast enlargement is also common in older men. Some estimates indicate that 40 percent or more of males over 50 years of age experience gynecomastia. Any trip to the beach in the summer will convince us of this. Several factors contribute to this effect. Although not understood, estrogen production in peripheral tissues increases as the male ages. In some cases the accumulation of adipose (fat) tissue with age is an important contributing factor. Adipose tissue contributes a substantial fraction of the circulating estrogens in males, and gynecomastia is seen more frequently in overweight or obese males.

Infrequently, gynecomastia can also be produced by disturbances in steroid hormone synthesis, various disease states, tumors, and other conditions that lead to an increase in the overall estrogen levels. In rare cases, breast cancer can develop. A few rather bizarre cases have also been reported. One interesting case concerned a mortician who began developing breasts. It turned out that the source of the estrogen was the cream that he applied to the face of the bodies to make them "look better." Such creams contain estrogens, and in the case of the mortician, when applied with the ungloved hand, estrogen in the cream was absorbed through the skin. The increased estrogen levels were responsible for the development of breasts in the mortician. Gynecomastia underscores the essential similarity between male and female breast tissue. Indeed, with proper hormonal stimulation the male breast could be made to produce milk.

Performance-enhancing drugs - the ergogenic aids dilemma

. . . think only of the ambition of men, and you will wonder at the senselessness of their ways, unless you consider how they are stirred by the love of an immortality of fame. They are ready to run all risks greater far than they would have run for their children, and to spend money and undergo any sort of toil, and even to die, for the sake of leaving behind them a name which shall be eternal (4, Diotima's dialogue in Plato Symposium)

Anabolic steroids and their cousins

No one who reads the sports pages or watches the sports networks nowadays can doubt that many elite athletes, as well as those who want to become elite athletes, are using what are often called performance-enhancing drugs. Everyone is shocked, shocked, as Chief of Police, Captain Renault of Casablanca fame would say by the almost daily new revelations, accusations, and emphatic denials. Today, performance-enhancing drugs come in a wide array of compounds and have quite different physiological effects.

In the clinical literature drugs taken by athletes in the belief that they will improve performance are referred to as ergogenic aids. It is estimated that athletes today can choose from an array of over 150 substances, with new ones are being introduced every year. A short list of the different types of ergogenic aids in use are the anabolic steroids, synthetic compounds that behave as testosterone agonists (that is, they mimic the effects of testosterone), human growth hormone (hGH), erythropoietin (referred to as EPO), creatine, ephedrine, amphetamines, androstenedione (known as Andro), and beta-hydroxy-beta-methylbutyrate (known as HMB). Many other not well-characterized substances are also being used. A short summary of the effects of a few of these compounds is given in the table below.

The modern history of ergogenic aids begins with investigations of the effects of testicular extracts the use of which, as we saw above, became increasingly popular towards the end of the 19th century. Recall that injection of testicular extracts to restore sexual function was commonplace in the latter part of the 19th century. However, a report by two Austrian physiologists in 1896 on the effects of bull testicular extracts in increasing muscle strength may be considered as the first step in opening the anabolic steroid floodgates. The final sentence of their paper – **"The training of athletes offers an opportunity for further research in this area and for a practical assessment of our experimental results" (5)** - can be said to have laid the groundwork for the current widespread use of anabolic steroids. But it was not until 1935 that the active component in the testicular extracts was identified as the hormone testosterone. It took only two years before the first synthetic testosterone analogs made their appearance. During these early years these synthetic testosterone analogs were reserved primarily for treating men who had suffered testicular damage.

Biochemical research reports of the early 1940s began sounding the two themes that dominate much of the discussion regarding androgen use today – *"whether the endurance in man for muscular work could be increased by testosterone" and "whether the reduction of working capacity with age might proceed differently if the sex-hormone concentration could be artificially maintained at a higher level" (5, J.M. Hoberman and C. E Yesalis The history of synthetic testosterone).* The first theme has become what is now the proscribed use of anabolic steroids by athletes, and the second is the promotion of testosterone replacement therapy (TRT) in older males. This latter theme we will tackle Chapter 5.

In the U. S. bodybuilders in the West Coast were perhaps the first group to begin experimenting with different testosterone analogs (compounds that behave like testosterone), probably as a consequence of the publication of Paul de Kruif's book *The Male Hormone* in 1945. News of the effects of these compounds spread quickly to other strength-intensive sports. Despite the bans and fines established for different sports in the 1970s, the use of these compounds has become commonplace not only among Olympic and other professional sports athletes, but also among college and even high school athletes. Anabolic steroids, being testosterone analogs, stimulate protein synthesis in muscle, leading to an increase in the size of muscle cells rather than their number. The primary observed effects are an increase in lean body mass and weight, and a decrease in body fat. An increase in muscle strength is assumed to take place as well, although definitive evidence for this is lacking.

It is interesting to contemplate that in the near future the boundary between the illegitimate and legitimate use of anabolic steroids may blur significantly. The legitimate uses of anabolic steroids since their beginning have been as therapy for testicular dysfunction. Another legitimate use – as a male contraceptive – may be a possibility. If a drug regimen of this type is eventually approved as a contraceptive, it will be relatively easy for athletes to claim that they are using anabolic steroids as contraceptives. In one easy step, the illegitimate use of an anabolic steroid will have been converted to legitimate use.

Most of the other ergogenic aids are used because of their purported effects with respect to increased oxygen utilization from the blood, boosting metabolic rate, or increasing endurance. It should be stated that although these compounds may have the physiological effects indicated in the table below, there is little evidence from controlled studies that they improve performance. Athletes take them with the hope or conviction that their use will improve their performance.

Table 3.3 ***Ergogenic (Performance Enhancing) Compounds***

Name	Desired effect	Adverse Side Effect
Anabolic steroids	Increase muscle mass, strength decrease body fat	Liver damage, hypertension, cardiac damage, testicular atrophy, aggression, depression, atherosclerosis
HGH	Stimulate body growth	muscle damage
Erythropoietin	Increases endurance, depression, increases oxygen-carrying capacity of blood	heart attacks, pulmonary embolism
Creatine	Increased strength /Performance	Dehydration, long-term effects not known
HMB	Suppresses protein Breakdown	Uknown
Amphetamines	Increased endurance	Anxiety, hypertension, hallucinations, heart Damage, addiction, death
Ephedrine	Increases alertness, Increases Endurance, increases metabolism	Anxiety, hypertension, hallucinations, addiction
Andro	May lead to increased Testosterone	Unknown, possible cardiovascular risk

The important question about these substances from a medical perspective is - are they harmful or not? Or, perhaps a better way to phrase the question - what is their risk / benefit equation? Unfortunately, since the use of these compounds is officially banned, no comprehensive large-scale studies have been carried out to evaluate their side effects. Nevertheless, the information from many individual case studies and a few small-scale studies that is available indicates that the side effects can be serious. Their severity of the effects varies widely among individuals, probably depending on the particular compound, the dose, the length of time they use it, and the mixture of substances that they may be using. The side effects are generally well known among athletes, but probably everyone who contemplates taking one or more of these substances thinks he/she will be the exception, or that the perceived benefits will outweigh the risks. Many who used these types of substances in the past, such as Arthur Schwarzenegger, former bodybuilder and movie star, and former governor of California, have no regrets.

The use of ergogenic aids will probably continue into the foreseeable future despite the bans, the testing, and negative commentary from many sports writers. Most obviously, the financial rewards, the fame that comes from excelling in a particular sport, and the adulation by sports fans may be a sufficient incentive. Diotima had it right. But there may be an additional motivation – the all too human desire to push physical performance and endurance to its limits. How else to explain physically disabled and even blind individuals who want to climb mountains that would difficult for the ordinary person, or those who swim in extremely cold waters, or sail around the world in flimsy boats. Our history is full of adventurers, intrepid souls, and even assorted lunatics who have pushed themselves to their limits, and quite often societies reward them with fame and remembrance. This desire to extend our limits is universal. Maybe the term ergogenic aids is an appropriate one – aids that help us extend our limits.

Gene doping – the next frontier

We all know that athletic ability is more than simple discipline and hard training. If it were that simple, many more of us would become star athletes. From our high school days, for example, we may remember the ones who excelled as sprinters, or as long distance runners, or as gymnasts, or as weight lifters. Most of them had not earned their ability, but in fact had been born with it. You may recall the story of Hercules who in protecting himself from the goddess Hera strangled a snake in each hand while still an infant. We probably dismissed this story as a fable, but we may have reconsider after we learn that the *New England Journal of Medicine* in 2004 published the description of an unusually muscular young boy.

At birth he was "extraordinarily muscular, with protruding muscles in his thighs and upper arms". At four years of age he continued to have a significantly enlarged muscle mass, and was much stronger than the average 4-year-old. Several member of his mother's family are all very strong as well, and his mother was a former Olympic athlete. The child and the other members of his family are strong because they carry a mutation in the myostatin gene, a gene whose effects were already known from studies in the 1990s of two lines of cattle – Belgian Blue and Piedmontese – with exaggerated musculature. These "double-muscled" cattle also carry naturally occurring mutations in the mysostatin gene. In these cases, the mutation knocks out the function of the myostatin protein. The child of the 2004 article carries the first disabling myostatin mutation known in humans.

It is important to keep in mind what is meant by this. For example, all of us have a myostatin gene. Only a mutation in the gene that results in a defective myostatin protein is associated with increased muscle mass and strength. This explains why most of us have normal musculature. We don't yet fully understand why the absence of myostatin function leads to increased muscle mass. With this understanding clinicians working with muscle degenerative disorders, such as muscular dystrophy, are testing compounds that inhibit the action of the normal myostatin protein. Animal experiments have shown that muscle mass can be increased in animal models of muscular dystrophy.

Those interested in performance enhancement have not been left behind, and several products claiming myostatin inhibition, none of them FDA approved, have appeared on the market. None of them have been validated, but it is quite likely that they will soon enter the ergogenic aids formulary.

These examples tell us that athletic performance is to a very large part determined by genes that enhance speed, endurance, strength, and power. A systematic search for genes that influence muscle structure, composition, and function began in the 1990s, and since then more than 90 candidate genes have been identified. Most of these are still "candidates" because the full complement of studies that would really demonstrate their function has not been carried out yet. About 6 – 8 of these genes have been studied further, and they fall into two types – cardiorespiratory and skeletal muscle function genes.

One of these has an interesting history. Eero Mäntyranta, the Olympic gold medalist (two medals in 1964) Finnish cross-country skier, was known for his extraordinary endurance. In fact, several members of his family were also champion endurance skiers. Many years later, they were all found to carry mutations in a gene that provided excessive response to erythropoietin, which resulted in very high numbers of oxygen carrying red blood cells, and hence, explained their endurance ability. The effect of this mutation greatly exceeded those that have been measured in tests with EPO taken by many athletes.

Other genes that have been associated with individual athletes are ACTN3, associated with enhanced muscle function, ACEI/D, two variants of the ACE gene associated with endurance and sprint power, CKMM, M235T, and Ar2B2 associated with cardiac output and oxygen uptake. We will probably be hearing much more of these and other genes in the next few years. It seems likely that elite athletes owe a large part of their success to having inherited the enhanced variants of some of these genes.

Much of the current research on some of these genes has a therapeutic rationale, particularly in the treatment of muscle degenerative diseases. The focus is on "gene therapy", that is, the introduction of genes into the damaged tissue to replace non-functional genes. Although this type of work is in its infancy, the expectations are that in the next few decades gene therapy will become part of the arsenal for a variety of diseases due to non-functional genes, not only muscle disorders.

You can see that it is only a short step to pass from therapeutics to enhancement – gene therapy to enhance muscle strength, muscle agility, cardiac output, or any other function that will improve athletic performance. Once the technical hurdles have been worked out, gene therapy for athletes is inevitable. Will it be permitted? If not, how would you prevent it? How would you detect it?

What will be the long-term consequences of gene therapy? We tend to focus on the positive, but in fact there may be serious health risks and unpredictable effects. At this stage we don't have enough information to be able to predict in a reasonable way the severity of the risks.

Much of the sentiment against the use of ergogenic aids has been based on the ideal of a level playing field for all competitors. This has been a constant theme of many sports commentators and many politicians. This ideal is really an illusion - athletic and other types of ability have not been distributed uniformly – the playing field was always stacked in favor of those who had an intrinsic, usually genetic advantage over others. *"Is it really reasonable that athletes should make do with bodies that have not been enhanced?" (6, A sporting chance)* is a question that has been asked over and over.

Those who support performance enhancement with drugs or gene therapy argue that ergogenic aids and gene therapy provide a way of leveling the field. Recent calls for allowing ergogenic aids in sport have pointed out that legislation of drugs in sport may be fairer and safer than the clandestine drugging that occurs now, and that like earlier prohibitions on women and remuneration which in retrospect made no sense, drug prohibitions also makes no sense.

Chapter 4

The Pubertal Coming of Age

Why the long drawn-out process of childhood growth before the final physiological frenzy of the adolescent growth spurt and reproductive maturation? (1, Peter T. Ellison On Fertile Ground)

How many of us remember our own puberty? Momentous and remarkable changes take place in our bodies and also in our brains, but possibly because the changes take place so imperceptibly our memory of them escapes us. If we do remember something about our puberty, what is it that we remember? Females may remember especially the first menstruation – known as menarche. The loss of blood may have been quite scary and possibly even slightly traumatic, even if her mother or sisters had prepared her for it. Boys do not experience anything like menarche, certainly nothing as overt and public. Perhaps the nearest equivalent would be the nocturnal ejaculations – the so-called "wet dreams" – that characterize the pubertal transition in boys. Most boys don't understand them. What we were told and read in pamphlets provided by our parish church was that they were due to 'impure thoughts'. And, of course, no matter that I resolved to abolish impure thoughts from my mind, I knew the next morning that I had not been successful.

The enigma of puberty

The more we come to understand about puberty, the more we come to appreciate what a momentous change it represents. In fundamental ways puberty is a metamorphosis, perhaps not as visibly dramatic as the transformation of a caterpillar into a butterfly, but a metamorphosis nonetheless, for we literally shed our childhood skin and take on the adult skin. The pubertal metamorphosis is not only irreversible (for we can never recover the child that we once were), but often we emerge as someone unrecognizable, almost as if the adult had no past in the child. How these mind-boggling changes take place remains the true enigma of puberty.

Our understanding of puberty has progressed in two stages. The first stage has involved a description, or a cataloguing of the visible changes that take place, for example, in the reproductive tissues, the changes in hormones, and way in which our growth and the shape of the body is modified. We understand now that these changes are a consequence of a cascade of events that begin with the maturation of the gonads in preparation for fertility, the large increase in gonadal steroid hormone levels, which in turn orchestrate the transformation of the child's body into an adult's. These are the physical changes. No less important are the behavioral and psychological changes, probably also driven by the action of gonadal steroid hormones in the brain, that take place during a fairly long drawn-out period generally referred to as adolescence. The cataloguing of the physical and behavioral changes is fairly straightforward.

What is much more difficult is the second stage - to understand their causes, and the details of how the changes come about. Some progress has been made, and we do know a few things. We know, for example, that the proximate trigger for the initiation of puberty comes from the hypothalamus in the form of the reactivation of the gonadotropin-releasing hormone (GnRH) pacemaker after a long quiescent period during childhood, but for the most part we don't know how the activation is brought about (see Appendix 1 for a discussion of the GnRH pacemaker, the master regulator of the reproductive system). We have a reasonable understanding of the conditions that need to be met before puberty can begin, but we know very little about how those conditions are translated into the hormonal signals that initiate puberty, or what the ultimate trigger for puberty is. We don't really know if a central 'puberty clock', hard-wired into our brain, as has been suggested by some neuroscientists, controls the initiation of puberty and regulates the metamorphosis. This is the main challenge today.

So let's begin our exploration of the puberty drama.

The puberty drama – preparation for fertility

In the female

"I can never forget my experience. It was that day when I realized that I could not escape from the fact that I am a woman. All my life I tried to show others that I am very tough. I wore pants, trousers all the time. When I got my period, I used to hide it badly. I did everything to prove that it's not an issue at all. I didn't want anyone to know" (2, Ayse K. Uskul Women's menarche stories from a multicultural sample)

The first signs of puberty in the female are the growth of the breasts and appearance of pubic hair. These changes take place gradually over a period of about four years. In the initial years these changes are due to increased secretion of estrogens and androgens from the adrenal glands, and not the ovaries. Clinicians divide these changes into five steps, known as the Tanner stages, with pre-puberty being stage 1, puberty itself, stages 2-4 and post-puberty, stage 5. Table 4.1 summarizes the features that characterize the Tanner stages in girls. Although there is a mean age for each Tanner stage, every individual follows her own "puberty clock". That is, the timing of these stages can vary greatly from one individual to another without being considered abnormal. For example, the normal variation in the timing of Tanner 2 is from 8 – 15 years.

Table 4.1	Tanner Stages of Breast and Pubic Hair Development

Breast

	Stage	Mean age	Range (years)
I.	Prepubertal; slight elevation of papilla		
II.	Elevation of breast and papilla; areola diameter increases	11.2	9.0 - 11.3
III.	Enlargement of breast tissue; no separation of breast and areola	12.2	10.0 - 14.3
IV.	Areola and papilla form a secondary mound above the level of the breast	13.1	10.8 - 15.3
V.	Mature stage; erect papilla projecting above areola	15.3	11.9 - 18.8

Pubic Hair

	Stage	Mean age	Range (years)
I.	Prepubertal; no pubic hair		
II.	Sparse, curly, pigmented hair appearing along the lower labia	11.7	9.3 - 14.1
III.	Spread of darker, coarser hair across the lower pubis	12.4	10.2 - 14.6
IV.	Abundant adult type hair, but limited to labia area	13.0	10.8 - 15.1
V.	Spread of pubic hair to form an inverted triangle; spread of hair along the upper inner thigh	14.4	12.2 - 16.7

Reference: Tanner, 1962; Marshall and Tanner, 1969.

The ovaries also mature during this period, and they begin to prepare for the production of the egg. In girls, this occurs in two stages, first menstruation and then ovulation. The age at menarche, the first menstruation, marks the time at which the ovary has begun its cyclic production of estrogen and progesterone. Recall from Chapter 3 the roles of estrogen and progesterone in menstruation. For all traditional societies menarche has been a source of fascination, and in many cases has been celebrated in elaborate ways.

The age at menarche is also quite variable, varying not only from individual to individual, but from one population group to another. For example, the current average age at menarche for all girls in the U. S. is 12.43 years, while the menarcheal ages for Caucasian, African-American and Mexican-American girls are 12.55, 12.06 and 12.25 years, respectively. There has been much concern in the last two or three years about what appears to be a trend toward earlier initiation of puberty in the U. S., especially among African-American girls. The reports indicate that Tanner 2 stage is being seen in girls as young as 6 or 7. However, the age of menarche does not appear to show this downward trend. Since the early stages of puberty are due to adrenal steroid hormones, it is not at all clear how to account for the early stimulation of adrenal function in these girls.

The initiation of menstrual cycles does not mean, however, that the girl is fertile. This is because the menstrual cycles during the first year after menarche are anovulatory, meaning that no ovulation takes place. True ovulatory cycles, and therefore fertility, begin to be established about 1 - 2 years after menarche. Even then, not all cycles are ovulatory. Ovulation requires a fairly stringent collaboration between the ovary, the pituitary, and the GnRH pacemaker, and this takes some time to be established.

In the male

Tell me why this hair grows out of my face,
my stupid face with its big nose
and volcanic skin breaking out in moon-size craters . . .?
And what should I do about the shaggy flower
that blooms around my balls, or my secret risings and fallings? (3, Alan
Soldofsky Thirteen)

The Tanner stages in boys, summarized in Table 4.2, focus on the growth of the penis and scrotum, and the growth and development of pubic hair. As with girls the age at which the initial pubertal changes take place varies considerably from boy to boy, the norm being 9 – 15 years. Fertility in boys also develops gradually. Boys begin to experience spontaneous erections at about the age of 12, spontaneous nocturnal ejaculations at 13. During the next year or two, the ejaculate contains no sperm. Sperm production begins to take place on average at about 15 years. Again it is important to keep in mind that these are mean ages. The "puberty clock", that is, the ages at which the different events take place varies from one person to another. However, the sequence of changes is the same in all persons.

Table 4.2	Tanner Stages of External Genitalia and Pubic Hair in Males

External Genitalia

	Stage	Mean age	Range (years)
I.	Prepubertal		
II.	Enlargement of scrotum and testes; scrotum becomes pigmented	11.6	9.0 - 14.7
III.	Growth of penis; continued growth of scrotum and testes	12.9	10.3 - 15.5
IV.	Increase in length and breadth of penis; growth of glans penis	13.8	11.2 - 16.3
V.	Adult size and shape	14.9	12.2 - 17.7

Pubic Hair

	Stage	Mean age	Range (years)
I.	Prepubertal; no pubic hair		
II.	Sparse growth of slightly curled hair along the base of the penis	13.4	10.8 - 16.0
III.	Spread of darker, coarser hair above penis	13.9	11.4 - 16.5
IV.	Abundant adult type of hair, but limited to genitalia	14.4	11.7 - 17.1
V.	Adult hair in type and quantity;	15.2	12.5 - 17.9

The puberty drama – secondary changes

Somatic changes, skeletal growth and maturation

Other important changes not involving the breasts and reproductive tissues also take place, and these are called the secondary sex characteristics. These are summarized in Table 3. One of the most unusual is the growth spurt, a two to three year period of accelerated skeletal growth. The growth spurt is unusual because it seems to be unique to humans. In other mammalian species puberty is accompanied by weight gain, but not in skeletal growth. Although the growth spurt occurs in both sexes, we see from Table 4.3 that females initiate their growth spurt typically on the average about two years before boys (10 years versus 12 years). We see this quite vividly by observing students at any junior high school. However, girls reach their final height at about 16 years, while boys may continue growing into the late teens.

Table 4.3 Secondary Sexual Characteristics in Females and Males Associated with Puberty.

Individuals can vary greatly in the timing of these changes without being abnormal.

Females

Change	Mean age
Initiation of growth spurt and deposition of fat	10
Widening of the pelvis	11
Growth and maturation of the internal genitalia and vagina	12
Axillary hair begins to appear	13
Skeletal growth decreases; sweat and sebaceous gland development, sometimes accompanied with acne; first ovulation	14
Voice deepens slightly	15
Adult height reached	16
Males	
Initiation of androgen production after childhood quiescence	10
Fat deposition begins	11
Skeletal growth begins; spontaneous erections; growth of seminal vesicles and prostate gland	12
Spontaneous nocturnal ejaculations begin	13
Growth of vocal cords and deepening of voice; appearance of axillary hair and hair on upper lip	14
First fertile ejaculation	15

Appearance of chest , body, and facial hair; sweat and sebaceous glands develop, often with acne; loss of body fat	16
Muscle growth and increase in muscle strength; broadening of shoulders	17
Adult height may be reached; although often growth may continue into the early twenties.	18
Reference: Marshall and Tanner, 1969; Marshall and Tanner, 1970; Reynolds and Wines, 1948; Reynolds and Wines, 1951.	

In both sexes the growth spurt is initiated by androgens, although estrogens probably also have an essential role. Androgens and estrogens are produced in the initial stages of puberty by the adrenal glands. The main function of the adrenals is to secrete the glucocorticoids hormones, such as cortisol, that are necessary for metabolism of carbohydrates. However, the adrenals begin estrogen and androgen production before the ovaries or the testes, and adrenal sex steroids are responsible for the initial growth of the breasts, penis and scrotum, and the appearance of pubic hair. Gradually, the ovaries and the testes begin to take over production of these hormones.

In girls the growth spurt occurs earlier because in the early stages of ovarian maturation the ratio of androgens to estrogens is high. Although the most obvious feature of the growth spurt in girls is growth in height, skeletal growth also involves the restructuring and widening of her pelvis. Pelvic widening may be one of the really critical events that prepare a girl for reproduction. Androgens are also responsible for the appearance of pubic and axillary (underarm) hair, and the development of sweat and sebaceous glands. As the ovary matures estrogen levels increase and bring to an end to the growth spurt. In boys skeletal growth is also accompanied by changes in the body – broadening of the shoulders, increase in muscle mass and strength, appearance of axillary, facial, and chest hair, and deepening of the voice – all of which are due principally to androgens.

Ovarian estrogens are responsible for changes in body composition and shape, particularly the deposition of fat and subtle rounding of the body contours that eventually convert the body of a girl to that of a woman. Fat deposition also takes place in boys in the beginning stages of puberty, but in later stages a loss of fat takes place. Androgens stimulate muscle growth in both sexes in the initial stages of puberty, but because of their higher androgen levels, boys accumulate significantly more muscle tissue.

Final cessation of growth in both sexes, known as skeletal maturation, depends on estrogen. The earlier pubertal spurt in girls and also the younger age at which skeletal maturation occurs is due primarily to the fact that estrogen levels begin to increase earlier and reach higher levels earlier than in males. Female or male patients with a deficiency in estrogen action exhibit continued skeletal growth, and they continue increasing in height long after the normative ages when skeletal growth ceases in either sex. Their bone age is younger than their chronological age. Patients with deficiency of estrogen action also suffer from osteoporosis, that is, very weak and brittle bones due to the loss of calcium from the bone, demonstrating the essential role of estrogen in bone mineralization.

Patients with an excess of estrogen, on the other hand, have an advanced bone age and are short, due to early skeletal maturation, and also have increased bone density. All these studies make evident the multiple roles that estrogen plays in skeletal growth and bone metabolism in both males and females.

Nutrition has important effects on pubertal growth. Malnutrition leads to the inhibition of skeletal growth as well as the pubertal growth spurt. In obese individuals growth increases even though growth hormone levels decrease below normal levels. Indeed, there are cases of patients with an absolute growth hormone deficiency that still continue to grow. The mechanism for this effect is not well understood.

Acne – universal rite of passage?

In fact, acne may be a secondary sexual trait, albeit one that is temporary, and acting in the opposite direction from that normally encountered. (4, Dale F. Bloom (2004) Is acne really a disease?)

We all welcome the pubertal changes because we see them as signs of becoming adults. One change that isn't welcomed, however, is the scourge of all adolescents - acne. For many of us acne makes our life (and our mother's) miserable, and much money is spent in seeing dermatologists and trying different remedies. Most of the time we just have to suffer it out.

Probably most adolescents (estimates range from 85 – 100%) suffer from acne at some time during their teenage years. Persistent acne affects 23 to 50% of the teenage population, but males are more likely to suffer from moderate to severe cases of acne. However, females are more vulnerable to the negative psychological effects of acne. This is not unexpected given the greater importance for females in having unblemished skin. The common type of acne peaks at about 18 years and has generally disappeared by the mid-twenties. Some types of acne persist into the 40s. Acne is also expensive – probably over a billion dollars a year is spent in the U. S. on acne treatments.

We don't yet understand fully the causes of acne (there may be several), but a likely possibility is that acne arises from an abnormal response of the sebaceous glands in the skin and associated hair follicles to the surge of androgens during puberty. The sebaceous glands produce an oily secretion – sebum - for the skin and hair. They are formed during fetal life, but they develop and mature during puberty, and they tend to predominate in the forehead and face. In the skin the localized conversion of circulating testosterone by the sebaceous glands to DHT (dihydrotestosterone) stimulates the secretion of sebum. Excess production of sebum leads to a localized inflammatory reaction, and secondarily, to the proliferation of a skin bacterium (known as Propionibacterium acnes).

Hence, acne may be seen as an inflammatory response, and the proliferation of the bacteria P. acnes is not the cause of acne, but a consequence of it. Individuals with moderate to severe cases of acne probably do not have higher levels of DHT, but rather may be more sensitive to its stimulatory effects. Treatments for acne are aimed at interfering with the different processes through which acne develops. For example, antibiotic therapy is aimed at eliminating the proliferation of the skin bacterium.

Although we tend to think of acne as a disease, its near universality has suggested to some evolutionary biologists that it may be a normal physiological process. But if so, what is its significance? One interesting suggestion is that because acne appears during the adolescence period and distorts the appearance of the sufferer, making them less attractive to a potential mate, acne may function as a device to scare them off, until the adolescent period is over and the person is sufficiently mature to be a parent. This idea is quite likely completely wrong, but at least now you know what to tell your adolescent when he or she is going through the agony of acne! Will it be any comfort, however?

Adolescence – when does it end?

A well-known quip from the 1990s – adolescence before the 1990s began at 13 and ended at 19, but in the 1990s it begins at 13 and ends at 30.

Although this was a tongue-in-cheek commentary on the times when adult children were returning to live with their parents, it may have held more than a grain of truth. The reference was to the relatively long time after puberty that seems to be required for full adult maturity, the period generally referred to as adolescence. Adolescence, then, is not the same as puberty. Puberty defines the physiological maturation of the reproductive system, and for many reproductive biologists puberty ends when bone growth ceases. Adolescence, on the other hand, encompasses a physiological, psychological, behavioral, and social transformation whose purpose is to convert us into adults. Because of the multitude of changes it is more nebulous, and we can only describe it in very general terms.

In evolutionary terms adolescence is a new kid on the block, appearing probably less than half a million years ago with the emergence of our own species. Perhaps the most striking change that takes place during adolescence is the growth and development of the prefrontal cortex part of the brain, a region very undeveloped in our primate relatives and also in children. Many crucial aspects of adult cognition and behavior are rooted in the prefrontal cortex – memory, complex problem solving, goal-directed behavior, planning and organization, control of impulses and emotions, responding to danger – and changes in our brains that give us those properties are acquired during the adolescent period. In our hunter-gatherer past, adolescents even if reproductively mature, remained dependent on parental or tribal resources until they became neurologically mature, and able to function independently. Half a million years later, this still appears to be true.

For neuroscientists the major challenge is to understand how this growth and remodeling of the prefrontal cortex is controlled. The standard view is that the rising sex steroid hormone associated with the maturing gonads initiate a tremendous proliferation of new neuron pathways and extensive neuronal wiring and rewiring of neuronal pathways in different parts of the central nervous system as well. Although this neural growth and remodeling may initially be dependent on the sex steroid hormones, very quickly environmental and social interactions may in fact become the dominant players - accelerating, intensifying, and modulating the remodeling in infinitely variable ways, so that the particulars of the adolescent transition may be as unique as our genetic inheritance. At this stage we can only guess at the underlying mechanisms.

The adolescent development and growth of the brain has visible and dramatic consequences. We can list some of the changes that developmental psychologists and neuroscientists have noted.

Early adolescence: beginning of concrete thinking and development of moral concepts; progression of sexual identity development (sexual orientation); possible homosexual peer interest; reassessment of body image; start of emotional separation from parents; start of strong peer identification; early exploratory behaviors (smoking, violence)

Mid-adolescence: Beginning of abstract thinking; growing verbal abilities; diminishing ability to learn foreign languages; identification of law with morality; start of fervent ideology (religious, political); increased capacity for making judgments and reasoning ability; strong peer identification; increased risk taking (smoking, alcohol, etc); heterosexual peer interest; early vocational plans.

Late adolescence: Complex abstract thinking; identification of difference between law and morality; increased impulse control; further development of personal identify; development of sexual activity and motivation; expression of sexual orientation and gender identity; further development or rejection of religious and political ideology; development of social autonomy; intimate relationships; development of vocational capability and financial independence

The changes associated with the adolescent transition often lead to conflicts within the family and with other adolescents. Experimenting with drugs, alcohol, sex, challenging the moral and social structures of society also lead to conflicts with the authorities. It is sometimes said that we suffer adolescence twice – once as adolescents ourselves, and later when our children go through it.

When does adolescence end? Given the complexity of the adolescent transformation it is no wonder that there is little agreement about when adolescence ends. Unlike puberty, we don't have a physiological parameter that marks its end. A recent publication, however, makes an interesting, and unexpected proposal. The authors begin by reminding us of something all of us are familiar with – ***"One conspicuous property of adolescence is the apparently unsaturable capacity to stay up late and to sleep in." (5, Till Roenneberger et al A marker for the end of adolescence)*** Eventually this property disappears. They examine this property by focusing on a person's sleep-wake chronotype – the extremes are the late "owls" who stay up late, and the early "larks" who go early to sleep. Then, of course, there are all the in-betweens.

Children are predominantly larks and as they grow they become owls, reaching the maximum owl score at about the age of 20. After 20, they begin to shift back in the direction of larks. Females begin their chronotype shift before males and become maximum owls at 19.5 years, while males do so at 20.9 years. Males typically also continue to be later chronotypes during their adulthood until about the age of 50 (average age of menopause) when the chronotypes of both females and males is about the same. After 65 years the chronotypes of both females and males varies considerably.

The authors suggest that the chronotype transitions reflect changes in the structure and nature of sleep, which in turn is a consequence of the brain remodeling taking place during adolescence. Hence, they suggest that the end of adolescence and the beginning of adulthood occurs at the age when the chronotype stops increasing and begins its downward change, that is, the transition from an owl to a lark, which on the average is about 20 years. This turn around point is variable, which means that some may delay their entry into adulthood past 20.

Possibly these authors have a point.

The puberty drama – the reawakening

Puberty is such a normal process that we may not think of it as mysterious. However, in science, it is generally the most normal of events that turn out to be the most difficult to understand. This certainly applies to puberty. To frame the issue properly we need to remember that puberty is but one stage in the developmental history of the reproductive system, a history that begins early in gestation. During the period from about the end of the sixth to the twentieth week of gestation, all of the components of the reproductive system are formed – the gonads, the pituitary and its secretion of the hormones LH and FSH, and the hypothalamus and its secretion of the master hormone regulator, gonadotropin-releasing hormone (GnRH).

Hence, the most remarkable feature of puberty is that it doesn't a start from scratch, from nothing. In fact, puberty represents the 'reawakening' of the reproductive tissues that were active before we were born and which then entered a long quiescent period. Although it is useful to use the term 'reawakening', in reality the reawakening is not a simple matter at all. Let's consider what happens.

The post-natal sex steroid hormone surge

First, recall that the fetal ovary and testis are active during a good part of gestation. They reach their maximal activity in producing estrogen and androgen around the middle of the second trimester of pregnancy. After that their activity is progressively inhibited so that hormone production by the ovaries and testes decreases to very low levels by the time of birth. Within a few days after birth, however, the ovaries and testes come dramatically to life again. The consequence is a surge of testosterone levels lasting about 6 – 8 months in boys and estrogen lasting 1-2 years in girls. After this post-natal surge, after testosterone and estrogen levels decline to very low levels. They remain low during the rest of infancy and throughout childhood until the beginning of puberty when the ovary and testis begin to awaken from their long childhood slumber.

What is the significance of the post-natal sex hormone surge? Unfortunately, at present we have only a limited understanding of its function. However, a few recent observations indicate that it is necessary for future reproductive success of the individual. In boys, for example, the post-natal androgen surge is absolutely required for the maintenance of the penis and scrotum. In infants in which it does not occur, the penis and scrotum begin to regress and shrink in size shortly after birth, and the testes even retract into the abdominal cavity. Luckily, administering testosterone to the male infants can reverse this regression. In girls the importance of the post-natal estrogen surge is less well understood, but observations indicate that it may represent a 'priming' of the ovary to ensure the later fertility of the girl.

The childhood slumber and reawakening the GnRH pacemaker

Reproductive activity depends ultimately on the synchronous pulsatile release of the hormone GnRH from the hypothalamus (see Appendix 2). This coordinated release of GnRH, known as the GnRH pacemaker, involves perhaps no more than 1000 neurons in a small region of the hypothalamus. Hence, an almost infinitesimally small number of cells, compared to the trillions of cells that make up the body, control one of the most important aspects of our physiology. We now know that the post-natal sex hormone surge, the subsequent inhibition of gonadal activity in later infancy and childhood, and the pubertal activation reflect the activity of the GnRH pacemaker. GnRH does not stimulate the testis or ovary directly, but instead stimulates certain cell groupings in the pituitary to produce the hormones LH and FSH, which in turn the testis and ovary to produce their hormones.

Perhaps one of the most interesting aspects of the reawakening of the GnRH pacemaker is that it begins while we are asleep. During the early Tanner stages, 1 and 2, the hypothalamus begins to fire off its pulses of GnRH as soon as we fall asleep. The pulses of GnRH continue as long as we sleep, and then stop when we awaken. In girls, the GnRH pulses begin to stimulate the ovaries to produce estrogen and progesterone. Estrogen and progesterone then begin to orchestrate the changes in the endometrium that will lead to the first menstruation. In boys the GnRH pulses stimulate the release of testosterone from the testes, and activate other brain centers to produce the spontaneous erections and the nocturnal ejaculations, the "wet-dreams", that all boys experience. As Tanner stage 3 begins the pulses of GnRH begin to appear during our waking hours as well. Gradually, by the end of Tanner stage 4 the adult rhythm of GnRH release is established. Full fertility is established when GnRH is being secreted during the entire day. In girls, ovulation will begin, and in boys, sperm production begins.

The puberty drama – the timing

Anthropologists have long wondered about the interval between birth and puberty in humans, much longer comparatively than in our nearest primate relatives. Why such a long interval? One early response was that it takes the human child a long time to become autonomous. Human societies, even the most primitive by the standards of modern industrialized societies, are extremely complex. Both sexes need to develop the social, linguistic, and intellectual skills to participate in the protection of the offspring. It would make sense then to postpone sexual maturity until all individuals have attained the psychological maturity necessary to participate in the society to which they are born.

Although this idea seemed plausible (perhaps we would like to be true), we know it can't be correct. In most countries in the world now, puberty occurs at least 10 years before the intellectual and psychological maturity necessary for full participation in a society is attained. We have to look elsewhere to understand the timing of puberty.

The short answer is that we don't know. This simple question really defines the profound mystery of puberty. We are still a long way from answering it, but, particularly in the last 30 years or so, some of the important pieces of the puzzle have been identified and we have a general sense of how to approach the question. A reasonable way to begin is to consider two different aspects to the question.

First, what conditions need to be met before puberty occurs? In females, it is fairly clear now that at least two processes - skeletal maturation and energy readiness – are critical determinants of the long birth-puberty interval in humans. The situation for males is less clear. There may be other conditions that also affect the timing of puberty – for example, stress during the childhood period – but these are secondary conditions.

In the female, skeletal maturation and energy readiness define the physiological parameters that permits her to carry a pregnancy to term and have a successful birth. They are permissive conditions for puberty, meaning that puberty will not be initiated unless they are met. Let's consider each in a little more detail.

Skeletal maturation

Skeletal maturation in the female and in the puberty context refers to attaining the appropriate pelvic size that will permit a normal birth. Because of the large head of the human infant, normal birth has always been problematic for females because pelvic size, or more precisely, the size of the birth canal is just barely adequate for the passage of the head. The size of the birth canal is difficult to measure directly, but a useful indirect parameter is the biiliac diameter - the distance between the tops of your hipbones. For adult females the average biiliac diameter is about 27 centimeters, while the threshold diameter for the initiation of puberty appears to be 24-25 centimeters, and menarche typically occurs within a year of reaching the threshold.

The growth of the pelvis takes place as part of skeletal growth, but it includes a remolding of the pelvis to prepare for birth occurs toward the end of skeletal growth. In the long history of the human species, the size and architecture of the birth canal has been the most important structural constraint for a normal birth. The requirement for a threshold pelvic size may be sufficient to account for the long interval between birth and puberty in humans. Our nearest primate relatives, with much smaller infant heads, have comparatively much shorter birth-puberty intervals.

What about males? Boys also undergo enormous skeletal growth during childhood but it would be hard to argue that for them pelvic size is important. Yet, it also appears that the onset of puberty in boys parallels skeletal maturation. For example, conditions that delay skeletal maturation in boys also tend to delay the onset of puberty, whereas conditions that accelerate skeletal maturation tend to hasten the onset of puberty. In population surveys the skeletal parameter most closely correlated with puberty is bone age. In a recent study of disorders that delay or advance puberty boys with the greatest bone age began puberty at the earliest chronological age, whereas boys with the greatest skeletal delay began puberty at the latest age. Furthermore, the magnitude of the skeletal advancement or delay matched the magnitude of the pubertal advancement or delay. In contrast, other maturational processes such as weight, height, or body mass index were not correlated with the onset of puberty.

Energy readiness

Pregnancy is expensive energetically, and a successful pregnancy requires that the female be able to allocate a substantial fraction of her energy stores to the development of the baby growing inside her. The energy requirements for a successful pregnancy are so critical that we can surmise that our successful female ancestors must have been those who had the energy resources – and this means fat - to sustain a pregnancy. Why fat? Well, fat is a very useful way to store energy. During gestation and early childhood, girls and boys generally accumulate fat at the same rate. At puberty, however, males experience a significant decrease in fat content, while the percentage of body fat in females increases significantly. For the female in particular, a fat reservoir may be seen as critically important for the success of a pregnancy.

These considerations led in the 1970s to the "critical weight" hypothesis for the onset of puberty, which proposed that a necessary signal for initiating puberty depended on a critical metabolic parameter in some way related to weight. The critical weight was set at 47 kg (106 lb) because of the observation that the body weight at the time of menarche had remained remarkably constant, at about 47 kg (106 lb) in populations that had experienced a decrease in the age of menarche. Later, critical weight became "critical fat", and the proposal was that a fat reservoir threshold (around 22% - the percentage of body weight due to fat) was necessary before puberty could be initiated.

The hypothesis was eminently plausible, and much circumstantial evidence could be brought in its support. Moderately obese girls tend to have an earlier menarche than thin girls. On the other hand, conditions that reduce her energy reservoir would be expected to delay puberty. Malnutrition, for example, is generally associated with delayed menarche. Puberty is delayed in pre-pubertal anorectic females, but in a re-feeding program the onset of puberty is often correlated with attaining the critical weight.

In historical surveys the importance of adequate food intake and its effects on reproduction had been noted in experimental studies with animals and in observations in humans. Consider a few examples. In Europe and the U. S. since the earliest times that records had been kept the average age of menarche has decreased from 16-17 years to the current 12-13 yeas, a change which generally been attributed to better nutrition. The Lapps are a nomadic people who live in the Arctic regions of Scandinavia. They did not experience the general improvement in living conditions and nutrition as the other people of Scandinavia in the years between 1870 and 1930. And the mean age of menarche did not decrease as it did with other Scandinavians. In the rural areas of Bangladesh, where malnutrition is widespread, menarche occurs 4 to 5 years later than in the more affluent areas. Puberty has occurred at a relatively early age during periods characterized by affluence and prosperity at least for the upper classes. In the fifth and sixth century in Rome, females and males reportedly went through puberty by 12 and 15, respectively. Similarly, wealthy females in seventeenth century Austria underwent puberty between 12 and 13, while their poorer counterparts from the rural areas did so at 17.

There is no doubt then that energy readiness is an important parameter for the initiation of puberty. But it should also be clear that skeletal maturation takes precedence. If it didn't, what would prevent a six or seven year old plump girl from going through puberty or giving birth? The size of the birth canal takes priority over energy because until the birth canal reaches a size that makes a normal birth possible it doesn't really matter whether the female has enough energy stores. Moreover, in epidemiological surveys menarche is more closely correlated with skeletal maturation than with weight or fat content. Energy readiness becomes important once the proper pelvic size has been attained.

The trigger(s)

Identification of the permissive conditions that permit the onset of puberty leads us to the second question: how does the body know when these conditions have been met? Or, what is the mechanism by which the meeting of these conditions is converted into the appropriate hormonal signals that eventually lead to the reactivation of the GnRH pacemaker, subsequent release of LH and FSH from the pituitary, and finally activation of the ovary and testis?

Recall from the previous section that after birth the GnRH pacemaker goes through three stages – post-partum activation, inhibition during childhood, and finally pubertal reactivation. Hence, to understand the pubertal activation we really need to understand the other two parts of the pacemaker's life history. We are still a long way from that. We have a few clues about the hormonal signals required for the pubertal reactivation.

The best known is the hormone leptin, discovered in 1994. Leptin is made in fat cells, and its levels are a measure of the fat content of the body. Obese individuals have high leptin levels, whereas very lean ones have very low leptin levels. The critical fat hypothesis discussed above received strong support with the discovery of leptin since we now had a way of translating fat content into a hormonal signal.

Leptin is involved in regulating food intake and energy expenditure, although we don't yet understand precisely the detailed mechanism. Studies in animals and observations in humans tell us that it must have a role in controlling the onset of puberty. Other studies tell us that leptin must be only one of several signals required for the initiation of puberty. This makes sense, of course, given our understanding for example of the importance of skeletal maturation in both sexes. Hence, we can imagine that in addition to the energy readiness signal(s) – leptin being one of these – there should be a skeletal maturation signal. We don't know yet what that is, but one of the current ideas is that the developing bone secretes an inhibitory signal that prevents the reactivation of the GnRH pacemaker. Once skeletal maturation takes place the inhibitory signal disappears permitting GnRH activation if other conditions have been met, for example, energy readiness.

More than likely there are many other neural signals, independent of skeletal maturation and energy readiness, and recent studies are beginning to identify them. The components of the "puberty clock" are slowly being uncovered.

The puberty drama – too early or too late

Recall that the timing of puberty varies considerably from one person to another. For girls the normal variation is taken to be from 8 to 15, and for boys, 9 to 16. Puberty onset before 8 years in girls or 9 years in boys is known clinically as precocious puberty. Typically in girls this means breast development and growth of pubic hair, and in boys the enlargement of the penis and scrotum and growth of pubic hair. There are documented cases of puberty onset as early as 8 months of age, and there is even one case of a girl of 5 giving birth (stillborn, by Ceasarean section). For unknown reasons, precocious puberty occurs more frequently in girls than in boys.

Many cases of precocious puberty are being reported in the U. S., especially among African-American girls. The features are early breast development and growth of pubic hair – both of which appear to be due to premature adrenal gland activation, the causes of which are unknown. It does not appear, however, that these early signs of puberty also lead to a premature menarche. Obesity may also result in early pubertal features.

Most cases of precocious puberty are due to intrinsic abnormalities in the hypothalamus, pituitary, or gonads. Although the detailed clinical features of individual cases of precocious puberty are quite variable, it is possible to classify precocious puberty into two easily distinguishable classes -

GnRH-dependent and GnRH-independent.

GnRH-dependent precocious puberty arises from the premature activation of the GnRH pacemaker. Normally, the reactivation of GnRH pacemaker takes place only when all of the conditions for puberty have been met. However, infrequently reactivation of the GnRH pacemaker occurs independently of any of the normal conditions. This type of precocious puberty is referred to as GnRH-dependent because puberty is being initiated by the pacemaker, but now at a very young age.

The causes of most cases of GnRH-dependent precocious puberty are unknown. In a few cases the cause can be traced to the development of tumors or other types of lesions in the hypothalamus or other sites in the central nervous system that lead to premature release of GnRH. The good news is that even if the cause is not known this type of precocious puberty can be treated successfully.

Let's consider one concrete example to illustrate how sometimes this condition is recognized and treated. A young boy, 4 years old, is referred to a pediatric endocrinologist (a doctor specializing in hormone disorders in children). The parents have a distressing story to tell. Their son has been expelled from his pre-school because he was creating a disturbance in the classroom that went beyond the limits of the acceptable. He was masturbating, and even ejaculating. Although the other children were fascinated by this display, the teacher was horrified – this was clearly unacceptable behavior.

The clinical examination shows that the young boy is already in Tanner stage 3/4 (the parent's must have been aware of the changes in their son, but had not reported them to his doctor). Biochemical tests reveal that the boy's GnRH pacemaker is pulsing as would be expected for his Tanner stage of puberty. What is taking place in this very young boy is what normally takes place in a boy that around the age of 13-14. So what can be done?

The boy is placed on GnRH agonist therapy. GnRH agonists are synthetic compounds that mimic the action of the naturally occurring GnRH. However, they are taken in oral form and are long lasting, which means that a high level of the synthetic compound is maintained in blood system. The amazing effect of such compounds is that they lead to suppression of the hormones LH and FSH from the pituitary, and in turn, suppression of gonadal function. The administration of GnRH agonists suppresses the onset of changes that typically occur during puberty, so that external genitalia regress to the pre-pubertal state.

Administration of the GnRH agonist can be continued until, for example, the mean age of puberty for boys is reached, at which time the endogenous GnRH reinitiates the onset of puberty, which has been held in abeyance for several years. Hence, the GnRH agonist is really a powerful medication – not only does it provide a way of treating CPP, but think about it, it is also a method of postponing the normal onset of puberty.

GnRH-independent precocious puberty occurs when secondary sex characteristics appear without GnRH stimulation. That is, the GnRH pacemaker is not reactivated, but nevertheless varying levels of pubertal changes take place. This type of precocious puberty can arise from many causes - isolated adrenal gland, pituitary, or gonadal activation, often due to tumors, resulting in increased secretion of adrenal sex steroid hormones, pituitary hormones, or gonadal steroid hormones. Therapies will depend once the cause has been determined

Precocious puberty is not a lethal condition but if untreated does have consequences. For example, although the person may be taller than their peers when young, they will end up much shorter. This is because skeletal maturation will take place before the long bones have had a chance to grow. There may be psychological problems as well, particularly for girls. Girls will appear mature way too young, and they may be the targets of sexual advances when they are not yet ready for them. Boys may like the fact that they are developing earlier than other boys, but they may regret later when they discover that they will be significantly shorter than other boys.

Delayed puberty

A delay in puberty is not always easy to diagnose properly. Many cases are due to what is referred to as a "constitutional delay in growth", meaning that for unknown reasons the onset of puberty takes place at a later chronological age. This type of delay appears to be more common in boys. But when puberty occurs, the progression of changes is normal. In other words, no intrinsic abnormality is present.

In other cases, the delay in puberty can be due to involuntary food restriction, for example, during periods of famine, war, or imprisonment, or the consequence of an eating disorder. Chronic illness or severe psychosocial stress, especially in females, can also retard the onset of puberty.

Other cases of delayed puberty may reflect an underlying abnormality in hypothalamic, pituitary, or gonadal function, for example, failure of the GnRH pacemaker to be reactivated at the normal time, or failure of the pituitary or the gonads to respond to hypothalamic or pituitary stimulation, respectively. Many different types of lesions have been identified, and appropriate therapies with varying degrees of success have been developed.

Delayed puberty leads to short stature during the period when peers are getting taller, but when the pubertal condition is restored, normal height can be achieved. A significant risk, especially for girls is osteoporosis, due to the estrogen deficiency.

Loss of self confidence, being treated by adults and peers as less mature than the chronological age, and more difficulty in getting a job are common complaints especially among boys. Clinical psychologists also report that separation from parents is more difficult.

Chapter 5

The Reproductive Twilight

Reproductive aging in both females and males has become a topic of immense interest. Widespread public interest in female reproductive aging in the U. S. began in the 1950s, although concern about the consequences about the cessation of menstruation – the menopause - were being voiced two centuries earlier. Interest in this period of a woman's life, if anything, appears to be increasing. In the last two or three years alone thousands of articles discussing this topic have appeared in newspapers and magazines, and hundreds of radio and television stations have carried programs focusing on female reproductive aging. In August 2001, the American Society for Reproductive Medicine (ASRM) launched their Prevention of Infertility Campaign, a public health information forum that focused on four themes – smoking, body weight, sexually transmitted diseases, and reproductive aging. According to the ASRM, reproductive aging was an important focal point of discussion in a campaign that led to over 24,000 radio and television airings, and dozens of articles in prominent newspapers and magazines with a nationwide distribution. In a word, the media blitz found a receptive audience.

Widespread interest in male reproductive aging began later perhaps in the 1970s, although men have been concerned about their loss of sexual drive as they age for a long time. What is interesting is that already in the 1930s and 1940s the terminology used in describing female reproductive aging began to be applied to males, and terms such as "male menopause", and "male climacteric", began to appear not only in the clinical literature, but also in popular writings. The current favorite today is "andropause".

Is reproductive aging a disorder, or is it simply a normal physiological process? Although a good case can be made for the latter, the conflating of hormonal changes with our cultural and psychological neuroses has transformed reproductive aging into a condition that requires medical attention and seemingly an increasing share of the resources of the medical establishment.

So let's begin and see what we can sort out.

The female

The menopause – a witch's brew of biology and culture

When women go through menopause, where do men go? (1, Title of video Elizabeth Sher)

Strictly speaking the term "menopause" refers to the last menstrual period in a woman's life, and represents the final cessation of ovarian activity. In the U. S. natural menopause occurs between the ages of 40 and 55, with a mean age of about 50. As far as we can tell, the mean age of menopause has probably not changed significantly since our hunter-gatherer past. Menopause is the consequence of a genetically programmed process that has not changed in many millennia. One particular challenge to our understanding of menopause is why it occurs so early compared to the human life span. We will come back to this question below.

Interest in this period of a woman's life is fairly recent. We know the menopause has been recognized and documented for at least 1500 years. However, throughout most of that history many women never experienced menopause since they died before they reached it. If it was given any consideration menopause was probably seen as part of normal aging, of no special importance or consequence. No special rites or festivities appear to have celebrated or announced menopause as they have birth, puberty, marriage, or death.

Interestingly, some women were considered to experience a renewed sexual passion during menopausal period. Hamlet chastises his mother who remarried immediately after the death of his father, for he finds her passion for her new husband unseemly:

You cannot call it love, for at your age
The heyday in the blood is tame, it's humble
And waits upon the judgement
Shakespeare, Hamlet)

For reasons that remain obscure the final cessation of menstruation began to be linked in the eighteenth century to a number of organic and emotional problems in women. The litany of symptoms characterizing this period in a woman's life was both rich and somber - flushes of the head, face, neck and chest, profuse sweating, sensations of cold in the hands and feet, dizziness, headaches, irritability, depression, insomnia, palpitations, feeling of numbness, itching and tingling of the sexual organs, constipation.

Most of these symptoms are very similar to the symptoms that women report today, which is perhaps why many clinicians viewed them as evidence of a neurotic pathology. The clinical literature of the late nineteenth and early part of the twentieth centuries routinely expressed the view that the cessation of menstruation led to a form of insanity, known as involutional melancholia. Clinicians have always excelled in coining frightful terms for newly perceived disorders. Fortunately, involutional melancholia has disappeared completely from the physicians' lexicon.

Even when such extreme views were not being expressed, menopause was beginning to be seen as more than a physiological process. One clinician, for example, writing in 1887 gave voice to the sense that menopause was more than the mere cessation of menstruation.

The perimenopause, or so-called change of life in women, presents, without question, one of the most interesting subjects offered to the physician, and especially to the gynecologist, in the practice of his profession. The phenomena of this period are so various and changeable . . . so ill-defined are the boundaries between the physiological and the pathological in this field of study, that it is highly desirable in the interest of our patients of the other sex, that the greatest possible light should be thrown upon this question. (3, F. Borner The menopause)

Much of the writing on menopause began to focus on the experience of menopause, meaning not only the symptoms themselves, but also the way in which the symptoms were interpreted by the confluence of a complex mixture of social, cultural, and psychological factors. A few examples illustrate some of these different points of view.

By far the greatest hazards of the menopause are psychogenical or culturally induced, and these are not so simply dispelled by a few pills. A psychiatrist working in China reported to me that she had never seen a menopausal psychosis in a Chinese woman. This she attributed to the fact that in China the older woman has a secure and coveted position. (4, C. Thompson On women)

The changes that affect both the body and the mind at and after menopause are immensely complicated. Not only are there hormonal changes, but also emotional, social, and family changes, and no one really knows why in fact some women, albeit the minority, pass through their fifties and sixties with little physical or emotional disturbance

There may be many symptoms and signs associated with menopause but, especially in the well-balanced, educated, contented woman who finds her family, sexual and professional life fulfilling, there may be no symptoms whatsoever. (5, M. Anderson The menopause)

All women have to incorporate and adjust to changes as best they can, and some have preferred to see them as an unremarkable matter of course rather than to appear awkward, self-important, neurotic, and so forth. We have seen, for example, that in general some individuals label their internal sensations as important, and some do not. The point of interest is that profound changes take place in all women, including those who do not report them. (6, W. Cooper No change A biological revolution for women)

Perhaps more pernicious was the view that menopause represented a deleterious transition in a woman's life, in contrast to Hamlet's view, from a sexual to a nonsexual being. Prominent among the many clinicians who expressed this view was the American obstetrician and gynecologist, R. A. Wilson, a strong proponent of the view of menopause as pathology, a disorder with many nefarious consequences.

A large percentage of women . . . acquire a vapid cowlike feeling called a "negative state". It is a strange endogenous misery . . . the world appears as through a grey veil, and they live as docile, harmless creatures missing most of life's values. (7, R. A. Wilson and T. A. Wilson The fate of the nontreated postmenopausal woman)

The menopausal woman is not normal; she suffers from a deficiency disease with serious sequelae and needs treatment. (7, R. A. Wilson and T. A. Wilson The fate of the nontreated postmenopausal woman)

Estrogen deficiency is as much a disease as thyroid, pancreatic, or adrenal deficiency. No attempt will be made here to detail all of the unwholesome effects of this deficiency disease; a few will suffice, e. g. thinning of bones, dowager's hump, ugly body contours, flaccidity of the breast, atrophy of the genitalia... The estrogenic treatment of older women will inhibit osteoporosis and thus help to prevent fractures, as long as they continue healthful activities and appropriate diets. Breast and genital organs will not shrivel. Such women will be much more pleasant to live with and will not become dull and unattractive. (8, R.

Wilson and T. A. Wilson The basic philosophy of estrogen maintenance)

Views like these reflected deeply held and generally unconscious views of the nature of the female by male. And they also undoubtedly influenced the way in which women themselves began to experience the menopausal transition. Simone de Beauvoir in her book *The Second Sex* published in 1953 grasped clearly the way in which women's attitudes were shaped by men's views, and a natural physiological process began to be interpreted as a loss of femininity and loss of sexual attractiveness.

The "dangerous age" is marked by certain organic disturbances, but what lends them importance is their symbolic significance. The crisis of the "change of life" is felt much less keenly by women who have not staked everything on their femininity. (9, Simone de Beauvoir The Second Sex)

Many female writers complained that wide acceptance of this view led to the medicalization of menopause. Germaine Greer wrote in The Change. Woman, Aging, and the Menopause:

It is not quite forty years since eliminating menopause was first mooted. The idea did not come from women, but from men who thought that the cessation of ovulation was a premature death, a tragedy. (10, Germaine Greer The change: Women, aging and the menopause)

What about today? We don't generally read or hear expressed Wilson's rather extreme view of the menopause anymore, at least not as openly or vividly. The loss of femininity may not be the primary focus anymore, but the view that menopause is a medical problem still prevails. Probably three factors are driving this point of view – first, the perceived and actual health consequences of the menopausal changes, second, the desire to alleviate the menopausal symptoms that many women experience, and third, the recognition of the progressive loss of fertility as women enter their late 30s and early 40s. In the first two cases, the primary concern has focused on the consequences of the decline in estrogen levels – osteoporosis and the possible increased risk of coronary heart disease, for example. This concern has been exacerbated by conflicting studies regarding estrogen replacement therapy.

The third arises from the almost revolutionary change in reproductive behavior in women in modern societies, that is, the postponement of childbearing until later in their lives. This change comes as a consequence of the much greater educational and professional opportunities available to women, and their understandable desire to participate fully in arenas that in previous generations were reserved for men. During the 1990s women were led to believe that they could have their cake and eat it too. That is, they could have their successful career and still have children whenever they wished. What we have discovered is that children cannot be as easily scheduled as we may have been led to believe, even with all of the well-publicized advances in assisted reproduction technologies.

So, let's begin to try to sort out this significant period in a woman's life.

The perimenopause – sliding towards the menopause

Hormonal changes

We often hear and use the expression "going through menopause" to describe the approach to menopause, a period which in the older literature was referred to as the "climacteric" or the "change of life". This period, some 8 -10 years before the menopause, and including perhaps the year after the menopause, now referred to as the perimenopause, is marked by two significant changes – progressively decreasing estrogen levels and declining fertility. The decrease in estrogen is associated with changes in the pattern of estrogen and progesterone production during the follicular and luteal phases of the ovulatory cycle. Menstrual cycles may become irregular, but ovulation may continue until well into the 40s even as mean estrogen levels are declining.

We do not yet fully understand the ultimate cause of these events. The decrease in estrogen and progesterone clearly reflect an alteration in ovarian function, and many investigators suggest that the precipitating factor may be the depletion of follicles in the ovaries below some critical value. Recall from Chapter 1 that atretic loss of follicles begins during fetal life. The rate of follicular loss after birth is relatively constant until the late 30s, after which the rate of loss increases significantly. Successful follicular development and hormone production may depend on having a certain threshold of follicles – around 25,000 has been suggested. Ovarian function may begin to be perturbed once the follicular reserve falls below this critical level. For example, women who continue to menstruate regularly after the age of 45 have been found to have about 10 times more follicles than 45 year-old women who experience irregular menstrual cycles.

The progressive loss of ovarian function results in significant changes in the hormonal environment of the female. LH and FSH, the pituitary hormones, whose regulation is so important for ovulation, begin to increase during the latter stages of the perimenopause, and they increase to such high levels that they begin to be secreted in the urine. Indeed, LH and FSH extracted from the urine of menopausal women is known as human menopausal gonadotropin (HMG). HMG has been marketed and sold for many years, and has been used as a source for LH and FSH in countless experiments. The perimenopausal rise in LH and FSH levels is attributed to the progressive decrease in estrogen. Since estrogen exerts a negative feedback on the pituitary, as estrogen levels drop, the negative feedback decreases permitting LH and FSH to increase. The physiological significance of the rising LH and FSH levels remains poorly understood.

Although estrogen production declines precipitously as the follicle reserve is depleted, other cells in the ovary continue to produce a very weak form of estrogen, known as estrone. Adipose (fat) tissue also is a source of estrogen, and fat or obese postmenopausal women have higher estrogen levels than leaner ones. Testosterone production by ovary may also begin to increase and this can lead to a variety of side effects sometimes seen in postmenopausal women - hirsutism (growth of facial or body hair), thinning hair on the head, acne, deepening of the voice, and weight gain. These side effects vary greatly in severity and frequency. The extent to which we should interpret these changes as normal physiological changes, or as pathological ones remains unclear.

Eventually, when the number of remaining follicles falls below another critical threshold, perhaps around 1000, regular menstruation ceases. However, menses can reoccur occasionally even after several months have passed without a period. For example, the likelihood of menses after six months without a period is 52 percent if the woman is between 45 and 49 years old, and 20 percent if she is over 53. Approximately, 10 percent of women have a period more than one year after what they think was their last.

Decline in fertility

The decline in fertility as women age has been recognized for a long time. Elizabeth Barrett Browning expresses this recognition beautifully in one of her letters written to Robert Browning trying to discourage him from continuing to pursue her:

If you were justified, could I be therefore justified in abetting such a step – the step of wasting in a sense your best feelings of emptying your water gourds into the sand. (Elizabeth Barrett Browning, Letters to Robert Browning)

And in sonnet 18 from Sonnets from the Portuguese:

My day of youth went yesterday;
My hair no longer bounds to my foot's glee,
Nor plant I it from rose or myrtle-tree,
As girls do, anymore

As a society we have become acutely aware of the decline in female fertility with age by one important trend in all of the industrialized countries – the postponement of childbearing, and as a consequence the increasing number of sub-fertile or infertile couples. Most of us probably know of women in their late 30s who were menstruating regularly but who were unable to get pregnant or had great difficulty in getting pregnant. In general, fertility declines more rapidly than the decrease in ovarian function. For example, the end of fertility is reached at a mean age of 40 – 41 years, while menstrual cycles may remain reasonably regular until a mean age of 45 – 46, and menopause is reached at about 50 years. Fertility declines in a large fraction of women even when they remain ovulating normally.

Moreover, the development of the endometrium, the outer layer of the uterus where implantation takes place, during the cycle remains robust in women who continue menstruating regularly into the middle 40s and older. For example, in egg donor cases, the success of the pregnancy depends principally on the age of the egg donor, rather than on the age of the recipient. Even in women who have stopped menstruating, an endometrium able to support implantation and a pregnancy can be prepared successfully. Hence, the comparatively early loss of fertility does not appear to be due principally to ovulatory problems nor to endometrial insufficiency.

The loss of fertility appears to be due to an age-related decline in egg or oocyte quality. Recall from Chapter 1 that a female's store of oocytes was produced before she was born. By the time she gets to the perimenopausal age, the remaining oocytes in her ovaries are as old as she is. As a woman ages an increasingly greater fraction of her oocytes carry abnormal numbers of chromosomes. One study showed that almost 80% of the oocytes in women aged 40 – 45 are chromosomally abnormal. Such oocytes can be fertilized, but are unable to support normal embryonic development. The consequence is a significant increase in fetal loss (miscarriages). In many cases the miscarriage may take place within the first few days after fertilization, or in the very early stages of pregnancy, even before the females realizes that a conception has taken place.

Another factor that may contribute to the decline in oocyte or egg quality is attributable to the consequences of follicular development in a hormonal environment of accelerating atretic loss, that is loss of follicles. Normally, follicular development and oocyte maturation within the follicle are regulated fairly precisely by the coordinated activity between the follicular cells, whose activity is controlled by the pituitary hormones LH and FSH, and the oocyte itself. Proper egg maturation increases the likelihood of a successful pregnancy. The rising levels of FSH and LH during the perimenopause may result in an imbalance between follicular growth and oocyte maturation so that a not quite mature oocyte will be ovulated. Such an oocyte will not be ready to support normal embryonic development, and the pregnancy will terminate early in gestation.

Variability in the age of menopause

The factors or conditions that influence the rate at which follicles are depleted from the ovary during a woman's lifetime, that is, atretic loss, will determine the age at which at menopause occurs. Smoking, for example, decreases the age of menopause by 2 to 4 years depending on the length of time the woman has smoked and the intensity of smoking. A number of recent findings have shown that components in tobacco smoke accelerate the death of primordial follicles, hence, leading to an accelerated depletion of the follicular reserve. Menopause can also be induced in young women by several types of medical treatments for health problems, such as removal of both ovaries (clinically, bilateral oophorectomy), certain types of cancer chemotherapy, and pelvic radiation therapy. Removal of the uterus (hysterectomy) does not induce menopause (unless the ovaries are removed at the same time), although it advances natural menopause by 1-2 years.

Does an earlier age of menarche (the first menstruation) mean an earlier menopause?

There is no evidence that it does. An earlier onset of puberty does not affect the rate of the rate of atretic loss from the resting primordial follicular pool.

Does removal of one ovary (unilateral ovariectomy) lead to early menopause?

It depends on the age at which the ovariectomy is performed. If performed when the resting primordial pool has been greatly depleted, menopause may occur earlier because the size of the pool is the determinant of ovarian senescence. But if performed when the pool is large, the effect on the age of menopause will be minimal.

Does the use of steroidal contraceptives that inhibit ovulation delay menopause?

No. The contraceptives suppress ovulation but have no effect on the rate of primordial pool depletion.

Does increased parity (number of births) delay menopause?

Yes. This effect is thought to be due to high progesterone levels associated with pregnancy. Progesterone suppresses initial recruitment, permitting maintenance of a larger primordial reservoir.

Do females who have undergone ovarian stimulation in assisted reproduction experience a delay in menopause?

No. Assisted reproduction involves the use of the pituitary hormones, LH and FSH, to stimulate ovulation. The rate of atretic loss from the follicular reserve is not affected.

The menopause – its consequences

Menopausal symptomology

One of the things that really struck us ... is the fact that menopause is not a disease, yet at the same time there are subsets of women who clearly have disabling symptoms from menopause that affect their quality of life and their ability to function. (11, Carol M. Mangione, Chair, NIH panel on menopause)

A number of symptoms, singly or in combination, have traditionally been associated with the menopausal transition. Both physical and emotional symptoms are reported. These typically are short term and disappear 3-5 years after the menopause, although they can persist in some women for many years. The physical symptoms include loss of skin texture, dry and itchy skin, hair loss, facial hair growth, reduction in breast size, weight gain, vaginal atrophy (thinning of vaginal, urethral, and bladder walls, loss of vaginal secretions, shortening of the urethra), alterations in lipid metabolism and cardiovascular function, hot flashes (flushes), night sweats, sleep disturbances, numbness, backache, bloatedness, rheumatic pains, bowel disorders, fatigue, headache, palpitations, and dizzy spells. The emotional symptoms reported include irritability, nervousness, depression, excitability, diminished sexual drive, mood swings and panic attacks. All of these have generally been attributed to estrogen deficiency.

In some women the menopausal symptoms strike with a particular intensity.

In my case, when it arrived at 49, perimenopause was terrifying, and like nothing I had ever before physically experienced. It was not just the hot flashes, it was the mood swings, although the phrase mood swings sounds far too cartoon-like and teen-girlish. I would describe it as the sudden onset of a crippling, unreasoning gloom. It is like resting one's hand on the familiar wall of one's day—helping kids with homework, some grocery shopping, hurtling along on a favorite freeway, listening to Miles Davis—and then feeling the hand suddenly push through the wall, through foam spongy as the flesh of a drowned corpse, into ... nothingness. (12, Sandra Tsing Loh The bitch is back. Are menopausal woman mad, bad, or dangerous?)

However, a report by a National Institutes of Health Consensus Panel on Menopause (2005) found that only hot flashes, night sweats, vaginal atrophy, and possibly sleep disturbances are strongly associated with the decline in estrogen levels. These symptoms are most severe in women in whom menopause was induced by medical treatments.

Hot flashes, described as a collection of transient symptoms that include a sensation of being hot, sweating, increased heartbeat (tachycardia), anxiety, followed by rapid cooling or chilling have been associated in the public mind as a universal menopausal symptom. They occur with varying degrees of frequency (from one or two per day to as many as one per hour). Intensity is greatest during the first year after menopause and diminishes gradually so that in most women they cease by five years after menopause. However, only about 50 percent of menopausal women in the United States and Europe report having experienced hot flashes. Since the menopausal symptoms have been attributed to loss of estrogen, the standard therapy has been estrogen replacement. For women who choose not to take estrogen, or in whom it is contraindicated, a variety of other treatments are available, including anti-depressants, progestins, and herbal medicines. Symptomatic relief is highly variable. Hot flashes at night (night sweats), especially if they occur frequently, will invariably disturb sleep patterns. The sleep disturbances can lead to fatigue and irritability and possibly other disturbances. Estrogen therapy is effective in relieving sleep disturbances.

The vaginal lining begins to thin out after the menopause, leading to a decrease in the elasticity of the vaginal wall and vaginal dryness that in turn can make sexual intercourse painful. Systemic estrogen therapy is available, but for women who want to minimize systemic effects, a topical estrogen applied directly to the vagina is very effective. It turns out, however, that vaginal atrophy can be prevented by continuing sexual activity even without estrogen treatments.

In the U. S. some 50 to 60 percent of women seek medical attention for symptoms thought to be associated with menopause. A substantial fraction of women have no symptoms or suffer very mild symptoms. In a small fraction of women (10-20 percent), the symptoms can be severe and distressing. The origin of the other reported physical symptoms and emotional disturbances remain controversial and the subject of much debate, particularly because only some women experience these symptoms, and their severity is quite variable. The number and severity of the symptoms reported varies significantly not only from one individual to another, but also from one culture or society to another. For some scholars this variability suggests that menopausal symptoms are not always biologically determined, but rather are social constructs. A recent study comparing the experience of menopause in Tunisian and French women illustrates the importance of social influences. A three-part comparison was carried out: Tunisian women in Tunisia, Tunisian women in France, and French women in France. Working class Tunisian women in Tunisia and France experienced menopause with intense symptoms and strong feeling of social degradation. For middle-class Tunisian women in both countries menopause was associated with a severe decline in aesthetic and social value, but with mild symptoms. French women experienced menopause with few symptoms and little change in their social or aesthetic value. It would be interesting to find the roots of the changes in social or aesthetic value.

Medically important changes

Most menopausal symptoms, although vexing, troublesome, and perhaps embarrassing for women, are not life threatening, and cannot be considered serious medical problems. The truly significant consequences of estrogen depletion are osteoporosis and coronary heart disease.

Osteoporosis

A significant long-term consequence of estrogen deficiency after menopause is osteoporosis, defined as a severe loss of bone mass and disruption in bone architecture. As much as 5% of the bone mass can be lost per year during the first few years after menopause. The loss of calcium leads to brittle, easily fractured bones. Osteoporotic fractures contribute significantly to morbidity and mortality. In the United States, about 25 million people suffer from osteoporosis. Recent studies have shown that estrogen in addition prevents collagen being lost from the intervertebral discs, thus maintaining their strength and function. The loss of collagen leads to vertebrate compression fractures that account for about 50% of all postmenopausal fractures, and they result in loss of height, chronic back pain, and a bending of the upper spine (known as dowager's hump). Hip fractures are less common, but with a 20-30 % mortality rate they are more lethal. Many of the survivors of hip fractures remain permanently disabled.

Because most cases of osteoporosis are asymptomatic until a fracture occurs, the true incidence of osteoporosis is greater than the diagnosed cases. The cost of treating osteoporosis and its consequences is enormous (about $14 billion in 1995), more than the cost of cardiovascular disease ($7.5 billion). By any measure osteoporosis is a huge public health problem in the U. S.

Bone metabolism is a complex dynamic process involving a continuous interplay of bone formation and bone loss (the latter referred to as bone resorption). The critical role of estrogen is to stimulate bone formation and maintenance of bone structure. In both males and females bone formation exceeds bone resorption during childhood and adolescence, and bone mass reaches a peak in the late 20s. Males typically reach higher levels of bone mass. After the peak, bone resorption progressively begins to exceed bone formation. The bone mass at which the bones fracture easily is known as the fracture threshold, and is a useful marker for evaluating bone mass.

The relatively drastic reduction in estrogen levels that accompanies the menopause leads in many women to an accelerated loss of bone mass during the first 5 years after the menopause. Because women in general attain lower levels of bone mass than men, the accelerated loss after menopause means that in general they will reach the fracture threshold much earlier than men. In the United States, a woman at the age of 50 is estimated to have a 40% chance of experiencing an osteoporotic fracture. For this reason, osteoporosis has been considered a disease of women.

Since males normally reach a higher level of bone mass, and do not experience anything like a menopause, they tend to reach the fracture threshold 20-30 years after females. Osteoporosis in men in their 50s or 60s does occur, but the causes remain for the most part unknown. Additional bone loss will continue to take place especially if weight-bearing physical activity, such as walking, declines or if calcium and vitamin D intake is inadequate, both of which tend to occur as a person ages.

Osteoporosis, however, is not an inevitable consequence of menopause. Genetic and environmental factors are known to influence the balance between bone formation and bone resorption. Genetic factors include race, stature, and age at menarche. Osteoporosis is more common among Caucasian women than among Black women, where it is relatively rare. One explanation is that Black women reach a higher bone mass while they are young, why this is the case is unknown.

Environmental factors must also play a role. The increase in osteoporosis noted in many industrialized countries in recent years appears to reflect significant changes in life-style factors. British women today, for example, are twice as likely to suffer hip fractures as they were 30 years ago, a difference that is not due to differences in estrogen levels. Changes in diet, less exercise, decreased vitamin D and calcium intake, and increased incidence of alcohol consumption and cigarette smoking among younger females all clearly reduce the premenopausal bone-mass levels. Many investigators are convinced that attainment of high bone-mass values while young may be the best protection against osteoporosis.

Coronary heart disease

Coronary heart disease (CHD) is the most common cause of death for women in the United States. It accounts for about 53 percent of all deaths in women over the age of 50, about 500,000 deaths per year, about eight-fold more than deaths due to breast cancer. Despite its high mortality, it may be ironic to note that the public does not view CHD with the same dread as it does breast cancer. Women have a lower incidence of CHD than men, and this was attributed to their higher estrogen levels. CHD increased after menopause, and again the increase was attributed to the loss of estrogen. But skeptics pointed out that not all studies showed this correlation:

Japanese women tend to have lower levels of estrogen than women in the western countries, yet their incidence of CHD is much lower. The view that the rate of CHD is greatly accelerated at menopause was questioned in some studies. Skeptics also pointed to many life-style factors that could equally well predispose women in the industrialized countries to CHD. Despite these discrepancies in the reported studies, there is general agreement now that estrogen is cardioprotecive (see below).

Postmenopausal hormone therapy – an unfolding saga

The American gynecologist R. A. Wilson was the first to advocate estrogen replacement therapy forcefully. His message, promoted in his book *Feminine Forever* published in 1966 was simple, but powerful: the culprit, the cause of all the menopausal misery and medical problems was estrogen deficiency. The significant and widespread effects of the steroid sex hormones, estrogens in the female, and androgens in the male, were beginning to be widely appreciated by the public at large. It was a relatively easy leap of faith to consider that estrogen was the elixir of the 'fountain of youth' for the female. Estrogen therapy was heavily promoted not only for the prevention of osteoporosis, but also for the treatment of as many as twenty-six symptoms, among them depression, frigidity, alcoholism, absent-mindedness, and suicide.

The publicity was phenomenally successful: in the early 1970s about 50 percent of the women between the ages of 55 and 64, and about 33 percent of women between 65 and 74 were on estrogen or a combination of estrogen/progestin therapy. Hormone therapy very quickly became the standard therapy for postmenopausal women. Since then hormone therapy has had a complex and contentious history. The initial, hopeful, expectation that the adverse effects of menopause would be eliminated risk free turned out not to be fulfilled. Many studies during the 1980s and 1990s reported a perplexing dismay of adverse effects of post-menopausal estrogen therapy, including uterine bleeding, increased risk of blood clots, stroke, venous thrombosis, migraine headaches, increased risk of breast and endometrial cancer, and even loss of cognitive function, increased risk of dementia. As a consequence, many doctors stopped prescribing estrogen to post-menopausal women.

More recently a thorough assessment of the different studies has led to the recognition that the estrogen and progestin components of the hormone therapy formulation, the route of administration, and the timing of the therapy are critically important in developing a useful individual benefit-risk profile. There is general agreement that reported adverse side effects of hormone therapy – breast cancer, stroke, and heart attacks - occurred in women who started the wrong hormone therapy dose over the age of 60. The 'one size fits all' approach is never going to be effective. From now on a fairly specific hormone therapy regimen would have to be developed for each woman's circumstances. A few general conclusions and recommendations follow from this new understanding of the complexities of postmenopausal hormone therapy (HT).

Hormone therapy (HT) should be started before the age of 60. The health risks of HT between the ages of 50 and 59 are low. HT in older women carries greater risks.

Transdermal estrogen (in the form of a skin patch) is safer than oral estrogens; minimal doses and duration of progestins should be used.

Estrogen by itself is effective for treating hot flashes and vaginal atrophy and dryness and improving texture of the skin.

Estrogen is cardioprotective – the adverse effects found in the previous studies are attributed to the progestin component, the wrong doses and forms of estrogen, and the wrong age of the women. In general, estrogen alone is associated with a reduced number of heart attacks if started below the age of 60.

Estrogen increases bone density, prevents osteoporotic fractures, and protects the intervertebral discs. This treatment is very safe when started in women under the age of 60. Early start of estrogen therapy may lead to significant increase in bone mass that will reduce the incidence of fractures in later years.

It is important to keep in mind that we have not heard the last word. Newer studies and more research on the effects of genetics, lifestyle, and individual clinical characteristics should help in developing more effective and safer HT regimens.

One of the most important lessons from the hormone therapy debacle was that well-intended prescriptions might backfire if plausibility is the main argument to support them. The impetus for hormone therapy was the view that menopause is a pathological condition requiring medical intervention. Those who were skeptical of the benefits of the use of hormone therapy on a mass scale argued that we needed to know more about those women who do not succumb to the more serious of menopausal consequences. Germaine Greer put it this way *" . . the obstacle to understanding here is the defect that disfigures all gynecological investigation; we do not know enough about the well woman to understand what has gone wrong with the sick one." (10, Germaine Greer The change: Women, aging and the menopause)*

The menopause puzzle

Despite half a century of enquiry, the human menopause remains an evolutionary puzzle. (13, Daryl P. Shanley and Thomas B.L. Kirkwood Evolution of the human menopause)

Menopause occurs very early in the human female (50 years) compared to her life span (probably greater than 90 years), and this is highly unusual. In most other species, females appear to be fertile until they are very near the end of their life span. In our closest primate relative, the chimpanzee, female fertility ends at about 45, but in the wild the chimpanzee life span is about the same, so that very few chimpanzees survive past the end of their fertility. In the developed countries the postmenopausal infertile period of the human female constitutes about one-third of her total life span. It's important here to distinguish longevity (life span) from life expectancy. A significant increase in the latter has become most evident since the beginning of the 20th century. Before then, the postmenopausal period was masked because of the relatively short life expectancy due in large part to the inadequate control of infectious diseases. For example, in the early twentieth century, the life expectancy for women in the United States was about 48 years. Still even with such relatively short life expectancy, at least a third of females in historical and pre-historical populations lived past the age of 45.

The long life span that distinguishes humans from chimpanzees is a feature that we inherited from our hominid ancestors from around 6 million years ago when the hominid line diverged from the African apes. Hence, in contrast to the significant increases in life expectancy during the last 100 years or so, the human life span has been relatively constant for thousands of years. The reproductive life span of the human female and in our nearest primate relatives is a consequence of a limited oocyte supply. Recall from our discussion above that the age of menopause is determined by two factors, the size of the follicular pool generated early in gestation and the rate of follicular atresia, or the destruction of primordial follicles. A limited oocyte reserve has an ancient lineage being found in birds and mammals.

For evolutionary biologists who like to think about these things, the early menopause in human females is a conundrum - not that the reproductive span is restricted, but that the restriction occurs in the face of a long life span. Why should a woman cease reproducing halfway through her life span, especially when most other body functions have not yet begun to age? Would it not be better for her to continue reproducing at least until senescence really begins to take hold? This is clearly the case for almost all other species. In fact, the only other known mammalian species with an early menopause are toothed whales. In other whale species, such as baleen whales, the reproductive span is comparable to the life span. The question then is why the reproductive span of the human female has not adjusted to her increased life span.

There are several pieces to this puzzle that are worth reviewing. First, let's consider the restricted egg supply. In the overwhelming majority of vertebrates (fish, amphibians, and reptiles), females produce eggs on a continual basis, just as males do. The few exceptions are birds, mammals, and perhaps unexpectedly, sharks and rays. An unusual feature of sharks and rays is that the young develop internally, and give birth to a small number of live young. All of these species are characterized by significant maternal investment in a small number of progeny. A general hypothesis proposes that restricted egg production evolved concomitantly with an increased maternal investment in the young. A limited egg supply then would be advantageous in evolutionary terms because it would increase the likelihood of survival of the young.

In humans, however, the restricted egg feature was inherited along with an increased life span. What accounts for the increase in life span? We don't really know. Some scholars suggest that the increase was associated with the increase in brain size in hominid lineage from which humans emerged. Why didn't the egg reservoir expand to accommodate the increasing life span? Or alternatively, why didn't the rate of follicular atresia, or the destruction of primordial follicles, slow down. Most evolutionary biologists suggest that the ultimate explanation for the divergence between the reproductive span and the life span lies in the evolutionary biology of the human lineage. Several general hypotheses have been offered.

One – the *Mother hypothesis* – proposes that menopause is a consequence of the constraints of childbirth. The large head of human fetuses makes childbirth especially difficult for human females compared with other primates. The neonatal head is just at the limit compatible with reasonably safe delivery. Historically birth was associated with high maternal mortality. By various measures the risks of childbearing increase with maternal age. Human infants also require prolonged care in feeding and in training to ensure their survival. It seems reasonable to suppose that evolution would favor limiting reproduction to younger women when it relatively safer and the mother is likely to survive to care for the child. In this view then, two constraints unique to humans - the increased risk of childbirth due to the large head of human infants, and the prolonged care that human infants require - may have provided the selective advantage to premature reproductive aging.

The second hypothesis – the *Grandmother hypothesis* - is based on the observation that humans are unique in the extent to which close kin, and especially grandmothers, contribute to the care and training of the young. An early menopause evolved to permit the female to switch her investment to close kin rather than to reproduction. The decision between an early or late menopause involves a cost-benefit comparison of the advantages of females continuing to give birth up until they die, or forgoing some births in order to survive to care for her children and grandchildren.

The role of the postmenopausal woman has been explored in several anthropological studies carried out in existing hunter-gatherer societies. One well-known study examined the importance of foraging by women of different ages among the Hadza people, a hunter-gatherer society in Tanzania. The postmenopausal grandmothers, because they could work more hours unimpeded and were more efficient, were found to be better foragers than the younger women. The excess food they contributed was shared with their children and grandchildren. The food contributed by the postmenopausal grandmothers was critical precisely because it enhanced the probability of survival of her children and grandchildren. Hence, women gain more (in the sense of ensuring maximum survival of their genes) by withdrawing early from reproductive competition and devoting part of their postmenopausal period to the care of their children and grandchildren.

A couple of other hypotheses – *Male Longevity* and the *Reproductive Conflict* (between the younger and older generation) – have been examined as well. None of these, despite their plausible features, has found uniform favor among evolutionary biologists. For some scholars, it is not clear that there is a conundrum. The limited egg supply determined the reproductive life span of the female, and up until the last century, female human longevity matched her reproductive life span. Now that human longevity is increasing it is reasonable to suppose that over a long span of time, selection for a greater egg supply or decreased atresia will be taking place. At some time in the future, the reproductive span of the female will approach her life span.

The male

Every man desires to live long, but no man would be old (14, Jonathan Swift Miscellanies)

Andropause – a disorder in the making?

For males the main lament about aging has been the decline in sexual drive and activity. We read, for example, in the King James translation of the Hebrew Bible (Kings I:1–4) that King David, a prodigious womanizer "gat no heat", in his seventies The young woman sent to arouse him "cherished the king and ministered to him: but the king knew her not."

The desire to prevent or ameliorate the loss of sexual vigor was the impetus (as we saw in Chapter 3) in the nineteenth century for the testes transplants and injections of testicular extracts carried out in many clinics. These experiments were the forerunners of what is becoming a new growth industry - testosterone replacement therapy (TRT).

During the last 40 years or so the terms "male menopause" or "andropause" have been used increasingly to describe a collection of physiological and psychological symptoms that are reported in some men at 45 – 60 years of age. The terms are being used more and more frequently to replace and give a clinical patina to what was once called "the mid-life crisis". The symptoms list is long: loss of sexual drive, nervousness, depression, decreased memory and concentration, loss of self-confidence, fatigue, sleep disturbances, irritability, numbness, excitability, headaches, vertigo, constipation, crying, chilly sensations, itching, sweating, cold hands and feet, etc., symptoms very reminiscent of those used for menopause.

It is difficult to know how seriously to take the list of symptoms, but it is increasing clear that this whole package is being used to try to define aging as a deficiency disorder, and one that can be treated by testosterone supplementation. There are many skeptics, however. One presents the issue in very acerbic terms: *a man, 45 – 60, loses his sex drive and becomes depressed, irritable and constipated – it must be andropause. He then leaves his wife for a younger woman and regains his sex drive – what happened to his andropause? (14)*

Writing as early as 1994, John McKinlay, Director of the New England Research Institute in Watertown, MA, and specialist in aging, was quite straightforward about the andropause.

"I don't believe in the male midlife crisis. But even though in my perspective there is no epidemiological, physiological or clinical evidence for such a syndrome, I think by the year 2000 the syndrome will exist. There is a very strong interest in treating aging men for profit, just as there is for menopausal women" (15, Martha Weinman Lear (1973) Is there a male menopause)

Testosterone prescriptions for middle-aged men rose over 20-fold in the U. S. in the 1990s despite any convincing evidence that testosterone supplementation is safe or efficacious. Many skeptics are worried that the hormone debacle for women will now become a testosterone replacement therapy debacle for men.

Male reproductive health

The debate about the validity of a term such as andropause has conflated three different measures of the decline in male reproductive health with age – fertility, sexual function, and testosterone decline. Failure to make appropriate distinctions has often confused, more than enlightened the debates. Let's begin with fertility.

Fertility

Fertility in older males is difficult to measure as men age because men over 50 years account for less than 1% of births. Some population estimates do suggest a relatively modest decline in male fertility after the age of 50. Nevertheless, there are numerous examples of men in their 60s and 70s who father children, and apparently there is evidence of a 94 year old who fathered a child. We do know that spermatogenesis, once established at puberty continues essentially for the rest of the male's life. Clinical measurements of semen quality (sperm count, ejaculate volume, sperm morphology) in men over 50 are often inconsistent, and because they come from small-scale studies may not be representative of the male population in general. Nevertheless, overall, these studies suggest a small reduction, but the decrease is unlikely to reduce male fertility in any significant way.

Another way of estimating sperm production potential is by measuring testis size. Testis size is considered to be a valid predictor of spermatogenesis because about 90% of testis volume is due to the seminiferous tubules, the site of spermatogenesis. Post-mortem analyses have shown that testis size begins to diminish somewhat only after 70 years of age. In summary, fertility diminishes only minimally as men age, very clearly different from the abrupt loss of fertility in females at menopause. Moreover, we know that testosterone supplementation does not improve fertility in men at any age.

Sexual function

Impotence, or what is now referred to as erectile dysfunction (ED), increases with age especially after the age of 70. Although ED has often been attributed to decrease in testosterone as men age, the evidence connecting the two is inconsistent, except in those cases of severe testicular atrophy leading to severe androgen deficiency. Hence, hormonal deficiency is not generally the cause of ED. The most likely intrinsic cause of ED is considered to be due to age-related increase in atherosclerosis. A number of studies have shown that the most frequent form of erectile dysfunction has properties very similar to those of atherogenic cardiovascular disease. The apparent large increase in the prevalence of erectile dysfunction in the U. S. may reflect the concomitant increase in cardiovascular atherosclerosis.

Sexual function is also influenced by extrinsic causes, for example, the side effects of therapeutic drugs used in treatments of diseases associated with increasing age, side effects of recreational drugs, such as alcohol abuse, tobacco use, and illegal drugs, and sociocultural factors – loss of employment, anxieties about getting old, facing their mortality. It is not always easy to assess in a definitive way the relative importance of extrinsic versus intrinsic causes to loss of sexual function.

Testosterone and the aging male

There is a growing interest, as well as a booming industry, in the use of testosterone therapy for middle-aged and older men. (16, David J. Handelsman and Peter Y. Liu Andropause: invention, prevention, rejuvenation)

Aging men do show clinical signs of testosterone deficiency, in particular, loss of body mass and muscle strength (sarcopenia), and an increase in visceral (abdominal) fat. These features, when present in younger men, are known to be due to loss of testicular function, as a consequence of illness or physical trauma to the testes. In such cases testosterone replacement therapy is quite successful in restoring body mass and strength, vigor, and erectile function. In fact, the original testosterone analogs (anabolic steroids) were developed as therapy for disease-induced testosterone deficiency.

Numerous studies have shown that testosterone levels decline in men as they age. The decline, however, is quite variable, and most men remain in what are considered the normal range throughout their lives. The decline has until recently not been considered physiologically important because the mean levels are still above those that in younger men are required for maintenance of erectile function and sexual drive. Testosterone deficiency – denoted hypogonadism - is associated with several significant symptoms – shrinking or very small testes, reduced facial or body hair, decreased spontaneous erections, decreases sexual drive, osteoporosis, low-trauma fracture, breast enlargement, hot flashes and night sweats. According to the Institute of Medicine, about 250,000 men in the U. S. were diagnosed with testosterone deficiency in 2002, the only condition for which testosterone supplementation is approved. Yet, over 1.75 million prescriptions for testosterone were written by American doctors in 2002, a reflection of the persistent belief by men that testosterone is the anti-aging hormone.

The few, and very limited, studies that have evaluated testosterone supplementation have yielded inconsistent results. In some studies, it is relatively unsuccessful, while in others, some positive effects have been noted. The differences in response may depend on the general health of the individual, with healthy older men who maintain some level of physical activity responding better than others who may be in poor health and physical condition. The differences may also depend on the specific parameter used to measure response to the exogenous testosterone administration.

For some investigators, the risks of testosterone replacement may outweigh the meager benefits. Unresolved risks have been of special concern – prostate disease (benign prostatic hyperplasia - enlargement of the prostate gland - and prostate cancer), cardiovascular disorders, polycythemia (an excessive number of red blood cells), and obstructive sleep apnea (respiratory pause during sleep that can increase the risk of hypertension, heart attack, and stroke). The prostate is particularly sensitive to androgens, and the danger is that testosterone supplementation may increase the likelihood of developing prostate cancer, or other prostatic disorders. The cardiovascular safety of testosterone supplementation is also far from clear. A few studies suggest that sleep apnea (interruptions in breathing during sleep) can be aggravated by injectable testosterone.

Still, the possibility that testosterone supplementation might improve physical functioning, improve muscle tone, and prevent fractures seemed reason enough to look into this in more detail. The Testosterone in Older Men with Mobility Limitations (TOM) trial, randomized and placebo controlled, was designed to test the efficacy and safety of testosterone therapy in men who were considered to need the hormone. All of the participants were 65 or over, had low to low-normal testosterone levels, and had limited walking ability, and difficulty in climbing stairs. They were also overweight and the majority had hypertension. The TOM study planned for

252 participants and six months of therapy. The trial was halted after just 209 men had been enrolled (129 of whom had completed six months of therapy) because of an excess of cardiovascular events in the men who had received testosterone. A higher rate of respiratory tract and skin complications were also recorded in the men who took testosterone.

The TOM study is a cautionary tale, reminding us that testosterone therapy is not a simple matter and can carry significant adverse effects. Many experts suggest that testosterone therapy should be limited to men enrolled in closely controlled clinical trials. The real danger is that given the current climate of unbridled mass marketing and prescribing we will begin to learn about the detrimental side effects when the casualties start coming in.

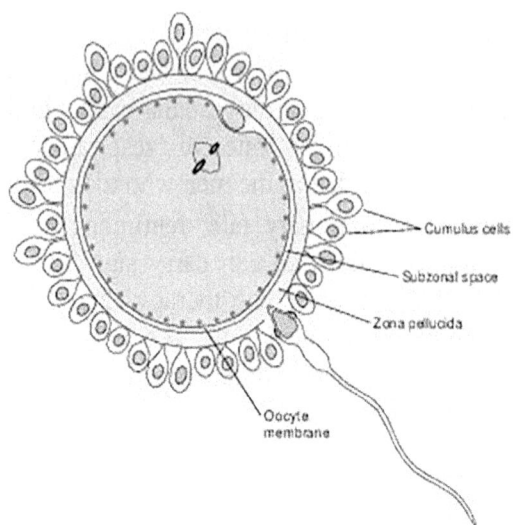

PART B

Glimpses of our pre-natal and early post-natal life

Chapter 6

How we begin

Fertilization – competition and female choice

Every human being begins with the meeting and fusion of the egg with the sperm, quite a remarkable process when we think about it. Consider what's required. The ovulated egg, expelled from the ovary, must be "caught" by the fimbriae of the uterine tube (also known as the fallopian tube, or oviduct). From there the egg is transported by the cilia of the inner lining of the oviduct to a special region known as the ampulla, after which it sits there waiting, very often in vain, for an occasional sperm to come by. The egg is a tiny microscopic object in a huge cavern. Remarkable pictures have been taken of the lonely egg, almost hidden by the gigantic folds of the inner lining of the oviduct, almost like a surfer being engulfed by a huge wave (see the beautiful images in A Child is Born, by Lennart Nilsson and Lars Hamburger). If not fertilized, the egg begins to self-destruct after perhaps 24 hours, and resorbed by the tissue of the oviduct.

Fig. 6.1 is a schematic diagram depicting ovulation and transport of the ovulated egg into the uterine tube, the deposition of sperm at the vaginal-cervical boundary, their transport up the uterus and through the uterine tube, finally reaching the awaiting egg.

The sperm that finally reaches the egg goes through hell and high water to get there. Think about it. It is also a microscopic object; it started its journey in the testis, was deposited in the upper parts of the vagina after intercourse, moved through the cervix, then traveled through the length of the uterus and into the oviduct, and finally to find and eventually penetrate the egg. How it does this is as yet poorly understood. It is a true survivor – it has bested millions of its compatriots and has managed to overcome the obstacles placed in its path by the female genital tracts. It is literally true that the female has the final say in selecting the sperm that will fertilize the egg.

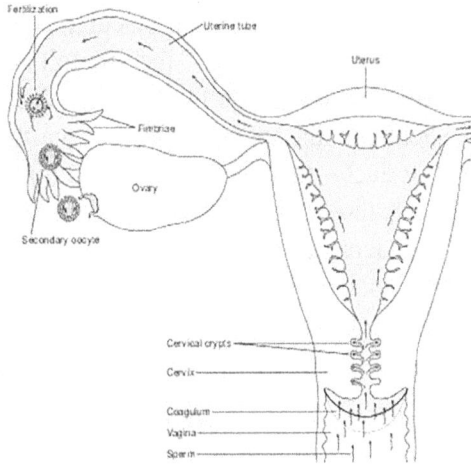

Figure 6.1

Each step in this process appears precarious. If fertilization did not occur as frequently as it does, we would probably predict that the conditions under which the egg and sperm must meet are so special and unique that fertilization would be rare. What makes fertilization highly probable is that you shower the female genital tract with millions and millions of sperm. Astronomical numbers of sperm is what guarantees success.

Fertilization sets in motion a series of transformations that convert the fertilized egg into a viable and functional human being in the space of some 38 weeks. These transformations are of such complexity that even today with the considerably dispassionate approach of most modern biologists, we cannot but marvel at their intricacy. It would take a massive volume to really cover the complete embryology of human being, way beyond the scope of this book. What I try to do here is to take a few snapshots – glimpses – of the initial and final stages in our intrauterine development, the long-lasting consequences of our time in the womb, and finally, a review of the system that makes us mammals.

Preparation of the sperm

If you were to take sperm directly from the testis (that is, from the seminiferous tubules) you might be surprised to find that such sperm, although fully formed, are unable to fertilize an egg. On the other hand, sperm taken from distal end (far end) of the epididymis have much better fertilizing ability (recovering sperm from an ejaculate). (Recall that sperm produced through the ministrations of the Sertoli cells within the seminiferous tubules are passed through the tube into a storage vessel, the epididymis. During ejaculation the sperm are taken from the epididymis and pushed through the long duct – the vas deferens – and into the urethra and finally to the outside). In fact, sperm once they leave their site of birth - seminiferous tubule - undergo a complex series of changes that prepare them for their ultimate goal in life – fertilizing the egg. Some of these changes take place in the male, and many others take place in the female.

Let's begin first with the preparation of sperm in the testis.

In the male – preparation for the rough road ahead

The first of these changes takes place during a 10 to 14 day sojourn in the epididymis. Many changes in the sperm have been noted, but the precise significance of some of them may not be clear. One of the most important visible changes is that sperm acquire the ability to move, that is, the ability of the sperm to move in a forward direction by the motion of its tail (flagellum). This type of movement is quite impressive, especially when compared to motility of sperm taken from inside the testis. When examined in a culture dish, sperm taken directly from the testis remain relatively motionless. However, after passage through the epididymis sperm exhibit two alternating main types of motility - movement in a more or less forward motion interspersed with a gyrating motion in which the spermatozoon moves in circles, a type of motion referred to as hyper-activated motility. Both types of motility appear to be required for normal male fertility.

Two other very important, but not as easily noted, changes also take place: first, the ability of the sperm to recognize the egg as being a human egg, and second, the ability to use components present in the seminal fluid to provide for the sperm's metabolism and survival. In a sense, seminal fluid functions as a portable survival kit for the sperm. For example, fructose, the main sugar found in honey, is present in seminal fluid, and serves as the sperm's primary energy source once it starts its journey in the female.

In the female – limiting the number of suitors

There must be a reinvigorated application of research to studying sperm interaction with the female reproductive tract. . . It is likely that we have been studying the spermatozoa in the wrong environment, in the wrong way and at the wrong time. (2, C.L.R. Barratt and J. Kirkman-Brown Man-made versus female-made environment)

It has been known for some time from animal studies that ejaculated sperm, that is, sperm after they have spent their prep time in the epididymis, still have not attained their optimal fertilizing potential. Their fertilizing ability improves only after they have been exposed to fluids and components of the female reproductive tract - the cervix, the uterus, and the uterine tube. The nature of these female fluid-dependent changes – technically known as capacitation – (think of it as a ripening process) remains incompletely understood, but it seems clear that ripening is akin to a quality control system – testing sperm, discarding those that don't pass muster, and also very importantly limiting the number of sperm that reach the egg.

Let's consider a few of the ripening landmarks.

Over 200 million sperm are typically deposited in the vaginal – cervical boundary. Because of a difference in the acidity between the seminal and vaginal fluids, a mucus coagulate forms trapping most of the sperm. This mucus plug appears to have two roles – it functions as a trap to keep the sperm from falling out, and it also functions as a filter, permitting the sperm with the best motility to move through the plug and into the cervix. Estimates suggest that about 0.1% of the sperm deposited at the vaginal – cervical boundary pass into the cervix, prompting the quip from the New Testament that "many are called, but few are chosen".

The cervix in turn seems to function as a policeman at an intersection, regulating traffic, stopping cars and letting them go through, because the sperm that enter the cervix continue into the uterus periodically in small numbers and not as a group.

Once the sperm enter the uterus, it in turn, begins to assume its role - facilitating sperm transport through a contraction mechanism beginning in the cervical region, propagating the sperm to the oviduct region. This mild contraction process is dependent on estrogen, and increases in frequency and intensity as ovulation approaches, hence, increasing the likelihood of sperm reaching the egg soon after ovulation. Interestingly, the sperm are also preferentially directed to the tube on the same side as the ovary in which ovulation will take place.

Movement into the uterine tubes requires motility. Keep in mind that this complicated passage is not passive. The fluids from the different tissues are interacting with the sperm – evaluating, modifying, saving a few, and eliminating most of them. The final stages of the ripening process take place in the uterine tube. The surviving sperm now have to negotiate their way through the tube. Most don't make it – they seem to get stuck along the way. Only a few are able to reach the vicinity of the egg.

In the final approach, the egg plays the last card of this complicated game – it secretes compounds known as chemo-attractants that guide the sperm to the egg – think of it as a homing system. The sperm that respond best to the attractants will have the best chance of fertilizing the egg. Sperm selection is absolutely ruthless and merciless - estimates suggest that out of the millions of sperm that started their journey, very few will arrive at the general vicinity of the egg, probably less 20. In fact, there is a critically important reason for this ruthless selection: fertilization by more than one sperm will lead to an inviable embryo.

The best time for conception

Is there an optimal time for conception? Much has been written about this, and there is an extensive literature on this topic, both scientific and non-scientific. The latest studies suggest quite clearly that the 5-6 days ending on the day of ovulation defines the fertility window, the best time for conception, in humans. The probability of conception during this interval is not constant, but varies from around 5 percent on day –5 to a maximum of 25 – 30 percent on days –2 to 0 (day 0 is the day of ovulation). The likelihood of conception decreases to zero the day after ovulation. The length of the fertility window varies from one female to another, from as short as 1 day up to 6 days. The shorter windows are seen in subfertile couples.

The whys and wherefores of the fertility window are straightforward. The beginning of the fertility interval corresponds to the initial rise in estrogen levels during the second part of the follicular phase. Recall from Chapter 3 that during the follicular phase the dominant follicle is the source of estrogen. Estrogen determines the cervical mucus quality that can be inferred indirectly from vaginal secretions. At about day -5, the vaginal discharge begins to change from a thick, creamy, yellowish, sticky consistency to the optimal (transparent, like raw egg white, watery) seen most consistently about day –2, roughly coincident with the estrogen peak which precedes ovulation. This is considered optimal because it reflects a cervical mucus consistency that permits the easiest passage of sperm through the cervix and into the uterus. After ovulation, the increasing secretion of progesterone from the developing corpus luteum results in a thick mucus that acts as a very effective physical barrier to sperm penetration. In fact, as we will see later, the efficacy of progesterone-only contraceptive regimens depend on this cervical mucus effect.

Hence, the best predictor of conception is the quality of the cervical mucus, and not the timing of intercourse relative to ovulation, as had been suggested from studies in the 1990s. Moreover, interestingly, there is no convincing evidence that frequency of intercourse affects probability of conception, or that the sex of the baby is related to the time of intercourse.

Implantation – the embryo makes its presence known

The embryo invades and establishes itself

Within a few hours after fertilization, the fertilized egg (the zygote) begins to divide successively into 2, 4, 8, 16 cells, and so on, and as it does so it is transported down the length of the oviduct. During these divisions the embryo looks like a blackberry, which is why it is referred to as a morula (Latin for "berry"). The cells of the morula are loosely associated and are held together by the zona pellucida (ZP). In humans, the morula reaches the uterus in 5-6 days (see Fig. 6.2)

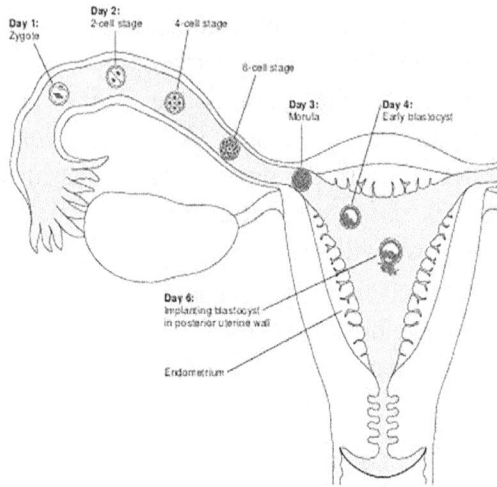

Figure 6.2

The pre-implantation stage of the human embryo as it moves after fertilization along the uterine tube and into the uterus. During this period the fertilized egg (the zygote) undergoes a continuing series of cell divisions and transformations until it is ready to implant in the endometrium.

At the 32- to 64- cell stage the morula, as it enters the uterus, begins to transform itself into the blastocyst. The cells of the morula rearrange themselves to form two functionally distinct tissues, the trophoblast and the inner cell mass. The trophoblast is one of the progenitor tissues for the formation of the placenta that will begin developing several days later, while the inner cell mass cells are the progenitors of all of the tissues and organs of the body. The blastocyst eventually "hatches" from the zona pellucida, meaning that the zona pellucida begins to decompose. Perhaps one of the very important functions of the zona pellucida at this stage is that it prevents the implantation of the blastocyst until it has reached the uterus. Hence, the transport of the embryo along the uterine tube follows a fairly tight schedule, the critical feature being that zona pellucida degeneration should begin to take place only after the embryo has reached the uterus.

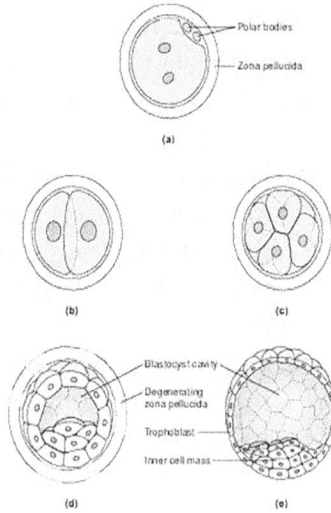

Figure 6.3

During the 5 – 7 days after fertilization – the pre-implantation stage, the embryo draws its nutritional support from the secretions of the uterine tube through which it is moving. Eventually, however, these secretions are inadequate to support further growth, and it is at this stage that implantation begins. The blastocyst attaches to the uterine endometrium, a preferred site being the back wall of the uterine cavity.

How does the embryo know where and when to begin its attachment? This is an old question and only recently have a few clues emerged. The blastocyst embryo, it turns out, is quite sticky – it can attach itself to diverse tissues. A successful implantation, however, requires a carefully coordinated interaction between the embryo and a properly prepared endometrium. There is only a short window of opportunity for this to occur. Recent studies suggest that proteins known on the surface of the trophoblast makes fertile contact with another set of molecules that appear on the endometrial surface. We can imagine that the embryo is "homing in" to find the appropriate site at which to begin its implantation, and finally "locks in". Many questions remain about this process, but at least some of the key molecules have been identified. Perhaps this type of information will be useful in those cases of infertility due to implantation failure.

The stable attachment of the embryo to the endometrium, the outer lining of the uterus, by the blastocyst initiates the invasion of the endometrium.

The invading force is provided by the rapid proliferation of a class of cells in the embryo known as the trophoblast cells, and their ability to penetrate the endometrial layers. The depth to which the blastocyst invades the maternal tissues varies with the species. In humans, implantation is highly invasive, and the blastocyst burrows its way completely not only into the uterine endometrium, but into the deeper layers of the uterine wall. By 12 days after fertilization the embryo is completely embedded in the maternal endometrium, and the advance cells of the invading embryo have begun to make intimate contact with the maternal circulatory system and hence to use the mother to support the continuing growth of the embryo.

Luckily we have a very reliable marker for the start of implantation. The invading cells of the embryo secrete the hormone, human chorionic gonadotropin (hCG), which is the earliest reliable biochemical indicator of implantation. Sensitive test kits that detect hCG secreted into the urine, easy to use at home, are now widely available for the early detection of pregnancy. The critical function of hCG is to stimulate the corpus luteum in the ovary to continue producing progesterone. Recall from Topic 4 that if fertilization does not occur, the corpus luteum begins to self-destruct. In fact, it is not fertilization that provides the signal to maintain the corpus luteum, but hCG. The embryo at this point is notifying the mother of its existence.

Implantation, in fact, occurs at about the time that the corpus luteum would start regressing if fertilization had not taken place. The continuing production of progesterone by the corpus luteum permits the implantation process to be completed. Beginning around week 8-10 the placenta begins to take over major production of progesterone, which is essential for the maintenance of the pregnancy. Progesterone also suppresses the release of GnRH from the hypothalamus, thereby, suppressing menstruation and ovulation for the duration of the pregnancy.

Implantation marks the stage at which the embryo begins to take over the maternal system for its own growth and development. This process begins initially with the deep penetration into the uterine wall, and is followed by the elaboration of the amazing tissue known as the placenta. The placenta begins to dominate the entire physiology of the maternal system by around week 8, when the embryo transitions into the fetus (Latin, meaning "offspring").

The gestation period for a human being is considered to be about 266 days or 38 weeks long beginning with fertilization, and is conventionally divided into three trimesters. The trimesters are measures of time, rather than being defined by precise developmental stages. Two other measures are also used: the embryonic period, the first eight weeks, during which all of the principal elements of the organ systems develop, and the fetal period, from week 9 to the end of the pregnancy, during which the organs and tissues grow and mature. Quite often a pregnancy is measured from the date of the last menstrual period. Using this measure, the normal length of a pregnancy is about 280 days (40 weeks). Hence, there is always a two-week difference between gestational age (measured from fertilization) and pregnancy age, measured from the last menstrual period). The standard way of estimating the expected date of delivery is to count back three calendar months from the first day of the last menstrual period, and then add a year and seven days. A moment's reflection should tell you why this method provides a reasonably accurate estimate of the expected date of delivery.

The fetal period is characterized by a high rate of growth. At week 8, the human fetus is about 45 mm long; at week 12, 150 mm; at week 25, 375 mm; and at week 38, about 500 mm long. To accommodate this growth, the uterus also has to grow, eventually quadrupling in size from its pre-pregnant state, and displacing the mother's internal organs and stretching the skin and the muscle of the interior abdominal wall.

The amniotic sac, the beginnings of which go back to the formation of the blastocyst, defines the region in which the embryo and later the fetus develops. The umbilical cord connects the embryo/fetus to the placenta. The cord is 1 to 2 cm thick, and 30 to 90 cm long. Very long or very short cords are uncommon. Long cords have a tendency to coil around the fetus, and this may create serious problems during delivery if the cord is compressed as it passes through the cervix. Damage to the baby's brain may result due to cutting off of the blood supply.

Multiple births – the conventional wisdom is toppled

The most common types of multiple births are twins, but the incidence varies significantly by geographical region – 6 per 1000 live births in Asia, 10 – 20 per 1000 live births in Europe and the U. S., and 40 per 1000 live births in West Africa, and regions of the Americas in descendants of people who were brought over as slaves from West Africa. The reason for these geographical differences remains unknown. Twinning appears also to run in some families, suggesting a significant genetic component in such families. Twins also have a higher frequency of birth defects – major malformations (neural tube defects, congenital heart defects, orofacial clefts), as well as low birth weight, premature delivery, and fetal, peri-natal, and infant mortality.

Until recently, the conventional wisdom was that there were two type of twins, commonly referred to as fraternal and identical. Fraternal twins were considered to arise when two dominant follicles were produced and two oocytes were ovulated simultaneously and each is fertilized individually, resulting in two fertilized eggs or zygotes, hence, the clinical term, dizygotic, or two-egg, twins. Because they arose from two different zygotes, the twins could be of the same sex or different sex, and genetically, they were related to each other, as are normal sibs. For dizygotic twins, placental organization would depend on how the two embryos implant in the endometrium. Most commonly the two blastocysts would implant separately, resulting in the formation of two placentas. However, if the two blastocysts implant very close together, the placentas could fuse and appear to be one placenta.

Identical, or monozygotic, or single-egg, twins were considered to have a more mysterious origin - they arose from a splitting of the inner cells mass into two groups of cells after the formation of the blastocyst. Each inner cell mass then could develop into a separate embryo, but because all the cells are derived from one zygote, both embryos would carry the same genetic information, and hence, would be identical. For monozygotic twins, there would be one placenta. Most of the birth anomalies seen in twins were attributed to monozygotic twinning.

A special type of monozygotic twinning were conjoined twins, commonly known as Siamese twins, thought to arise from a failure of the inner cell mass to separate completely into two separate masses. The result of this failure was that the twins shared many cells, tissues, and organs.

What is interesting is that the conventional wisdom regarding the origin of twins was based more on plausibility arguments rather than valid analysis. Recent thorough genetic analyses of what were considered monzygotic and dizygotic twins (for example, dizygotic twins are much more genetically alike than sibs), plus the finding of opposite sex monozygotic twins, has indicated that the origin of twins can be traced to a peculiarity of egg production in humans. A comprehensive review of these studies comes to a number of somewhat startling conclusions, among which are:

There is no evidence that any pair of natural dizygotic twins ever came from double ovulation.

Dizygotic embryogenesis happens the same way as monozygotic embryogenesis—defining and growing out two body symmetries from a single mass of cells

Dizygotic embryogenesis is at least as odd as that of monzygotic twins.

Every anomaly attributed to odd embryogenesis in monzygotic twins happens with equal or greater frequency in dizygotic twins. (3, Charles E. Boklage Embryogenesis of chimeras, twins and anterior midline asymmetries)

Ectopic implantation – mistakes in implantation

Although implantation usually takes place in the uterine wall, infrequently the blastocyst can implant at sites outside the uterus, and these are known as ectopic implantations (see Fig. 4). The most common of these ectopic sites are in the uterine tubes, and these give rise to tubal pregnancies. Such pregnancies never reach term because growth of the fetus is severely limited. They can be quite dangerous because rupture of the uterine tube wall produced by the rapidly growing embryo may lead to severe bleeding, which if uncontrolled, can be lethal to the mother.

Tubal implantations arise as a consequence of interference with the movement of the embryo after fertilization on its way through the uterine tube to the uterus. Recall that the development of the embryo after fertilization follows its own internal clock. If passage of the embryo through the uterine is delayed, the embryo may reach the blastocyst stage, the implanting stage, before it gets to the uterus. If this happens, implantation will take in the tube, but these implantations are doomed.

A significant increase in tubal pregnancies in the last few years has been associated with the large increase in the incidence of sexually transmitted diseases (STDs). The consequence of an STD is often the formation of scar tissue in the uterine tubes, which may impede the transport of the embryo on its way to the uterus.

Implantation at other problematic sites occurs with a much lower frequency. Implantations, for example, near the uterine - cervical boundary result in an abnormal development of the placenta, which results in severe bleeding during the latter stages of pregnancy, and a pre-term birth. Even rarer are implantations completely outside the uterus or the uterine tubes, such as the abdominal wall, or even on the ovary.

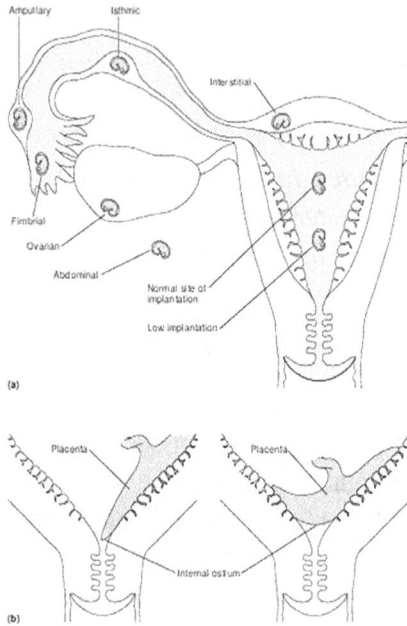

Figure 6.4

Fig. 6.4 Ectopic implantation sites. Implantation in the ampullary and isthmic sites account for over 80% of ectopic implantations.

The placenta has enormous genetic endowments, comparable to those of the brain and ovary. The molecular, cellular, vascular arrangements are designed for directing the traffic of biochemical and nutritional flow preferentially to the fetus. . . Thus, the placenta may be viewed as the third brain, which links the developed (maternal) and developing (fetal) brains. (4, S.S.C. Yen The placenta as a third Brain)

The placenta (Latin, flat cake) is commonly called the after-birth, because it is expelled from the uterus after the fetus. It is disc-shaped with a diameter of about 7.5 inches and weighs about 1.5 lb when fully formed. In many primitive societies the placenta was given special importance, and in some societies the ritual eating of the placenta was considered to bring good luck. Its function remained obscure, however, during all of classical antiquity. The fetal membranes associated with the placenta were recognized during Greek and Roman times, but no special term or appreciation of its function was evident. The term placenta did not appear until 1559, and it was perhaps a century later that some inkling of its function began to be appreciated.

The placenta was originally seen primarily as an organ for transporting nutrients from the mother and wastes from the fetus. More recently, its role as a complex neuroendocrine organ regulating maternal - fetal interactions, regulating the growth of the embryo and fetus, and preparing the mother for the feeding of the infant after birth, have been increasingly appreciated.

Placental secretions, more than those of the mother, dominate the hormonal environment of the pregnant female. Before pregnancy the ovary was the primary source of hormones such as estrogen and progesterone. During pregnancy, the placenta takes over this role. An essential function of the placenta is to ensure the well being of the developing fetus. It does so by regulating maternal protein and energy metabolism so that proper nutritional support for the rapidly developing fetus is provided continually. Many studies with primates in the wild indicate that pregnant females are quite judicious at food selection. For example, pregnant baboons in the wild can always balance their nutrient intake to what is seasonally available. In human societies, analysis of existing hunter-gatherer peoples has shown that food selection by pregnant females is quite purposeful, providing the energy-nutrient balance required for well-regulated fetal growth.

Food choices, food aversions or preferences during pregnancy, commonly joked about and experienced by many pregnant women, may not be psychological whims, but may reflect placental hormone-mediated physiological effects. Consider, for example, my wife's experience. She had never liked avocados, but one day while passing by a fruit and vegetable stand in Nijmegen, the Netherlands, where we were living in 1966, she developed an intense craving for avocados. She was about three months pregnant at the time. She found a ripe one and ate it with relish. She returned the next day for another one. After a few days the green grocer saved ripe avocados for her, and she ate one avocado every day the rest of the pregnancy, and she has loved avocados since then.

Birth posture observed by United States Army surgeon in the mid-nineteenth century of a young Sioux woman who retired to the bank of a stream at the onset of labor. She sat cross-legged, thighs widely separated, arms folded, and head bowed, especially during labor pains, until birth occurred 40 minutes later. (G. J. Englemann. 1977. *Labor among Primitive Peoples*. AMS Press, New York, NY. Reprint of 1882 edition, published by J. H. Chambers, St. Louis.)

Chapter 7

Our entry into the world

In our mother's pain

'We come into this world in our mother's pain, and leave it in our own' is an old adage. For most of our history, it was not only our mother's pain, but her death as well, for up until the beginnings of the 20th century, childbirth was the leading contributor to maternal mortality. Although the great advances in obstetrical medicine have reduced maternal childbirth mortality in the industrialized countries to historic lows, the specter of pain in childbirth remains to cloud the anticipation of a happy event.

The timing of birth

What triggers birth? We might expect that under normal conditions birth would be initiated when the fetal organs have matured to permit the baby to survive outside the uterus, and that labor is initiated by an internal signal when this maturational state has been reached. One early hypothesis was that the placenta was the source of the initiating signal. Given the undoubted importance of the placenta in regulating essentially all aspects of maternal-fetal interactions, a prominent placental role in the induction of labor was deemed eminently reasonable. It is interesting to note, however, that the ancient Greek physician Hippocrates suggested more than 2000 years ago that the fetus was responsible for initiating labor. He could provide no evidence to support his view, however.

In humans, the initiating signal appears to come from the placenta. Recent studies suggest that the timing of delivery is closely related to the rate at which the placental corticotrophic-releasing hormone (CRH) is released into the maternal and fetal circulations during the last few weeks of pregnancy. Women, for example, with the highest CRH levels between 16 and 20 weeks of gestation were the most likely to deliver prematurely, while those with the lowest levels tended to deliver late.

The rapid increase in placental CRH towards the end of gestation unleashes an entire cascade of events - the uterus begins to become contractile, the maternal pituitary gland begins to secrete oxytocin, the cervix begins to dilate (ripen), and oxytocin begins to induce uterine contractions. Placental CRH appears to function as pregnancy clock. A number of investigators have been trying to use placental CRH or other hormones triggered by its rise as predictive markers for the initiation of labor. It seems quite likely that in the near future "labor kits" will be available (just like pregnancy kits) that will be able to predict when labor will begin within a day or two. There will probably be a huge market for such kits.

Stages of labor

Labor (Latin, toil or suffering) refers to the sequence of events that begins with involuntary uterine contractions and ends with the expulsion of the fetus and placenta from the uterus. At least five physiological events can be distinguished: rupture of the fetal membranes (commonly referred to as "breaking the bag of

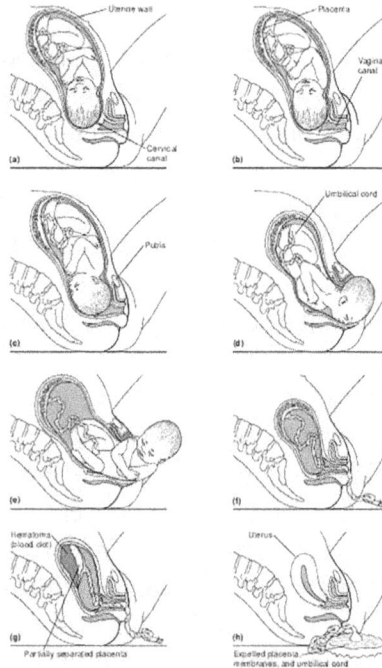

Figure 7.1

waters"); cervical dilatation, also known as cervical ripening; induction of contractions in the uterus and expulsion of the fetus; separation of the placenta from the uterine wall and its expulsion from the uterus; and involution of the uterus (contraction of the pregnant uterus to its former non-pregnant form).

The dilation stage begins with the onset of regular contractions of the uterus that are less than 10 minutes apart and culminates with the dilation of the cervix. This stage can be quite long, generally from 7 to 12 hours. The duration of this stage tends to be shorter for women who have given birth before, but it can be quite variable.

The expulsion stage begins when the amniochorionic membrane ruptures and the fetus passes through the dilated cervix and vagina. This stage is much shorter than the dilation stage, generally about one hour.

The placental stage refers to the expulsion of the placenta. After the fetus is delivered, uterine contractions begin anew, resulting in the contraction of the uterus. As the uterus contracts, the placenta and fetal membranes separate from the uterine wall and are expelled from the uterus. Although expulsion of the placenta takes place in about 15 minutes in the majority of deliveries, in a few, expulsion may take much more time or may need to be manipulated out. The separation of the placenta from the uterine wall results in bleeding and the formation of a large blood clot (hematoma) between the uterine wall and the placenta.

The recovery stage begins after the expulsion of the placenta. The uterus continues to contract and this restores it more or less to its pre-pregnancy form, and at the same time constricts the arteries to prevent excessive bleeding. This stage normally takes about 2 to 3 hours.

Preterm birth – unpleasant consequences

Labor is triggered prematurely in about 8 percent of pregnancies. This means that under certain circumstances the triggering signal for the initiation of labor can be uncoupled from the maturation of critical organs, and the cascade of birth signals can be generated before the fetus is able to survive outside. A number of conditions are associated with preterm labor, but the specific causes remain unknown. There is a sense of urgency in developing preventive or treatment strategies because preterm labor is a leading cause of fetal mortality. Our new understanding of the different factors that play a role in initiating labor should help us in devising intervention strategies for preventing premature labor.

Preterm birth is generally defined as the initiation of uterine contractions accompanied by appropriate cervical dilation between the 20th and 37th week of gestation. Many factors are associated with preterm labor – abnormalities of the uterus or cervix, diabetes, hypertension, obesity, blood-clotting disorders, uterine or cervical infections, smoking, drug use, and genetic factors. The incidence of preterm births in the U.S. is about 1 in 8 babies, a rate that has increased 27% over the last two decades. Life style factors may account for this increase.

Impressive developments in neonatal medicine enables the survival of many preterm babies, but many require intensive care lasting several weeks or months saddling families with enormous medical and non-medical expenses. Such babies are at significant risk for disabilities such as mental retardation, cerebral palsy, lung and gastrointestinal problems, and vision and hearing loss. Unfortunately, no clinically effective agents to delay preterm labor are available. An important question is: how do preterm births differ from normal term births? Because of the immense costs associated with the complications of preterm birth, there is an important need to understand parturition mechanisms.

The risks to the baby increase significantly the earlier preterm birth occurs, and the survival likelihood decreases dramatically for babies born before 26 weeks. The American Academy of Pediatrics guidelines propose that it is not appropriate to undertake resuscitation for fetuses younger than 23 weeks of gestation, or those whose birth weight is less than 400 gm (less than one pound). The rationale for the guidelines is the dismal prognosis for such infants. A recent article describes the outcomes at 6 years among infants born between 22 and 25 weeks gestation. The results:

Neonatal survival to discharge from hospital: 1% at 22 wks, 11% at 23 wks, 26% at 24 wks, and 44% at 25 wks.

Survival with no physical disability at 6 years: 0% at 22 wks, 1% at 23 wks, 3% at 24 wks, 8% at 25 wks.

Serious cognitive impairment: 41% in survivors. Only 20% had no appreciable neuromotor or cognitive disability at 6 years.

Breast-Feeding – control by the infant

In all mammalian species (except in humans since the adoption of breast-milk substitutes) postnatal survival of the newborn depends upon the milk provided by the mother. Indeed, the term "mammal" refers to the mammary gland, the milk-producing organ that defines mammals. The basic features of the mammary glands in different species are quite similar, although the number, size, shape, and location can vary considerably among species. Just compare, for example, the cow's udders with the dog or cat's teats.

The length of time that the young are dependent on the mother's milk also varies considerably from one species to another. In humans the nursing time varies from three months, the average for women who breast feed in the U. S., to two years seen in many underdeveloped countries. The two-year nursing period was probably the norm in our ancestors long ago. We infer that this was the case because two years is the normal nursing period in the few remaining human groups that maintain a hunter-gatherer lifestyle.

The long nursing period was of course necessary before milk substitutes were available. However, it is quite likely that another important effect of breast-feeding was recognized quite early in our history – its contraceptive effect. During most of humankind's history, this contraceptive effect was perhaps the main factor in the control of population growth. Even in some developing countries today, breast-feeding may prevent more births than modern contraceptive methods. With the emergence modern industrialized societies, and because of the availability of milk substitutes and birth control methods, breast-feeding was not seen as necessary, or even compatible with the new work-related demands placed on women. However, in recent years we have to come to recognize that breast-feeding has significant benefits not only for the baby but for the nursing mother as well. One welcome consequence of this recognition has been the development and success during the last twenty years of informational campaigns to encourage women to breast-feed.

Cultural dynamics of breast-feeding

Women at this daie are so curious of their comlinesse, or rather of their vanitie, that they hadde rather pervert the nature of their Children, then change the fourme of their firme, harde, and round pappes. (1, Taken from The ciuile Conuersation of mr. Stephen Guazzo, written first in Italian, divided into foure bookes, the first three translated our of French by G. Pettie, 1586)

Although milk production by the mammary gland is a fairly straightforward physiological process, in human societies the activity of breast-feeding has probably never been so. For example, problems in breastfeeding appear to be as old as history. One of the earliest documents about breastfeeding can be found in an Egyptian papyrus from around 1400 BCE describing how to stimulate milk flow: the woman is told to warm the bones of a Xra-fish in oil, and then have her back rubbed with the suspension. Other methods suggested sitting cross-legged while rubbing her breasts with a poppy plant. These methods may have had the virtue that they relaxed the nursing mother, but we don't really know how effective they were.

The more dependable alternative was to employ a wet nurse, a practice that also must have an ancient history. In the beginning, a wet nurse may have been used because the mother produced little milk, or perhaps did not want to nurse. Later, a wet nurse may be been used to protect the mother. For example, in the second century CE, the Greek physician, Soranus of Ephesus, recommended the use of a wet nurse "lest the mother grow prematurely old, having spent herself through the daily suckling". (1) Of course, little concern is shown for the wet nurse lest she also grow old prematurely.

Soranus also had very precise criteria for choosing a wet nurse, among which were that she should be between 20 and 40 years old, the mother of two or three children, large and swarthy – swarthy because dark women were considered to produce healthier milk than fair women. He also provided strict dietary guidelines, particularly foods to avoid, such as leeks, onions, garlic, and radishes, or highly seasoned foods because theses would make the milk taste bitter. He recommended what we recognize today as high protein foods – yellow of eggs, pigeons, chicken, freshwater fish, hard bread made from fresh wheat. From our modern perspective all of these dietary recommendations make sense.

The use of the wet nurse disappeared eventually, being replaced by a more egalitarian alternative made possible by the development of effective breast milk substitutes (formulas) and baby bottles around the beginning of the twentieth century. Their use began to be heavily promoted in the 1940s in the United States and several European countries. An implicit message in most of these promotional efforts was that breast-feeding was an antiquated custom, practiced in primitive societies, and somehow distasteful in a modern society. The consequence was that the percentage of breast-fed infants declined to 10 – 20 percent in the 1960s. The bottle-feeding campaigns have been particularly successful in many parts of the urbanized underdeveloped world. As a consequence breast-feeding has been undervalued not only as the most economical and beneficial source of infant nutrition, but also as an important contributor to fertility control.

Beginning in the 1970s, breast-feeding has experienced something of a revival so that currently in the U.S. breast-feeding has become more or less the norm – close to 75% of mothers breast feed – and in most European countries breast-feeding is universal. Interestingly, however, France and Ireland remain as the two holdouts. The French resistance, according to the French writer, Elisabeth Badinter, is based on their concept of freedom. Referring to the history of women's slow liberation: "The irony of this history is that it was precisely at the point that Western women finally rid themselves of patriarch that they acquired a new master in the home." (2, cited in Diane Johnson Mother's Beware!) She meant breast-feeding – a new symbol of women's oppression. In addition, the widespread belief that breast-feeding spoils the woman's breast has also contributed to the French resistance to nursing.

The Irish (Ireland is at the bottom the chart in breast-feeding) have their own complicated reasons for resisting the march to nursing. The Irish writer Ann Enright expresses her own distaste for it, which apparently may be wide spread in Ireland: *"I never liked being around nursing women – there was always too much love, too much need in the room. I also suspected it to be sexually gratifying. For whom? Oh, for everyone: for the mother, the child, the father, the father-in-law. Everyone's voice that little bit nervy, as thought it weren't happening: everyone taking pleasure in a perv-lite middle-class sort of way. Ick." (2, cited in Diane Johnson Mother's Beware!)*

Nothing seems simple.

The mammary gland

Two general cellular compartments make up the normal mature mammary gland: a fatty compartment permeated by fat deposits, blood vessels and nerves, and another compartment of lactiferous ducts and lobules, complex structures consisting of milk-secreting (alveoli) and a variety of non-secretory cells. The ducts extend radially out from the nipple toward the chest wall. Mammary gland development begins about the end of the fourth week of gestation, and fetal mammary gland formation is not completed until about week 30 to 32 of gestation. At birth, the nipples are poorly formed and depressed. At this stage, both the male and female glands consist of a few rudimentary ducts. Occasionally, within a few days after birth, the infant breast produces a milk-like secretion, known as "witch's milk", which subsides after about 3 weeks. Production of witch's milk is an indication of competence of the ductal tissue to produce milk. Essentially no further development takes place during infancy and childhood.

With the onset of puberty, the ducts begin to sprout and branch, and the precursors of the true alveoli begin to form at the end of the ductal branches. With increasing age and successive ovulatory cycles, more complex lobular structures begin to appear. One of these are the lactiferous sinuses, which in the breast feeding mother serve as small reservoirs for milk; they run through the nipple and directly onto its surface. The areola and nipple become pigmented and wrinkled, particularly in the late post-pubertal female. The different structures of the mammary gland continue to develop slowly during the post-pubertal period, but they do not mature until pregnancy. During pregnancy, the previously developed ductal-lobular-alveolar system undergoes extensive growth under the action of several placental hormones, and the mammary gland is fully developed for milk production by the end of the fourth month of gestation.

Milk production, milk release, and weaning

What prevents milk production and release during the latter months of gestation? Milk production requires the hormone, prolactin, which is secreted by the pituitary gland. During pregnancy, prolactin levels are high, but the milk-producing cells are not responsive to prolactin in the presence of the high placental estrogen and progesterone levels. After birth, the suppressive effects of placental hormones are removed. The initiation of milk production does not require infant suckling, but if the infant is not put to the breast by a few days after birth, milk production will cease.

Milk release is particularly sensitive to physical and emotional stress. Discomfort or pain, especially if the breasts are engorged, may prevent milk release even when the breasts are full of milk. Worrying about breast-feeding itself may also inhibit milk release. Hence, the importance of psychological factors in the successful initiation and maintenance of breast-feeding should not be underestimated.

If the breast is not emptied of milk frequently, an inhibitory compound produced in the milk will accumulate and suppress milk synthesis. This occurs normally as the infant is being weaned away from sole reliance on breast milk. With the decrease in suckling intensity, milk production gradually diminishes. Eventually, when suckling ceases altogether, the breast begins to decrease in size, primarily because of structural changes in and disappearance of many of the alveoli. The basic ductal network remains, however. Breast volume is reduced, but the breasts invariably remain larger after lactation than before pregnancy. The breasts enter a period of inactivity similar to the one that prevailed before pregnancy. With another pregnancy, the alveoli will again be induced to develop. At menopause, the entire ductal apparatus begins to atrophy.

Characteristics of breast milk

The milk produced during the first week after birth known as colostrum is a thick, yellowish fluid rich in minerals and immunoglobulin (maternal antibodies and other defense factors that protect the infant against a variety of infectious agents), but low in lactose (milk sugar) and protein.

Mature breast milk, which begins to appear after 10 – 12 days, is a complex mixture of fat, protein, carbohydrates, vitamins, and minerals. The primary energy source in breast milk is fat, but the fat is readily digestible because it is completely emulsified. The fat is also a good carrier of fat-soluble vitamins. Lactose, the main carbohydrate, is less sweet than table sugar and functions in promoting the proliferation of lactic acid-producing bacteria in the infant's intestines. One of the products of lactose breakdown, galactose, is important in forming the myelin sheath that envelopes nerve fibers.

Mature milk is also rich in various protective compounds, such as, antimicrobial agents, anti-inflammatory factors, and antibodies that protect the breast-feeding infant against diarrhea, respiratory and urinary tract infections, and viral infections. The protection may improve with the duration of breastfeeding, especially because breast milk contains factors that may stimulate the development of the infant's own immune system. Hence, there is good evidence that breast milk not only confers passive protection against infections during lactation, but that it also stimulates the development of the infant's immune system so that protection against a variety of other diseases is enhanced.

Suppression of milk production

It may be necessary to suppress milk production for a variety of reasons. The woman may simply decide not to breastfeed. If the fetus aborts after 4 months or if it is stillborn, breast-feeding will be unnecessary. If the mother is HIV positive, breastfeeding is contraindicated. A number of methods have been used to suppress milk production. Before hormonal therapy became available, tight binding of the breasts was common. Sex steroids, estrogen or progesterone, which inhibit the release of prolactin have often been administered. Probably the most common therapy today is bromocriptine. Bromocriptine suppresses prolactin release, and therefore, milk production decreases.

Insufficient milk supply

Difficulties in nursing and early cessation of breastfeeding are quite often attributed to insufficient milk supply (IMS). IMS is a condition that can arise from non-organic and organic causes. Organic IMS is very rare and is usually associated with a failure of mammary gland development. Non-organic IMS, on the other hand, is quite common and arises from a confluence of many factors: dietary deficiency (low calorie diets or diets low in protein), inadequate fluid intake, sore nipples, smoking, and excess use of alcohol. In industrialized societies a work schedule for the nursing mother that limits nursing frequency will clearly lead quickly to insufficient milk production. Emotional stress, unconscious negative attitudes about the act of breastfeeding, or using estrogen-containing contraceptive pills will also lead to less milk. Trying to breastfeed a preterm or critically ill baby presents a significant challenge for the mother. Preterm or ill babies may be unable to nurse or have difficulty in suckling and consequently milk production will diminish. Breastfeeding for such babies may be especially beneficial, and has been shown to increase their resistance to infection, improve cognitive and developmental progress as infants.

Perhaps the most common non-medication method for increasing or maintaining an adequate milk supply is to express milk from the breast with an electric breast pump. In the hands of a very committed mother and the use of double collection kits, this method can be quite successful. Other recommendations include skin-to-skin contact (commonly referred to as "kangaroo care"), non-nutritive suckling at the breast (encouraging the baby to continue suckling after the breast has been emptied), and avoidance of pacifiers.

If such methods are not successful, the use of medications that stimulate milk production may be advisable. These pharmacological agents function by increasing prolactin production, and two or three are available.

Other important benefits of breast-feeding

Breast-feeding as birth control

Breast-feeding induces a period of infertility, the length of which depends on the intensity of breast-feeding. The infertile period typically consists of two phases, an initial period characterized by the absence of menstruation, followed by a period in which menstrual cycles begin irregularly, and in which in the first few no ovulation takes place. The length of the first period can last for one, possibly even two years if the baby is breast fed exclusively. Possibly this was the norm in our hunter-gatherer ancestors.

However, in most modern societies under most circumstances full protection (98 percent) is normally considered to be effective for only the first five - six months postpartum of full breast-feeding. The resumption of menstruation clearly indicates the end of the infertile period. At this time, other forms of contraception are required to prevent a pregnancy.

Although the mechanism of suppression remains imperfectly understood, the intensity of suckling by the infant (frequency and duration of the suckling episodes) is thought to send a signal to the hypothalamus inhibiting the release of GnRH, the hormone that controls the functioning of the reproductive system. The generally intense suckling activity characteristic of the first few months of breast-feeding is responsible for the suppression of ovulation and menstruation seen during this period.

Despite the clear relationship between suckling intensity and infertility, it has proven extremely difficult to define a suckling parameter that can be used to insure a given period of infertility in any given female. A reduction in suckling frequency or suckling duration very quickly leads to resumption of normal ovarian activity. Reduction in suckling intensity typically begins when supplementary feeding is introduced, since the baby is no longer completely dependent on breast milk.

Breast-feeding and breast cancer

An important additional benefit of breast-feeding recognized recently is that it protects against breast cancer. Previous epidemiological studies have shown that childbearing protects against breast cancer, but the contribution of breastfeeding had been difficult to sort out. A summary of data from 47 different studies carried out in 30 countries and involving close to 150,000 women was published in 2002.

The women in these studies from the developed countries had 2-3 children and typically breastfed each for 2- 3 months, while women in the developing countries, where breast-cancer rates are four times lower, had 6-7 children and breastfed for about 2 years each. The analysis reveals that for every year a woman breastfeeds, her risk of breast cancer falls by more than 4%. This is on top of the 7% reduction for each child she bears, independent of other risk factors such as smoking, age of first birth, or genetic predisposition. According to this study, the incidence of breast cancer in the developed countries, could be reduced by more than half (from 6.3 to 2.7 per 100 women) by age 70 if women had larger families and longer durations of breastfeeding that have been typical of developing countries. Two-thirds of this estimated reduction is due to breastfeeding. Hence, breastfeeding per se is protective, and is independent of other aspects of childbearing.

Breast cancer incidence in some developing countries has begun to increase, apparently coincident with a fall in family size and reduction in duration of breastfeeding. Restricting families in China to one child, for example, has been accompanied by a rise in breast cancer incidence.

The mechanism of the protective effect of breast-feeding is not understood. Once it is understood, it may be possible to mimic its effects therapeutically. This would be especially beneficial since it is unrealistic to expect that women in the developed countries are will for having larger families

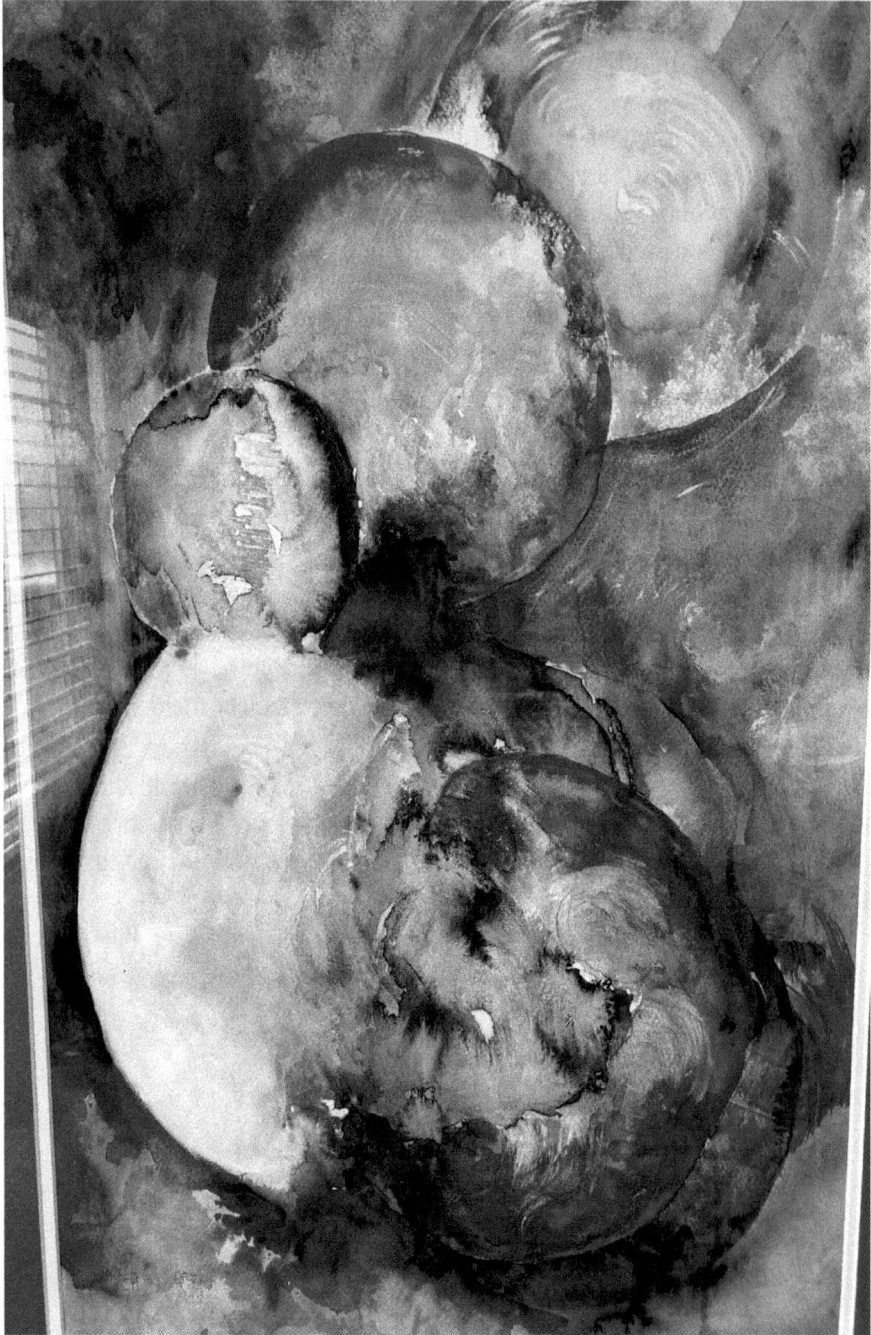

Chapter 8

Echoes of Our Life in the Womb

"You live in two worlds, the world of your mother and the world into which you are born." (1, David Barker, cited in Stephen S. Hall Small and Thin)

Most pregnant women nowadays are pretty much aware that smoking, alcohol, or other types of drugs can have dire consequences for the baby they are carrying. What may be less well known is that healthy habits during pregnancy may have long-term benefits: not only will the babies be healthier, but they will be more likely to become healthier adults. This is an important conclusion from a fast developing field of study, sometimes referred to as the "developmental origins of adult disease". The central idea is that the fetus responds to adverse environmental influences during pregnancy in different ways, depending on the condition or the period in gestation. This response "programs" the fetus in a way that may contribute significantly to the origin of a wide range of chronic adult disease, such as osteoporosis, cardiovascular disease, type 2 diabetes, high blood pressure, aging, immune disorders, and possibly even certain behavioral and psychological characteristics. Even more surprisingly, responses to certain environmental influences in one generation may carry over to several following generations.

Although many questions remain about the science behind this idea, enough supporting data has been marshaled that its general outlines have been widely accepted. The implications for the future are hugely important, because it means that the chronic adult diseases that are wrecking an untold number of lives and draining our health care resources may be to a large extent preventable.

To get a better idea of the significance of this concept, let's first look at how it developed.

Responding to adversity – the Barker hypothesis

A new global landscape of disease is emerging, in which the place where each of us stands is shaped not only by our genetic makeup and lifestyle, but also by the path we took to get here — our development. (2, Keith M. Godfrey, Peter D. Gluckman and Mark A. Hanson Developmental origins of metabolic disease)

The first suggestion that exposure to adverse environmental influences during pregnancy had profound effects long after birth came from a series of studies in the 1980s and 1990s led by David Barker at the University of Southampton. These investigators discovered that babies born small for their gestational age were more susceptible in middle age to coronary heart disease, type 2 diabetes, hypertension, and osteoporosis. These and similar studies in other countries led to the development of what became known as the Barker hypothesis for the origins of adult disease.

Briefly, the Barker hypothesis proposed that the risk of developing many chronic, adult diseases is influenced greatly by poor maternal nutrition during intrauterine life. The fetus in the womb responded to these adverse conditions in ways that tried to ensure its immediate survival. Depending on the severity of the malnutrition the response could include a reduction in total fetal growth, leading for example to lower birth weight. In other cases, the development of some organs might be impaired. The adaptation of the fetus generated a "survival phenotype", that is, a way of coping with the nutritional scarcity that permitted the fetus to survive.

The survival phenotype, it was proposed, had an ancient history, and probably was the norm for our hunter-gatherer ancestors, who lived under conditions of relative food scarcity. It resulted in a lean, small body still able to reproduce successfully. However, the survival phenotype, while effective for a deprived environment, became a disadvantage in an environment where food was abundant and physical activity diminished. The consequences of the "maladaptation" of the survival phenotype to the world of abundance was high blood pressure, type 2 diabetes, increase in cardio vascular disease, etc, all of the chronic adult disease that have increased in incidence all over the world.

But you ask: how does maternal nutritional limitation during pregnancy lead to chronic adult disease? Let's consider one example: the development of high blood pressure in middle age. In this case, the key tissue is the kidney. The functional unit in the kidney is the nephron, whose role is to extract waste from the blood as the blood circulates through the kidney. A typical adult kidney has about one million nephrons. Under conditions of nutritional limitation, the development of the kidney may be slighted, meaning that fewer nephrons are formed. Under these adverse conditions the energy extracted from the available food is preferentially channeled to the brain. Slighting the kidney can be done without endangering survival because, in the womb, the excretion of waste is carried out by the mother's kidney.

Now, a good measure of nutritional limitation is a low birth weight. If we then compare the number of nephrons in people who had a low birth weight with those who had a normal birth weight, we find that people who had a low birth weight have up to three times fewer nephrons than people who were larger at birth. Hence, according to the model, to ensure survival under nutritional limitation the growth of the kidney is compromised. But there is a price to be paid for slighting kidney development: in a kidney with fewer nephrons each nephron will have an increased workload. If the person gains weight rapidly in childhood resulting in a larger body, more waste to be extracted means that the wear and tear on the each nephron increases, hastening the death of nephrons that occurs with normal aging. As nephrons die, kidney function diminishes and blood pressure increases to maintain the proper level of waste removal. This in turn accelerates further nwephron death and setting in motion a self-perpetuating cycle of rising blood pressure and nephron loss.

For the scientists a low birth weight is an ideal parameter to use: it is easily available and it turns out to be not only a measure of poor maternal nutrition, but it is also a measure of other types of adverse environments to which the fetus responds. Consider, for example, the documented causes and consequences of low birth weight in the developed and in the developing countries summarized in Table 8.1 below.

Developed world	Developing world
Causes	*Causes*
Smoking	Smoking
Twinning/in-vitro fertilization	Poor maternal nutrition
Young maternal age	Young maternal age
Advanced maternal age (primigravida)workloads	Excessive maternal
Placental dysfunction syndromes, (stunting)	Poor maternal stature

e.g. pre-eclampsia	Infection (malaria, HIV)
Consequences	Consequences
Neonatal morbidity and mortality	Neonatal mortality
Enhanced risk of obesity	Infant mortality
Impaired cognitive development	Impaired cognitive development
Impaired postnatal growth	Stunting
Accelerated maturation	Lower tolerance for the nutritional deprivation
Prematurity	Impaired postnatal growth
	Enhanced risk of cardiovascular disease, type 2 diabetes, etc.

An important conclusion from these observations is that a general response of the fetus to many different adverse conditions is to limit fetal growth and alter the metabolic machinery to cope with the signals of distress. Moreover, the response varies with the time in gestation. One of the best-documented examples of the different responses to nutritional limitation is the study of the Dutch Hunger Winter, a brief but very severe famine during the 1944-1945 winter during World War II. Nutritional deprivation during the first trimester of pregnancy led to children who developed heart disease as adults. Deprivation during the second trimester saw an elevated incidence of kidney disease as adults. Finally, deprivation during the third trimester resulted in increased incidence of type 2 diabetes.

Predicting the post-natal environment –not always correctly

The original Barker model accounted for the observed consequences of a low birth weight, but it could not account for those cases in which chronic adult disease was associated with a continuum of birth weights, including normal and even at the high end of normal. In other words, how to account for adult disease developing even in a well fed fetus.

The latest and most well developed model that tries to incorporate many observations difficult to explain in the original Barker concept proposes that many of the adaptive responses made by the fetus are not for short term, immediate advantage, but rather in expectation of the future postnatal environment.

Disease risk in this "predictive adaptive response model", as it has been called, is a consequence of the degree of match or mismatch between exposures in two environments. First, the pre-birth or early post-natal period, that is, during the "plastic" period, during which it is possible to mold or program responses with long term consequences, and second, the post-plastic stage. The greater the degree of mismatch between the two environments, the greater the risk of disease. So that pre-natal nutritional abundance followed by post-natal limitation would also increase the risk of adult disease.

In other words, the fetus is making predictions about the post-natal environment and programming itself for this predicted environment. If it misjudges the situation, there will be problems. Hence, choosing the survival phenotype option, and then being confronted with nutritional overabundance after birth may lead to adult disease. This modification adds a very interesting twist to the dynamics of fetal responses.

The fetus isn't the only player in this game, the mother imposes her own limitations, and these are known as maternal constraint. The fetus, under conditions of nutritional abundance and if not restrained in its growth, would continue to grow so as to pose a threat to the well being of the mother. Hence, the mother has developed mechanisms to restrict the growth of the fetus to allow for a normal birth, for example, restrictions on the ability to accommodate a large fetus, and on the placenta to regulate the transfer of nutrients to the fetus. Maternal constraint is greater in first pregnancies, adolescent pregnancies and in mothers with shorter stature, in all of which the fetus tends to be of small size.

Fetal life as a futures stock market

We have all seen the remarkable images of a fetus in the womb that have appeared in many publications – the baby serenely floating in the amniotic sac, sometimes with its thumb in its mouth. There is a sense of calm and tranquility in these images, as if the baby in the womb was isolated from, impervious to, and protected from the outside world. In fact, as we have learned from the short discussion above, the opposite is true. The fetus is really a hot bed of activity, continually reacting to signals from the outside and making decisions that may affect the health of the baby long after birth. The fetus is engaging in what we could call "futures trading", similar to what the Chicago stock traders do predicting the price of hog bellies, soy beans, and many other agricultural products. And if the fetus, just as the Chicago futures trader, misjudges the future and make the wrong decision, it will pay a price for that mistake as an adult.

By "decisions" is meant remodeling genetic activity – turning some genes on, others off – in a way that the remodeling persists into adult life. The details of the programming will vary depending on the stage of gestation, and the type of adverse condition experienced. In some cases the genetic changes may be even more profound because they may persist into the following and subsequent generations. This type of effect is seen in some parts of India, where living conditions result in small women, who have small babies who also become small females, and so on.

We still have much to learn about fetal dynamics, but we know enough to imagine that we should be able to match pre-natal with post-natal conditions so that we could program the baby in the womb to grow up into a healthier adult. We have a real hope that the chronic adult diseases of the modern age may in the not too distant future be a thing of the past.

PART C

Our Perilous Beginnings

Chapter 9

Pregnancy Loss and Birth Defects

Inescapably, this is me – the diagnosis
Is cause for anger at those
Who brightly say we choose our destinies.
There is no store
of courage, wit or will
Can save me from myself and I must face
My children, feeling like
That wicked fairy, uninvited
At the christening, bestowing on my own,
Amidst murmurs of apprehension, a most
Unwanted gift – that
Of a blighted mind. No one
Could tell me of this curse when I
Was young and dreamt of children
And the graces they would bear. Later,
It seemed that a chill morning
Revealed deeper layers
Of truth. For my romancing
There is a price to pay –
Perhaps my children's children
Will pass this tollgate after me.
My grandmothers gaze down from their frames
on my wall, sadly wondering. (1, Meg Campbell, Heredity)

When things go wrong

A pregnancy evokes in us two conflicting emotions – the extravagant hope for a happy outcome, and simultaneously, a deep anxiety and perhaps even a dread that something will go wrong. For we know deep within us that not every pregnancy will be successful, nor will every newborn be healthy and strong. In some cases, the newborn infant may be severely deformed, an occurrence that can have devastating consequences for the family. Human societies have long been aware of the births of deformed infants. Images of deformities in the form of drawings, carvings, or sculptures have been left in the ruins of many ancient societies.

In previous times, severely deformed infants were termed monsters *(Latin, monstrum, meaning omen or warning)*, because these births were seen as a sign from the gods. In a book published in 1573 by A. Paré, titled **On Monsters and Marvels**, and which became widely known in Europe during the sixteenth and seventeenth centuries, the first two explanations for the birth of deformed infants were listed as the grace of God and the wrath of God. He didn't seem to be aware of the contradiction in these two explanations. Even today, in our secular and scientific world, these buried ancient beliefs may surface again when we are confronted with the birth of a child with abnormalities. When searching for an explanation the temptation to view the birth of a deformed child as punishment may be almost irresistible. And even if we do not see it as an omen, how do we assuage the guilt – as Meg Campbell says in her beautiful poem 'for my romancing there is a price to pay', a price to be paid by both the parent and the child.

As much as we might want to avoid thinking about things going wrong in a pregnancy, it is important to try to understand as much as we can about how they occur. The more we know or understand may possibly help us in preventing them. As devastating as they might be from a familial point of view, from a scientific perspective each case can be very informative. This was understood as long ago as 1882 when J. Paget, noted embryologist wrote:

"We ought not to set them aside with idle thoughts or idle words about "curiosities" or "chances." Not one of them is without meaning; not one that might not become the beginning of excellent knowledge, if only we could answer the question - why is it rare, or being rare, why did it in this instance happen? (2, J. Paget, cited in K. L. Moore and T. V. N. Persaud, The Developing Brain)

Let's begin by providing an overview of what is now an enormous field of study – fetal loss and birth defects. We will continue below with much more detail. This is not easy reading, but we hope you may begin to appreciate the complexities of pregnancy.

Fetal loss

Fetal loss refers to the termination of a pregnancy due to so-called natural causes, resulting in a spontaneous abortion, more commonly known as a miscarriage. A miscarriage is clearly distinguishable from an induced abortion, which requires the willful intervention on the part of the pregnant female herself or some other person. Fetal loss can occur at any time after fertilization. The ones we are aware of and which we call miscarriages are those that take place after the pregnancy have clearly been established. The incidence of reported miscarriages gives us a minimum estimate of post-implantation loss, or loss after a clinically recognized pregnancy has been established. Although post-implantation loss is in principle easy to measure (recall the hormone human chorionic gonadotropin (hCG) provides a reliable indicator of implantation), in practice, it is difficult to measure accurately since many losses go unreported or unnoticed, particularly if they occur very early in the implantation stages. Delayed menstruation in a woman who is sexually active may in fact represent a very early stage post-implantation loss, but is rarely reported as such.

Pre-implantation loss, which occurs before a pregnancy is established, can also occur, but this type of loss is more difficult to measure since no reliable measures of fertilization are yet available. Despite these limitations, a number of recent studies suggest that pre-implantation loss is quite high and that perhaps as many as 50 percent of conceptions are lost before or during the very early stages of implantation, while an additional 20 percent are lost between implantation and the end of the first trimester of pregnancy. In other words, most human conceptions are lost before implantation, before the woman knows she has conceived. Hence, only about 30 percent of human conceptions lead to a live birth. Humans have an amazingly high rate of fetal loss, maybe as much as 10-fold higher than in other mammalian species in the wild or in laboratories. We don't really understand why is the case.

Birth defects

Birth defects are abnormalities that may involve anatomical, metabolic, functional, or behavioral anomalies. They may be of major or minor clinical significance. Some involve an easily noticeable anatomical, physiological, or hormone abnormality that is detected at birth – these are referred to as congenital abnormalities. Other defects may involve more subtle alterations that may not necessarily manifest themselves at birth, and several months or even years can pass before the consequences of the defects can be established.

The incidence of birth defects depends on how they are defined. Congenital abnormalities (for example, major anatomical anomalies, spinal bifida, cleft lip, limb abnormalities, heart defects) are seen in 2 – 3 percent of newborn infants. They are the leading cause (more than 20 percent) of infant mortality in the U. S., and account for over 30 percent of admissions to hospital intensive care units. If we include other types of anomalies diagnosed after birth and within the first few years of life, the incidence of birth defects increases to 4 – 6 percent. In addition, a certain fraction of infants die within a few months after birth. These are known as perinatal deaths, and they occur in about 1 - 2 percent of all births. Hence, maybe up to 7 or 8 percent of newborn infants are born with some type of significant defect. By any measure this is a soberingly high number. How many of us are aware of these statistics when we begin to think about starting a family?

We understand now that birth defects are the tip of a large iceberg of abnormal conceptions. Most of these abnormal conceptions are eliminated before birth – only a few survive to birth. Elimination of abnormal conceptions is accomplished by a 'surveillance' system that functions right after fertilization. The surveillance system, although highly effective, is not perfect, and hence, birth defects represent its failures, cases that were missed by the surveillance system.

Why things go wrong

Fetal loss and birth defects are the result of disturbances in the developmental program that converts the fertilized egg into a fully developed infant. Perhaps an unappreciated aspect of modern biology is that we have come to recognize that developmental defects, tragic and unfortunate though they might be, are nevertheless to be expected. A moment's reflection will convince us that the development of an individual from the fertilized egg must be incredibly complex. There must be thousands of ways in which things can go wrong during the 9-month gestation period. Perhaps we should not be surprised when things go wrong, but instead should marvel that most people are born normal and healthy.

Disturbances in normal development can arise from many different factors. For our purposes, it useful to group these into two major categories: intrinsic (genetic), and extrinsic (environmental). In most cases, we do not understand precisely how these different factors produce specific disorders. Nevertheless, even our limited understanding has had important consequences, since it has led us to recognize that certain types of disorders can be prevented. Not all disorders are preventable, however, nor will they be in the near future.

Hence, even under the most ideal conditions, the incidence of fetal loss or birth defects cannot be reduced to zero. It is worth remembering that a measure of an advanced and humane society is how it treats its weakest and most defenseless members. J. Warkany, in his intensively detailed compendium Congenital Malformations put it well when he said

". . . to contribute to the care of the physically and mentally handicapped is the price to be paid by those who have normal children - the price to be paid for overcoming the barbarism and cruelty inherent in societies that eliminate the weak and dispose of the deformed. (3, J. Warkany Congenital malformations)

So let's begin our uneasy journey.

Intrinsic factors – the genetic lottery

Chromosome anomalies – the aging of the egg

Chromosome abnormalities, most commonly meaning abnormal numbers of chromosomes, are the major cause of fetal loss in humans, probably accounting for 70 percent of cases of fetal loss. Most of this loss occurs before implantation, that is, before the fertilized egg has begun to implant itself in the endometrium of the uterus, and before the woman even knows that she has conceived. These abnormalities arise from errors in the packaging of the chromosomes during oogenesis or spermatogenesis.

Let's consider what we mean by this. Under normal circumstances the egg will carry 22 autosomes and one X chromosome, while the sperm will carry 22 autosomes and an X chromosome, or 22 autosomes and a Y chromosome (refer to Appendix 1 for a discussion of the autosomes and sex chromosomes). Infrequent mistakes during the formation of the egg or the sperm may generate eggs that carry 22 or 24 chromosomes, rather that the normal 23, and similarly for sperm. The technical term for this condition is aneuploidy.

If a sperm with the normal complement of 23 chromosomes fertilizes an egg with 22 chromosomes (that is, one less than the normal number), the result is an embryo that has 45, rather than the normal 46, chromosomes. This condition is referred to as a monosomy. The monosomic condition is always lethal, that is, no monosomic embryos have been known to survive to birth. An embryo that has 47 chromosomes is known as a trisomic embryo, and this condition is almost always lethal, with one exception, and this is trisomy-21 (meaning these embryos carry 3 copies of chromosome 21).

Trisomy-21 leads to the clinical condition known as Down's syndrome, which probably most of you know something about. It occurs with an overall incidence of about 1 in 600 births. Trisomies for all the other chromosomes lead in most case to early fetal loss.

Aneuploidy, an abnormal number of chromosomes, is much more common in cogenesis (egg formation) than in spermatogenesis (sperm formation). For example, about 2 - 3 percent of sperm are aneuploid (that is, have a chromosome number other than 23), while around 25 percent of eggs are aneuploid in young adult women. Moreover, the percentage of aneuploid eggs increases markedly with maternal age, especially beginning after the age of 35. Aneuploidy in sperm does not appear to increase significantly with paternal age. This difference has important consequences.

First, this means that most cases of fetal loss are due to aneuploidy in the eggs. Second, aneuploidy increases with maternal age. Consider trisomy-21as an example: its incidence in women of ages 20 – 24 is about 1 in 1400; at 30-34, 1/700; at 35, 1/50; at 41, 1/85; at 43, 1/50, older than 43, 1/25. The substantial increase in the incidence of trisomy-21 with maternal age means that a significant fraction of trisomy-21 babies are born to older mothers.

But why should aneuplody increase with maternal age? This has been a hotly debated question, and we don't have a complete answer yet, but in some way it may due to the aging of the eggs. You may recall that in the female her stock of oocytes was produced by around the fifth month of gestation. We don't really know how to define 'aging' of the eggs in a precise way as yet, but it is possible that the long interval (years) from the time the egg was produced and when it is ovulated must be important.

Why is aneuploidy so lethal?

Another really important question: why does a missing chromosome or having an extra copy of a chromosome produce such catastrophic effects? Again, we don't have a complete answer, but the lethality associated with aneuploidy suggests that some genes on a given pair of chromosome have to be present in exactly two copies – one copy from the mother and one copy from the father. One of the really interesting discoveries of the last couple of decades is a category of genes known as imprinted genes. These are genes that are marked (i.e., imprinted) in a special way to indicate that they have come from the mother or the father. For this class of genes an exact balance of the maternal and paternal imprint is necessary for normal embryonic and fetal development. Any variation appears to result in an early term miscarriage. So consider: in a trisomic-16 embryo, for example, two copies of chromosome 16 come from one parent, and the other copy comes from the other parent. From the imprinted gene point of view, there is an imbalance between the maternal and paternal imprinted genes that happen to be located on chromosome 16. The lethality associated with the imbalance in imprinted genes appears to be due to a change in the way this class of genes function in the early stages of embryo development.

Errors in fertilization or embryogenesis

Two other types of chromosome anomalies contribute to fetal loss. One of them arises from errors in fertilization known as dispermy, in which two sperm fertilize the egg. This type of fertilization generates embryos with three complete sets of chromosomes, and these embryos are generally lost before birth. Estimates suggest that perhaps 1 to 2 percent of conceptions are dispermic conceptions.

The second type arises during the first few days after fertilization – errors in embryogenesis. These are not due to aneuploidy in either the egg or the sperm, but are due to mistakes in the very first divisions (the first few days after fertilization) of the fertilized egg. We know relatively little about how these errors arise, but the little information we have about them has come from studies of in vitro fertilization (IVF) – generated embryos (see Chapter 12). For example, about 50 percent of 3-day old IVF embryos are chromosomally abnormal and carry a very high risk of implantation failure. Investigators suspect normally generated embryos at the same stages are also chromosomally abnormal.

Chromosome abnormalities have a devastating effect during gestation, but they account for only a small fraction of birth defects noted after birth. This is probably because most embryos or fetuses carrying chromosome abnormalities are lost before birth. On the other hand, gene mutations, whether generated spontaneously or triggered by environmental factors, account for a large fraction of birth defects. The defects span a wide spectrum of severity.

Gene mutations

Developmental defects during embryogenesis can also arise from mutations in one or several genes. At present more than 10,000 disorders linked to single or multiple gene mutations have been catalogued. Fairly well known examples of monogenic disorders are sickle cell anemia, cystic fibrosis, Tay-Sachs disease, hemophilia, Duchenne muscular dystrophy, Huntington's disease, achondroplasia, neurofibromatosis, fragile X syndrome, familial breast and ovarian cancer, and phenylketonuria (PKU).

The contribution of gene mutations to prenatal loss cannot be estimated accurately, but it is significantly less than chromosome anomalies. On the other hand, single gene mutations account for about 7 – 8 percent of birth defects. For many single-gene disorders, we can make a direct connection between the disorder and a particular gene. There is no cure for most of the monogenic disorders, but palliative therapy is available for some: for example, clotting factor replacement for hemophilia, and dietary modification for phenylketonuria (PKU).

Disorders that arise from mutations in more than one gene, although much more difficult to categorize, may account for 20 – 25 percent of congenital disorders. Examples are neural tube defects, cleft lip, cleft palate, congenital heart disease, diabetes, and mental disorders such as schizophrenia and bipolar disease. In most cases the genes involved have not yet been identified.

Mutation rate is higher in males than in females

The older we are as fathers, the more likely we will pass on our mutations. The more mutations we pass on, the more likely that one of them is going to be deleterious. (4, Kári Stefansson, cited in Ewen Callaway, Fathers bequeath more mutations as they age)

Is the mutation rate the same in males and females? The British geneticist J.B.S Haldane suggested as early as 1930 that children inherit more mutations from their fathers than their mothers. Although at the time, he could not provide any evidence, he proposed a mechanism. The difference in the mutation rate in males and females arises from the difference in the way the gametes, that is, eggs or sperm, are produced in the two sexes. The mutation rate depends on the number of cell divisions from the fertilized egg (the zygote) to the gamete, the egg in the female and the sperm in the male. In the female, the eggs are formed only once, and these oocytes do not divide anymore. The number of cell divisions from the zygote (fertilized egg) to the egg is estimated to be about 24.

In the male, on the other hand, a stock of progenitor cells (spermatogonia) for sperm is produced during fetal life, and this stock serves as a self-generating source for spermatozoa that are produced continually once puberty begins. The continuous nature of cell divisions in spermatogenesis means that many divisions from zygote to sperm take place in the male, and also that more have taken place in an older male than in a younger one. It is estimated that the number of cell divisions between the zygote and the spermatozoon is about 197 when the male is 20 years old, 427 when he is 30 years old, and 792 when he is 45 years old. With over 100 million spermatozoa being produced per day, the testis is a "hot spot" of mutational activity. We might expect therefore that sperm would be at a much higher risk of transmitting heritable mutations to offspring compared to oocytes.

A comprehensive 2012 study of dozens of Icelandic families, the largest study of this type ever published, provides the most compelling confirmation of the mutation differences. The study found that fathers passed on nearly four times as many new mutations as mothers on average, and that the number of new mutations being passed on increases with the fathers' age. The study estimates that a 36-year-old male will pass on twice as many mutations as a man of 20, increasing to a factor of eight in a 70-year-old.

Although most such mutations are innocuous, this finding provides a way of understanding other studies that have shown that the risk of autism in a child increases with the father's age. Such a connection may also apply to other disorders such as schizophrenia. Since so many men delay fatherhood until later in most Western societies, what are the implications for future – increase in genetic disorders? Should we worry about this? But keeping in mind that mutations are the basis for evolution (see Appendix 1 for a discussion of mutations), the lead author of the study Kári Stefánsson commented *"Your could argue what is bad for the next generation is good for the future of the our species." (4, Kári Stefánsson, cited in Ewen Callaway,* Fathers bequeath more mutations as they age)

In summary, the male is responsible for a much larger fraction of genetic disease (that is, due to gene mutations) that leads birth defects than the female. The female, on the other hand, is responsible for most of the chromosomal anomalies that lead to fetal loss.

The Faustian bargain

There is a particularly interesting sidelight to all of this. In scrotal species like humans, the testes are a few degrees cooler than body temperature, and they operate in a very narrow temperature window: too low a temperature, and spermatogenesis and fertility decreases significantly; too high a temperature, and spermatogenesis also diminishes but the mutation rate goes up. Testes retained within the abdominal cavity (known clinically as cryptoorchidism) are extremely susceptible to the development of testicular cancer, especially cancers of the germ line. Hence, the evolution of the scrotum may have provided a convenient way to keep the mutation rate at some acceptable level. In nonscrotal species, special venous cooling mechanisms have appeared to insulate the testis from the core body temperature. Hence, in scrotal and nonscrotal species, cooling mechanisms that reduce the internal testis temperature appear to be an important aspect of testicular function.

Hence, the testis appears to have negotiated an uneasy Faustian bargain. In order to ensure the propagation of the species, it has to produce spermatozoa at a prodigious rate. A high price is paid for this, however: a much higher germ line mutation rate, and consequently, a high rate of genetic disorders. This is the price paid for maintaining fertility.

Maternal factors – additional complexity

The inability of the mother to support a pregnancy to term can also be due to maternal defects or deficiencies. These include, for example, endometrial defects resulting in an unstable endometrium, a whole variety of endocrine disorders, malformations of the uterus, or adverse immunological interactions between wife and husband, and placental disorders. Placental disorders, caused by abnormal implantations, are relatively common, and some studies suggest that they occur perhaps in as many as 1/3 of human pregnancies. The degree of severity can vary from relatively minor to very severe, often resulting in a spontaneous abortion (miscarriage). One common type of placental disorder that has been studied intensively in the last few years is pre-eclampsia. This disorder, characterized by very high blood pressure and proteinuria (presence of protein in the urine), generally becomes apparent at about 20 weeks gestation, and carries a high risk of mortality for mother and baby.

Pregnancy places special dietary demands on the mother. Metabolic adjustments to pregnancy are met by adjustment in the food intake, or nowadays, by supplementation with vitamins and other essential dietary requirements. Deficiencies in certain compounds can lead to growth retardation and other, more serious disorders. One of the best-documented examples of the association between a dietary compound and a serious disorder is that of neural tube defects (NTDs), disorders affecting the spinal cord and the brain. In the United States, the two most common NTDs are spina bifida (incomplete closing of the spine) and anencephaly (failure of the brain to form). Anencephalic infants die shortly before or after birth, while spina bifida infants will suffer from varying degrees of paralysis and disability. One important discovery of the last decade is that 50 – 70 percent of these two disorders can be prevented by folic acid supplementation during pregnancy. The U. S. Public Health Service recommends that all women of childbearing age consume 0.4 mg of folic acid daily because over half of the pregnancies in the United States are unplanned, and because these two defects occur about 3 - 4 weeks after fertilization, before most women are aware that they are pregnant.

Extrinsic factors – environmental agents

A broad category of external conditions or agents (with respect to the embryo or fetus) can disturb normal development. These agents are known as teratogens, and they come in many forms. Teratogens may be biological agents (infectious organisms such as bacteria or viruses), biochemical agents (therapeutic or recreational drugs), or environmental toxins (industrial chemicals, household chemicals, pesticides, heavy metals).

It is important to recognize that different tissue and organ systems develop at different times during gestation. The sensitivity of a particular organ system to teratogenic factors will not be the same at all periods of gestation. During the first two weeks, encompassing the pre-implantation and the peri-implantation stages, the embryo is particularly sensitive to genetic (typically chromosomal anomalies) factors, but may be relatively insensitive to environmental teratogens.

Weeks 3 – 8 of gestation, during which all of the organ systems develop, is the period during which the embryo is most sensitive to teratogenic effects. However, for each organ system, there are periods of major sensitivity followed by a period of lower sensitivity. Exposure to teratogens during the periods of major sensitivity may lead to severe abnormalities, while exposure at other times may have no effect or only minor consequences. The central nervous system, for example, appears to be continually sensitive to the effects of teratogens, with major sensitivity during the first 16 weeks of gestation, and less, but still significant sensitivity during the remaining time. This may account for the observation that defects of the brain and brain function account for the largest fraction of malformations of human organs. Heart, kidney, and limb abnormalities account for a significant fraction of major abnormalities as well.

Biological agents - viruses and bacteria

The embryo and fetus are susceptible to infection by the microorganisms to which the mother is exposed. Fortunately, the maternal immune system is able to eliminate or inactivate the large majority of infectious agents. However, a few may escape destruction and enter the fetal circulatory system through the placenta. The fetal central nervous system appears to be particularly sensitive to the effects of these agents. The consequences of these infections is generally quite severe, and include spontaneous abortions, stillbirths, premature births, multiple tissue damage, congenital abnormalities, mental retardation, and sensitivity to disease after birth.

The teratogenic potential, that is, ability to produce a birth defect, of the rubella virus, the causative agent for German measles, was probably the first well-documented example of the teratogenic effects of a virus. The risk of fetal infection is about 20 percent if the mother is exposed to rubella. However, the sensitive period for teratogenic damage by rubella infections occurs between the week 3 and week 12 of development, and the effects can vary greatly in severity. This example illustrates again the important principle that sensitivity to teratogenic agents is not uniform during gestation. Since a vaccine is available for the prevention of German measles, rubella-caused teratogenesis is very rare in the developed world.

A few examples of other infectious organisms that have been consistently associated with developmental disorders include the chicken pox virus - cataracts, hydrocephaly (water in the brain), neurological defects; Venezuelan equine encephalitis virus – microcephaly (underdeveloped brain), degeneration of central nervous system tissues; *Toxoplasmosis gondi* – microcephaly, mental retardation. Several others are organisms responsible for sexually transmitted diseases - herpes simplex virus, which causes genital herpes, human immunodeficiency virus (HIV), which causes AIDS, and *Treponema pallidum*, which causes syphilis.

Therapeutic and recreational drugs

A wide variety of biochemicals can be transferred from the mother to the embryo or fetus. Two categories of such compounds are therapeutic drugs (prescribed for controlling or treating disease or pathologies), and recreational drugs, whether licit or illicit. The placenta is not as effective a barrier to the passage of many chemicals as was once thought. The effect of these particular compounds depends on the dose that the conceptus experiences, not the dose experienced by the maternal system, and also on period of gestation. Some may produce quite severe effects, death, major malformations, mental retardation, and functional disorders.

Others may not produce clear-cut morphological or physiological defects, but may result in intrauterine growth retardation (IUGR). IUGR is a consequence of disordered fetal growth that may have serious consequences post-natally. One important diagnostic criterion for IUGR is prematurity and/or lower-than-normal birth weight. IUGR, for example, is a common condition in infants whose mothers were on drugs during pregnancy. IUGR has been associated with varying degrees of neurodevelopmental impairment, from learning and cognitive defects and behavioral difficulties to epilepsy, cerebral palsy, and mental retardation, as well as being a risk factor for diabetes, hypertension, and cardiovascular disease. Assessing the consequences of IUGR remains a difficult enterprise.

The use of prescription and nonprescription drugs during pregnancy is surprisingly high. Some studies indicate that 40 to 90 percent of pregnant women take at least one drug, and some take as many as four, during the first trimester of pregnancy, the most sensitive period for teratogenesis. A good number of these are known to have teratogenic effects. A few examples: methotrexate has been prescribed as an anticancer drug and for palliative therapy for rheumatic diseases. A few children with an uncommon and characteristic pattern of congenital anomalies have been born to women who received the drug during the first trimester of pregnancy. The effects of methotrexate have been attributed to the fact that it is a folic acid antagonist, meaning that its administration results in folic acid deficiency, which can have serious consequences.

Phenytoin is one of several drugs prescribed for seizure disorders, and a characteristic pattern of congenital abnormalities (heart disorders, and facial clefts) has been seen in among children of epileptic women treated with drugs of this type. Phenobarbitol, a barbiturate, is an anticonvulsant, and there is some limited evidence for teratogenic risk, but the risk is considered to be small to moderate.

A recently recognized class of teratogens is the retinoids, vitamin A analogs, prescribed in the treatment of dermatologic diseases such as acne and psoriasis (Accutane, the trade name for isotretinoin, is one of more popular retinoids). Children born to women treated with isotretinoin during the first trimester have been born with severe craniofacial abnormalities and cardiovascular defects. Based on the data collected, the teratogenic risk associated with retinoids is high.

Recreational drugs

Alcohol

The clinical characteristics that are now known as fetal alcohol syndrome (FAS) were first described by the French pediatrician, Lemoine, in 1968, and these included the following: growth deficiency, microcephaly (very small head due to lack of brain tissue development), anomalous facial characteristics, cardiac defects, limb deformities, hyperactivity, attention deficit disorder, delay in psychomotor and language development, poor visual memory, psychosocial maladjustment, low IQ, and mental retardation.

What is interesting about alcohol is that its effects have been suspected or known for a long time. Aristotle pointed out in his writings that women drunkards often gave birth to abnormal children. Drinking alcohol by the bride on her wedding night was prohibited in ancient Greek custom. During the English gin epidemic (1720 - 1750), a sharp decrease in the price of gin led to enormous problems in the health and well-being of infants. When the cause was identified, the English government raised the price of gin high enough to control the amount of gin consumption. The National Institute of Medicine estimates that in the United States 20 percent of women who drink continue to do so while they are pregnant. As a result, about 1 infant in every 1000 born has symptoms of alcohol damage.

Exposure to alcohol during the embryonic period is considered to produce the most severe defects. However, exposure to alcohol at all stages may be dangerous, particularly since the central nervous system remains sensitive to teratogenic action throughout gestation. Defects produced during the latter stages of pregnancy may not result in obvious abnormalities, but some evidence suggests that cognitive ability may be impaired. How much alcohol is safe? No precise answer can be given to this question. The safest course is to avoid it altogether.

Tobacco

Tobacco smoke contains over 3500 different compounds, many of which are mutagenic. The most abundant, nicotine, carbon monoxide, and hydrogen cyanide, have been considered to be the most toxic during pregnancy.

Maternal smoking

Many studies have shown that maternal smoking is associated with a number of adverse effects and complications of pregnancy, including spontaneous abortions, preterm delivery, lower birth weight (200 – 377 gm less than gestation-matched controls). Low birth weight is associated with higher rates of infant mortality and morbidity. In the offspring, increased risk of ADHD, externalizing behavior, decreased general cognitive function, and deficits in learning and memory tasks have been reported in recent studies. Recent studies indicate that smoking impairs placental function and morphology – nicotine and other components of tobacco smoke lead to hypoxia (restriction of oxygen flow due to competitive inhibition by carbon monoxide) and vasoconstriction resulting in reduced flow of uterine blood to the placenta. Hypoxia-induced damage can occur at very low exposures to tobacco smoke, and hence, second hand smoke is considered to be very detrimental. Exposure to tobacco smoke during the first trimester when placental development is taking place differentiation will likely have the most detrimental effects.

Paternal smoking

Up until recently much less attention had been paid to paternal smoking, but it has been recognized that its effects may be no less significant. In a report published in 1986 by the National Research Council, paternal smoking was associated with increased risk of peri-natal mortality, lower birth weight, increased risk of congenital malformations, and increased risk of childhood cancers. For example, the neonatal death rate for infants of smoking fathers was 17.2 per 1000 live births, while it was 11.9 per 1000 live births for infants of nonsmoking fathers. The rate of major malformations in newborns was 2.9 percent for smoking, and 0.8 percent, for nonsmoking fathers. Maternal smoking has little effect on the incidence of childhood cancers, while there appears to be a clear correlation with paternal smoking.

The paternal smoking effects are now considered to be due to mutagenic effects of tobacco smoke in the testis. Tobacco smoke contains many mutagenic compounds that are easily absorbed into the blood, and therefore, eventually reach the testes. The continual production of spermatozoa during the male's reproductive lifetime means that paternal smoking may increase the mutation rate in sperm. The risk that an embryo will be carrying genetic lesions with the potential to disturb normal development or that may result in childhood cancers is increased if the father is a smoker. The contribution cannot be estimated with great precision, but there is significant evidence that damage to the fetus may be as important as that of maternal smoking. It is no wonder that tobacco has been called *"the most significant reproductive poison in current use." (5, R. Forman, S. Gilmour-White, N. Forman)*

Cocaine

Cocaine is a topical anesthetic and a powerful central nervous system (CNS) stimulant. No controlled study on the effects of cocaine on the fetus has been carried out. However, a variety of malformations (microcephaly, kidney defects, cardiac defects, and limb deformities) have been reported in

169

children of mothers known to have used cocaine during pregnancy. A few case studies have also indicated that cocaine taken during pregnancy may lead to IUGR and behavioral abnormalities during infancy and childhood. The most reliable information suggests that premature expulsion of the placenta, and cocaine-induced fetal CNS hemorrhaging may be the most important types of damage due to cocaine exposure.

Environmental toxins – an important and continuing concern

It is estimated that more than 60,000 chemicals are used in manufacturing processes, and 500 or more new ones are being introduced yearly. These include organic solvents, heavy metals, and pesticides (over 21,000 of these are registered) Exposure to most of these chemicals is generally confined to the workers in the manufacturing plants that use them. However, a few may get dispersed widely, and in some circumstances can pose a possible threat to pregnant women. For example, the effects of exposure to heavy metals such as lead, chromium, and mercury to the people who live in the vicinity of refineries and other types of manufacturing plants are well documented. The teratogenic effects of exposure to polychlorinated biphenyls (PCBs) used in the manufacture of plastics, paints, and other products led to the worldwide ban on their manufacture or use. The PCBs have a long half-life will be around for 100 years or more. Although PCBs have been banned, they appear to have permeated the environment. They can be detected in the food chain and in almost all tissues of the body. Whether the low levels of PCBs detected in the environment have significant teratogenic potential remains a hotly debated topic.

A number of environmental chemicals turn out to be weak estrogen agonists or weak androgen antagonists, which means that exposure to them at a critical time in gestation could disrupt normal development of the male internal and external genitalia. One of the best-documented examples is DDT, used very effectively to control mosquito populations. One of the breakdown products of DDT has anti-androgenic properties, which accounts for the major effects of DDT exposure – abnormal development of the male genitalia. DDT is now banned in most countries, but it has a half-life of about 100 years, and significantly levels are still found in the rural areas of the American South where it was used most extensively.

Over 3000 environmental agents have been tested for teratogenicity and developmental toxicity, categories that include significant tissue and organ malformations, embryo and fetal lethality, intrauterine growth retardation (IUGR), and different types of functional impairment. About 1200 of these agents are known to produce congenital anomalies in experimental animals, but only about 40 are known to cause defects in humans. The criteria for establishing an agent as a teratogen or developmental toxin are quite stringent, since it is important to establish a convincing connection between exposure, consequence, and mechanism of action.

The number of environmental chemicals with teratogenic potential is large, but exposure of the general population to most of these is considered to be below the threshold needed to have significant developmental effects. There is widespread concern by the public that environmental chemicals are responsible for many developmental defects, functional impairment, childhood cancers, and even cognitive disorders, conditions for which no obvious cause can be found. Particularly troublesome have been the "cancer clusters" that have received much publicity over the last few years. These are cases in which an unusual number of cancers are seen in certain communities. Generally, some aspect of the environment, such as contaminated groundwater, the soil, the food, or the air, is blamed for the observed increase in cancers. However, despite intensive and exhaustive investigation by public health officials, not one of the cancer clusters found in the United States has been shown to be due to an environmental cause. In other parts of the world, in only a handful of clusters among the hundreds reported, has an environmental cause been convincingly identified.

In most cases, we don't know what doses are dangerous for any given compound, and we don't have an accurate measure of the average dose to which the average person is exposed. Many investigators suspect that for most toxins the average exposure levels are probably below the levels that would be expected to have a teratogenic effect. This is a question that has been hotly debated in the scientific literature, but we don't yet have a general or conclusive answer. We don't yet have accurate measurements of the extent to which environmental toxins account for human congenital abnormalities in the general population.

What can we conclude from all of this?

It is clear that many chemicals produce very obvious and severe malformations or abnormalities, and we properly do everything we can to minimize exposures to such compounds. The information we have at present indicates that alcohol and smoking may be responsible for a large fraction of developmental abnormalities due to external agents. Many of the defects produced by alcohol and smoking may be subtle. The most insidious of these are those that perturb brain development and affect cognitive and psychological function. The cumulative cost of such defects to the individual and to the society is incalculable.

On the other hand, it has been very difficult to demonstrate convincingly that normal exposures to the large number of environmental chemicals to which we are exposed contribute significantly to the overall rates of fetal loss or birth defects. It is ironic that up until recently we as a society have been much less concerned about alcohol and smoking, about whose effects in the general population there is no doubt, than we have been about environmental chemicals, whose contributions to developmental abnormalities, at least at this time in our history, are likely much less important.

Prenatal screening and diagnosis

What does prenatal screening involve?

Reproductive medicine both heals and harms women; it both produces and destroys fetuses; it is both palliative and iatrogenic; it both opens and closes reproductive possibilities; it is both a consumer choice and a form of social control; and it both shapes cultural meanings and it is a product of culture. (6, M. Casper The making of the unborn patient)

During the last decade prenatal screening for chromosome abnormalities and genetic disorders has become the standard in obstetrical care, especially if pregnant woman is over 35 years old. In other cases it is offered as an option for families that belong to certain ethnic groups in which certain types of disorders are much more common than in the general population. For single gene disorders, for example, Tay Sachs disorder in Ashkenazi Jewish parents, recently extended to Cajun and French-Canadian parents; cystic fibrosis in parents of northern and western European ancestry; sickle cell anemia in parents of African and African-American ancestry. The American College of Medical Genetics has suggested that prenatal screening should be mandated for 29 disorders, but from a health policy perspective this recommendation remains difficult to implement.

Prenatal screening and diagnosis has been widely accepted by the public at large, and has been considered valuable for several reasons. An often-stated long-term goal is to be able to identify an abnormal prenatal condition so that treatment for the condition before birth can be devised. We are still a long way from being able to do this in any efficacious way.

Prenatal screening and diagnosis may also be very useful in assessing the status of the fetus in cases where the method or timing of birth needs to be planned. For many parents identifying embryos carrying chromosomal aberrations or other severe disorders early in gestation may give the parents an opportunity to prepare for the birth of a baby with birth defects, or perhaps provide them with the option of terminating the pregnancy early. This area of reproductive medicine has evolved rapidly in the last decade and has become almost an esoteric field loaded with the language of statistics and probability, making it difficult for the average person to understand. We'll try to simplify it so that the main lesson comes through.

Screening versus diagnostic testing

First, it's important to distinguish between screening, which does not yield simple yes or no answers, and diagnostic testing, which does. Prenatal diagnostic methods are invasive in that they require tissue from the fetus. There are several invasive diagnostic methods currently used - amniocentesis, chorionic villus sampling, (CVS), cordocentesis, fetal biopsy, and preimplantation embryo biopsy.

Amniocentesis, introduced in the 1970s, involves puncturing the uterus and amniotic sac with a fine needle to remove a sample of amniotic fluid. Cells from the fetus are normally found in the amniotic fluid, and these are then subjected to chromosome analysis. The earliest time in gestation that amniocentesis can be performed successfully is 16 to 18 weeks. CVS is a placental biopsy in which cells are taken for analysis from chorionic villi, the invading tissue of the placenta. CVS can be done earlier than amniocentesis towards the end of the first trimester. Cordocentesis involves sampling blood from the umbilical cord. This has been useful in evaluating the blood status of the fetus or detecting prenatal infections. Fetal biopsy involves removal of fetal tissue, usually skin, liver, or muscular tissue, that can be analyzed directly for several disorders. Preimplantation embryo biopsy can be carried out as part of an in vitro fertilization program, and not carried out in a normal pregnancy. We will discuss this type of testing in Chapter 12.

Diagnostic testing is highly reliable, but also more costly, and because it is invasive there is an increased risk of inducing a miscarriage, the risk varying with the gestation time and the skill of the physician performing the procedure.

Prenatal screening, on the other hand, carries no risk to the embryo or fetus because it relies on maternal blood analyses and ultrasound imaging. For example, the standard second trimester test for Down syndrome and other chromosome abnormalities is known as the Quad Screen, because it looks at four biochemical markers in the mother's blood, and particular values of these are correlated with a Down syndrome fetus. The Quad Screen is also useful for neural tube defects (such as spinal bifida), as well as trisomy-13 and trisomy-18. The actual risk calculation is very complicated because it depends on a number of variables – the particular spectrum of values for the four biochemical markers, maternal age, weight of the mother, race or ethnicity, gestational age.

First trimester screening for two maternal biochemical markers is also becoming fairly standard, and useful information about the pregnancy status can be obtained as early as the seventh week of gestation.

Ultrasonic imaging has become one of the essential tools for following the pregnancy, and is now used as an essential adjunct of biochemical screening. Although originally used during the second and third trimester, continuing technological improvements are making it possible to obtain useful information about the developing conceptus in the first trimester. Ultrasound can locate the placenta, determine fetal cardiac activity, detect multiple pregnancies, identify sex, detect some types of structural abnormalities, and evaluate fetal well being. In the case of Down syndrome, for example, ultrasound can detect an increased collection of fluid under the skin, known as nuchal translucency, and together with the biochemical markers becomes an essential component of calculating risk.

Calculating risk and interpreting what that means is not as straightforward as we might expect. The tests are not foolproof, and false-positive and false-negative probabilities are evaluated by complex statistical formulas. Very often, then, instead of a definitive result, the parents are presented with an uncertainty. How to evaluate that uncertainty may not be easy for the non-expert.

Women as moral pioneers

Prenatal screening is not value free, for it brings with it unprecedented ethical, moral, and religious dilemmas. The patient will have to face making decisions that bring to the fore her core beliefs and values. Quite often in these circumstances ultimate questions have to be faced: when does life begin? What is a person? Should I intervene and try to preserve a life that would be burdened with a severe disorder? Is a life with a deformity better than no life at all? How can I make that decision for someone else? Under what conditions do I have the right to terminate a pregnancy?

Consider the thoughtfulness of the views offered by women when confronted with these decisions:

For me, having looked after a lot of children with special needs and having a reasonable understanding of the impact without obviously being in that situation myself, of the implications for the whole family, I personally would not choose to have a child if they were to have Down's syndrome, or any sort of defect which—it's not that I want a perfect baby, and if I didn't get a perfect baby—I've seen complications at birth, so what you're given is what you've got sort of thing. I don't know whether it's wrong to think like that, but I would rather know but having said that, I don't know what I would do if somebody said, 'you've got something wrong with your baby'. I would have to have a long, hard think about what the condition was, as to how severely the baby's quality of life was affected, as to whether I chose to carry on the pregnancy or to terminate. (7, Clare Williams et al Women as moral pioneers?)

This is why I panic, because where do you draw the line, because people get things wrong with them at different severities don't they? And I think if you've got a baby, you love it—whatever it's got wrong with it, you still love it and protect it, don't you? I know people who would say, 'no, that baby's got something wrong with it, I'm not having it', but that's why the test would be hard for me, because I wouldn't be straightaway, 'oh, if there's something wrong, I'm not having it'. (7, Clare Williams et al Women as moral pioneers?)

I think every woman's concerned whether everything's forming as it should and I know that Down's children can lead normal lives and everything else, it's just a matter of treatment and their life expectancy isn't usually that great, I think it's about 40 or something like that—I mean, life just begins then I think, it's an ethical reason really isn't it, whether it's right to terminate a life just because you feel it would serve no purpose only having a limited life span. I don't know, it's a hard question I think. (7, Clare Williams et al Women as moral pioneers?)

If things were going to be wrong, I would rather know, I'd rather they were to happen now rather than waiting until 23 weeks, and you've got a fairly viable pregnancy if the baby was to be born then. They'd probably end up in intensive care for a little while, but the fact is that it's more of a baby then, and therefore if something was wrong and you did decide to terminate, you'd have to go through the birth. That would be the most empty experience to me that I think there could be. (7, Clare Williams et al Women as moral pioneers?)

I would much rather know at this early stage because I couldn't imagine carrying a baby for 20 weeks, getting bigger, or 30 weeks and then miscarry. That would be so—especially after 24 weeks, when life is viable. Or even having a stillbirth. (7, Clare Williams et al Women as moral pioneers?)

I mean, at 16 weeks you're starting to really notice that there's a baby there, and if you're going to do anything about it, you don't have much time, because after 24 weeks, you absolutely have to deliver the baby, and I would HATE to do thatythere's noway I could choose to terminate a pregnancy at that stage it would be easier if I could just go to the hospital and have a little D and C [surgical termination] and that's it, but if you actually have to go through the whole process of actually giving birth to a child, no, I couldn't possible terminate. (7. Clare Williams et al Women as moral pioneers?)

I suppose the biggest thing for me about the scan because it's so early, it would mean if you was gonna make a decision like that no one would know unless you wanted them to know, whereas at 18 to 20 weeks everybody would know whatever you decided to tell them, and so as hard as it might be it would make it easier for you. (7, Clare Williams et al Women as moral pioneers?)

And the assumption [of screening] that I would select, based on the baby, was, you know, it's obviously helpful for some people, but I found it morally not so, we both did. When we first talked about having a baby, we knew that if it was a Down's baby, then it's a Down's baby, you know. No one wanders round hoping for a Down's baby but to me, to us, it was about taking on this sort of vulnerability of human life, and morally I just think that pregnancy and having a baby is such a wonderful gift, that no one has the right to either end a pregnancy, or—not that I'm saying, you know, I don't judge other people, it's just that I couldn't do it. . . but if the baby had cardiac problems and if there was something they could do about that, something positive they could do, then I would be happy for that, you knowy I mean, you hear of babies being operated on their hearts before they're even born and things like that, I mean, obviously I would do anything to improve it, if an improvement could be made. So that's why I agreed to have the scan done. (7, Clare Williams et al Women as moral pioneers?)

Inadvertently, as the views above demonstrate, and as a number of bioethicists have pointed out, women have become the arbiters of many of the technological advances in reproductive medicine. The professionals are responsible for the technical advances, but it is women who explore the ethical and moral dimensions of those advances. Men are not really challenged in the same profound way. It is women who make the final decisions, not the professionals. In their willingness to submit to prenatal screening, making and accepting responsibility for life and death choices, they are functioning as 'moral pioneers', or as 'moral philosophers of the private'. The ways in which we as a society view and think about the advances in reproductive medicine are fashioned by the collective, but individual, decisions that thousands of women are making every day. It is worth remembering that the advances in reproductive medicine are like a double-edged sword.

MOTHERS!

Can you afford to have a large family?

Do you want any more children?

If not, why do you have them?

DO NOT KILL, DO NOT TAKE LIFE, BUT PREVENT

Safe, Harmless Information can be obtained of trained Nurses at

46 AMBOY STREET

NEAR PITKIN AVE. — BROOKLYN.

Tell Your Friends and Neighbors.   All Mothers Welcome

A registration fee of 10 cents entitles any mother to this information.

מוטערס!

זייט איהר פערמעגליך צו האבען א גרויסע פאמיליע?

ווילם איהר האבען נאך קינדער?

אויב ניט, וואָרום האָט איהר זיי?

מערדערט ניט, נעהמט ניט קיין לעבען, נור פערהיט זיך.

זיכערע, אונשעדליכע אינסטרוקציעס קענט איהר בעקומען פון קרשאולעטע נורסעס אין

46 אמבאי סטריט נעֶר פּיֶטקין עוועֶניוּ ברוקלין

באזאגט דאס בעקאנטע צו אייערע פרינד און שכנות.   יעדע מוטער אֶ יוֶלֶקאֶמעֶן

ג׳ן 10 סֶעֶנֶט אֶיֶנֶשֶרֶיֶבֶצֶעֶלֶד גֶיֶט אֶיֶהֶר בֶעֶרֶעֶכֶטֶיֶגֶט צֶוֹ דֶיֶזֶעֶן אֶיֶנֶפֶאֶרֶמֶעֶיֶשֶאֶן

MADRI!

Potete permettervi il lusso d'avere altri bambini?

Ne volete ancora?

Se non ne volete piu', perche' continuate a metterli al mondo?

NON UCCIDETE MA PREVENITE!

Informazioni sicure ed innocue saranno fornite da infermiere autorizzate a

46 AMBOY STREET   Near Pitkin Ave. Brooklyn

a cominciare dal 12 Ottobre. Avvertite le vostre amiche e vicine.

Tutte le madri sono ben accette. La tassa d'iscrizione di 10 cents da diritto a qualunque madre di ricevere consigli ed informazioni gratis.

179

PART D

Fertility – Two Sides of One Coin

Chapter 10

Modern Birth Control

A contentious history

If a country has one dollar to spend on population, family planning, and development, that dollar should be spent on educating young girls. (1, Sheldon J. Segal Under the Banyan Tree)

Human societies in ancient times appear to have oscillated between too few or too many people. The threat of extinction faced periodically by many societies may explain in part why many religions have supported the dictum – "Be fruitful and multiply". According to the historian William LaFleur, ancient religions *"turned reproductivity into a mode of being godly. The multiplication of one's kind became both an index of divine favor and a way of receiving such favor". (2, Angus McLaren* Contraception and its discontents) At the same time, however, controlling or limiting fertility to protect scarce food resources was a crucial aspect of a society's ethos. Anthropologists tell us that hunter-gatherer societies try to control their numbers so as to ensure that the existing members have sufficient food resources.

One of the earliest written records addressing the concern regarding overpopulation was found in 3500-year old tablet from ancient Babylon. It's not a pretty story, and it goes something like this:

humans were originally created by the Gods to do all the menial work the Gods didn't want to do, and they made it easy for humans to reproduce. In time there were too many humans for the Gods to stomach, and so they sent plagues and other disasters to reduce their numbers. To keep the population in check, they imposed a religious obligation on the humans to ensure the limitation on their fertility.

Later societies didn't depend on the Gods to reduce their numbers, but took matters into their own hands. They fashioned their own potions and devices for limiting the number of births. Documents recovered in archeological excavations reveal a variety of means to prevent undesired births. Prescriptions for contraceptives and abortifacients (agents that induce an abortion) have been found in surviving ancient Egyptian, Chinese, and Indian texts. Most such prescriptions were probably not very effective, but some make sense. For example, part of an Egyptian text found in the Ebers Papyrus (1550 BCE) describes a medicated tampon made with ground acacia seed. When placed in the female, the acacia seed would ferment, releasing lactic acid, which is toxic to spermatozoa. Lactic acid has been used in many commercially available spermicides (or "sperm killers").

Hence, the Egyptian tampon may have functioned as a spermicide, although the designers of the tampon had no idea how it worked. The Romans made a significant contribution to the field of birth control by developing the condom, which was fashioned out of goat or fish bladders. In addition, hundreds of herbal recipes to prevent conception or to induce abortion were available in the Roman pharmacopoeia. Coitus interruptus, or withdrawal before ejaculation, was apparently a very common method of birth control. Infanticide, exposure of the newborn, or abandonment, especially of infants with birth defects were common practices as well.

More effective methods began to appear in Europe in the 19th century. Contraceptive sponges (roughly equivalent to the diaphragm today) began to be mass-produced at the beginning of the 19th century, while the development of vulcanized rubber in the 1880s made possible the mass-production of condoms. Since women were the users of sponges, their widespread use in Europe during the 19th and 20th century before the advent of the Pill indicates clearly that women were taking an active role in birth control. Condoms were used not only as contraceptives but also for protection of syphilis and gonorrhea. In addition, to sponges and condoms, the other two birth control methods were coitus interruptus and induced abortion. Together they are considered to account for what demographers call the "demographic transition' in Europe, the rapid change from a high birth rate to a low one. The average six-children family during the mid-19th century was replaced by the two to three children family by the time of World War I. This trend continues to the present day where in many countries in Europe the birth rate is below the replacement rate.

Despite the widespread acceptability world wide of modern birth control methods, a fundamental ambivalence about their use has remained in some countries. For some religious denominations the fundamental issue is that birth control separates reproduction from sex. Sigmund Freud, in 1915, expressed what one might call the conservative view, which still represents the position of the Roman Catholic Church and others who oppose birth control: *"We . . . describe a sexual activity as perverse if it has given up the aim of reproduction and pursues the attainment of pleasure as an aim independent of it" (2, Angus McLaren Contraception and its discontents).*

But Freud, much earlier in 1898, also expressed a very different view, a view that eventually became the hallmark of the birth control revolution that began in the latter half of the 20th century.

"It cannot be denied that in any marriage Malthusian preventive measures (what we would now call birth control) will become necessary at some time or other; and, from theoretical point of view, it would one of the greatest triumphs of humanity, one of the most tangible liberations from the constraints of nature to which mankind is subject, if we could succeed in raising the responsible act of procreating children to the level of a deliberate and intentional activity and in freeing from its entanglement with the necessary satisfaction of a natural need. ... But, as we know, we posses at present no method of preventing conception which fulfills every legitimate requirement – that is, which is certain and convenient, which does not diminish the sensation of pleasure during coitus and which does not would the woman's sensibilities. . . Whoever fills in this lacuna in our medical technique will have preserved the enjoyment of life and maintained the health of numberless people: though, it is true he will also have paved the way for a drastic change in our social conditions." (2, Angus McLaren Contraception and its Discontents)

The most persistent opposition to contraception has come from the Roman Catholic Church, despite the fact that a majority of catholic women around the world use some form of birth control. In the U. S. the most recent flare up has come under the guise of protesting the inclusion of contraception in employer provided health insurance plans, an issue long thought to have been settled. Although no woman is forced to use contraception, the Roman Catholic Church is now arguing that the inclusion of contraception in health plans is an assault on religious freedom. Socially conservative legislators in many states have joined forces with the Church on a wide-ranging assault on contraception rights. Since 2011 many bills have been proposed or passed in Congress and state legislatures that seek to limit women's contraceptive choices – excluding contraception in health plans, requiring vaginal ultrasounds before abortion, counseling and other protocols designed to discourage having an abortion, redefining rape and personhood.

This legislative assault, clearly aimed at women's rights, is eerily reminiscent of the series of 19th century legislative statutes known as the Comstock Laws. The force behind the assault then was Anthony Comstock, a devout Christian, who was appalled by what he considered the licentiousness of life in New York City. His crusade led to the passage of the Comstock Act in 1873 that made it illegal to send any obscene, lewd, and/or lascivious materials through the mail, including contraceptive information. For Comstock, the availability of contraceptives promoted lust and immorality, especially in women. The act also banned the distribution of information of abortion for educational purposes. It was not until 1965 that the Supreme Court finally overturned the last vestiges of the Comstock laws.

For some observers, the new legislative assault is another reflection of an intensifying religious and political fundamentalism that has characterized the United States since the 1970s. But there may something else at work. The American anthropologist Sarah Blaffer Hrdy, in her book, *Mother Nature: Maternal Instincts and How They Shape the Human Species (1999)*, may be closer to the truth when she argues that both the religious and social impulses to control fertility are based on a primal male impulse to control female fertility. Female sexuality has been a particular source of anxiety for men in most societies. Controlling a woman's fertility is really a way of controlling her sexuality. Contraception removes the burden of reproduction on women, leaving her free to express her sexuality. Young American women, Hrdy notes, are in danger of losing their hard-won rights because *"they see no connection between innate male desires to control women in earlier times and the attitudes toward women and family that. . . motivate elected officials to debate endlessly over who has the right to choose whether and when a woman gives birth". (3, Sarah Blaffer Hrdy Mother Nature: Maternal Instincts and How They Shape the Human Species)*

Modern Birth Control - different strategies

The development of modern efficacious birth control methods had to await a much better understanding of the complexities of the reproductive system, especially that of the female. The major breakthrough came in 1960 when the first birth control pill was introduced. Since then, a number of methods have appeared, and today birth control is a multi-billion dollar industry. It may be difficult for the average person to understand how one method differs from another, why one may be better than another, etc. We can bring some order into this marketplace by understanding that all the methods / products rely on one or two of four strategies:

- Prevention of gamete (either egg or sperm) formation,
- Prevention of fertilization,
- Prevention of implantation, or
- Prevention of a live birth (induced abortion).

A few examples will illustrate what we mean by this classification. What is generally referred to as the "pill" is used to prevent ovulation (egg formation) and so falls under strategy (1). The "pill" is no longer a single method, but in fact encompasses different hormonal protocols, some of which combine strategy (1) and (2). The condom, both the original male version and the newer female version, is used to prevent fertilization and falls under strategy (2). We can refer to both of these as true contraceptives, since the aim is to prevent conception. Many of the other methods used today—for example, sterilization, the intrauterine device (IUD), the diaphragm, the spermicides, and sexual abstinence—have strategy (2) as their rationale. Methods using strategy (3) are still by and large in initial stages of development, although the recently approved emergency contraceptive protocols use this strategy. Strategy (4) involves inducing an abortion. Both surgical and medical methods of abortion are available in the countries that permit induced abortions.

The acceptability of these strategies varies considerably from country to country. Strategies (1) and (2) are widely accepted in the United States, although they may be proscribed by certain religious groups; while strategies (3) and (4), which rely on interfering with development after fertilization, are much more controversial. For example, the licensing of RU-486, referred to as the "abortion pill", widely used in Europe for early term abortions, was denied in the United States until the year 2000 because of opposition by religious groups even though abortions have been legal since 1973.

Modern birth control methods have found wide acceptability on a worldwide basis. According to a 1994 United Nations report, about 60 percent of couples in the world were using some form of birth control. In 2003 the percentage was 61%, and nine of ten couples used modern methods – 39% favored sterilization, 23% used the intrauterine device (IUD), 12% used the contraceptive pill, 8% the condom, and 4% withdrawal. The intrauterine device, efficacious and less inexpensive than other forms of birth control, is widely used in China. In the U. S. about 64% of the 60 million women of childbearing age (15-44) use some form of birth control. Among women who are sexually active, 93% use contraception. Today, no one would doubt that the availability of safe and effective birth control methods represents one of the most far-reaching and momentous developments in the history of human societies.

Hormonal contraception in the female

But there is one categorical answer that can be given to the question of the Pill's benefits versus its risks, and that one is so overpowering that it alone justifies the continued existence of the Pill. I am referring to the numbers of unwanted children and abortions – the sheer mass of human suffering – prevented over the years. (4, Cited in Carl Djerassi This Man's Pill. Reflections on the 50th Birthday of the Pill)

The Pill – the first social, rather than therapeutic drug

The development in the 1950s of an effective hormonal method to suppress ovulation initiated the modern era of birth control research. The idea for a hormonal contraceptive dates back to experiments in rabbits by Ludwig Haberlandt who in 1921 reported that an ovarian product was able to suppress fertility. Haberlandt suggested that this effect could be developed into a method of sterilizing women for short periods. Hormonal contraception was discussed publicly for the first time at the Seventh International Birth Control Conference in Zurich, Switzerland, in 1930. These initiatives were premature because at the time relatively little was known about ovarian function and the chemical nature of the putative ovarian products.

A new impetus for reconsidering hormonal contraception came after the end of World War II, when three social movements coalesced—birth control, population control, and eugenics. The common element in all three movements was the desire to control human reproduction by separating sexual intercourse from reproduction. By the late 1940s two important advances had taken place: first, an understanding that estrogen and progesterone (first discovered and characterized in the 1930s) were able to suppress ovulation, and second, the development of techniques for the laboratory synthesis estrogen and progesterone analogs that would retain their potency when taken orally.

These two advances laid the immediate scientific basis for hormonal contraception. To convert the scientific understanding to a product something else was needed – the marshalling of the social and financial resources to test, market, and promote the development of an efficacious contraceptive pill. The story of how all this came about is immensely complicated, replete with bad guys, good guys, inflated egos, complex motives, and driven personalities. Perhaps the most balanced and exhaustive account of this convoluted history is given by Lara V. Marks in her book Sexual Chemistry. A History of the Contraceptive Pill, published in 2001.

In the U. S. the principle protagonists were the scientists and physicians Gregory Pincus, John A. Rock, and C. R. Garcia, who developed and tested the first combination of estrogen and progestin analogs, and Margaret Sanger and Katherine McCormick, two powerhouses of feminist passion and concern for the rights of women, who provided the moral, social, and financial resources for successful completion of the project. Testing began in 1956, and the Federal Drug Administration (FDA) approved the first birth control pill for use in the U. S. in 1960.

There is no doubt that the Pill in its various incarnations has had a revolutionary impact on modern societies. In contrast to most other medications it is prescribed not to prevent or to treat an illness, but rather, its purpose is social. Some commentators have called it the first "designer drug". But as social medication it has had an enormous beneficial impact in improving the health and welfare of millions of women and people all around the world. It has also contributed significantly, although not exclusively, to the drop in birth rate in many countries. Yet, it has also generated untold controversies in all societies, controversies about sexual freedom, separation of reproduction from sexuality, the proper role of women, and the role of governments in regulating the reproductive practices of its citizens that appear to plague all countries, developed and developing.

Combined oral contraceptives (COCs)

Pills containing both estrogen and progesterone became known as the combined oral contraceptives (COCs), and they have been by and large the standard for many years. The efficacy of COCs lies in their suppression of ovulation. These formulations take advantage of the negative feedback effects of estrogen and progesterone on pituitary release of LH and FSH. Recall from Chapter 3 that the pituitary hormones LH and FSH are both necessary for ovulation to occur. Hence, the estrogen and progesterone components work in concert to suppress LH and FSH release by the pituitary, and the combination is more effective in suppressing ovulation completely than either one alone

The newer formulations are said to be multiphasic because the estrogen and progestin dosage is varied periodically during the cycle. For example, the biphasic COCs provides altering doses of estrogen and progestins during the first half of the cycle, while only progestins at higher levels are given during the second half of the cycle. The dosage regimen of the triphasic formulations alters the estrogen and progestin concentrations throughout the cycle. Both are generally prescribed in 28-day packs, which deliver the hormones for 21 days, and these are followed by 7 days of inert tablets, containing iron and/or vitamins.

Yasmin, one of the newer of the 28-day-regimen COCs on the market, combines estradiol with a new type of progesterone analog called drospirenone that acts as a diuretic. Drospirenone is chemically related to the potassium-sparing diuretic, spironolactone (Aldactone) and thus has been touted as being effective in minimizing adverse side effects such as weight gain and bloating that typically accompany menstruation. Although controlled studies have not confirmed these effects, the use of Yasmin has grown appreciably especially among young women.

Who Needs a Period Anymore?

The idea that a woman can actually forego their monthly menstrual cycle along with the treacherous trials of premenstrual syndrome and the burden of feminine hygiene products is not entirely new. Physicians have known since the introduction of the pill that women could eliminate their monthly periods entirely by simply continuing their regimen - rather than stopping or taking the placebos for seven days. This neat little trick – recommended to brides wanting to delay menstruating on their honeymoons or to women athletes on the eve of a competition - has not generally been an accepted practice among medical circles.

Interestingly this concept of hormone manipulation has been recently been studied and consequently FDA-approved in 2003 in the form of an extended cycle COC named Seasonale. It's one of the newest weapons in the birth control arsenal that will suppress the number of yearly menstrual periods from 13 to 4, or once each season, making this option quite attractive for many women. This is accomplished by taking Seasonale for 84 consecutive days, then skipping a week

In actuality, Seasonale is merely a new take on an old off-label use of traditional birth control pills. The difference now is that studies on safety and efficacy have been performed on Seasonale, while lacking on others. The benefits of this kind of regimen go well beyond PMS and the obvious convenience. It can help minimize anemia and endometriosis associated with menstruation as well as decrease the risk of ovarian and cervical cancer by 50 and 40 percent respectively. Occasional spotting seen with traditional birth control pills, may also be experienced with Seasonale.

Although there is no evidence that menstruation provides a woman any benefit, critics argue that menstruation is a natural part of a woman's monthly hormonal cycle and should not be eliminated. While the verdict is still out on whether menstruation should be obsolete, it's clear that a period-free future may abolish those terrible premenstrual syndrome jokes.

Important benefits that come from regular use of COCs include the prevention of iron deficiency anemia, a reduction in dysfunctional uterine bleeding and dysmenorrhea, a lower incidence of ovarian cysts, ectopic pregnancy, benign breast disease, and pelvic inflammatory disease. Interestingly, COCs are also associated with a reduced risk of cancers of the endometrium and ovary of which the benefit is detectable within 1 year of use and appears to persist for years after discontinuation. Women can also benefit from the convenience of menstrual regularity.

Since combined oral contraceptives can raise sex hormone binding globulin and testosterone concentrations, women can also expect an improvement in acne breakouts. The COCs, however, are not free of side effects, and this has been their most important drawback. The early COCs had a relatively high estrogen content, and consequently more significant side effects, which included nausea, bloating, fluid retention, weight gain, irritability, nervousness, headaches, breast tenderness, increased blood pressure, and increased risk of blood clot formation. The major progesterone-related side effects included increased appetite, erratic menstrual bleeding, and breast shrinkage. Newer generations of oral COCs containing the lowest levels of estrogens and progestins compatible with high efficacy have in general reduced, but not eliminated, the incidence of side effects. The side effects given as reasons by many women who discontinue the oral COCs are irregular bleeding (12%), gastro-intestinal disturbances (7%), weight gain (5%), mood changes (5%), breast tenderness (4%), and headache (4%). Moreover, the COCs are contraindicated in a small but significant percentage of women, for example, those with thromboembolic or cardiovascular disorders, impaired liver function due to hepatitis, deep varicose veins, known or suspected breast cancer, hypertension, epilepsy, and for smokers over the age of 35.

Is the "pill" safe?

In 1960, the Pill created a revolution that liberated millions of women worldwide from clumsy and often unreliable mechanical methods such as diaphragms and IUDs to the ability to control fertility hormonally. However, tugging on the coattails of this revolution has been the questionable cardiovascular risk, particularly with the advent of the Women's Health Initiative clinical trial that advised six million post-menopausal women in 2002 to stop hormone replacement therapy due to an increased risk of heart attack and stroke. But the same Women's Health Initiative now provides reassurance to women of reproductive age that oral contraceptives are safe. According to the findings presented at the 2004 American Society for Reproductive Medicine Conference, 67,000 women on the pill enrolled in the study, had a surprisingly 8 percent lower risk of heart disease and stroke and no increased risk of breast cancer. Older COCs containing more than 50 mcg of ethinyl estradiol have been associated with a significantly higher risk of heart attack and stroke particularly in smokers or uncontrolled hypertension. However, newer COCs have considerably less estradiol with a cardiovascular risk that is also less.

In December 2012 the American College of Obstetricians and Gynecologists published an official position paper concluding that given their proven safety record it was appropriate for birth control pills to sold without a doctor's prescription. Oral contraceptives, if used improperly, do pose minor risks, but the danger they pose less danger than many other medicines available over the counter, such as nonsteroidal pail pills, such as Motrin (which can cause stomach bleeding), or decongestants like Sudafed (which raises the blood pressure). Dr. Eve Espey, professor of obstetrics and gynecology at the University of New Mexico, one of the authors of the position paper commented: "Nonsteroidal medicines kill far more people than birth control pills. For most women, the absolute risk of taking the pill is far less than the risks incurred in pregnancy". The position paper argues that making oral contraceptives easily available over the counter is "a potential way to improve contraceptive access and use, and possibly decrease the unintended pregnancy rate."

However, given political and religious climate with regard to contraception, it seems unlikely that the recommendations of the position paper will be accepted.

Progesterone-only contraceptives (POCs)

Progesterone-only contraceptives were developed initially for women for whom estrogen was poorly tolerated or contraindicated, such as women over 35 who smoke. An additional important advantage of the POCs over combined oral contraceptives (COCs) is that they do not interfere with milk production, and hence, may be used by breast-feeding women who desire extra protection during the lactation period.

Progesterone injectables (DMPA) containing the progesterone analog depo-provera, were developed first. A single high-dose injection of the synthetic progesterone provided sufficient protection for about three months. The need for repeated injections could be a disadvantage for those who dislike injections. On the other hand, these three-month injectables were an advantage in that the problem of compliance with daily pill taking was dispensed with. In addition, the necessity to visit a doctor's office every three months provides a built-in monitoring system. However, one of the major side effects of Depo-Provera was the disruption of menstrual bleeding patterns, and this was the main reason for their discontinuation by users. Long term usage of Depo-Provera also leads to loss of bone mass and amenorrhea. In addition, the return to fertility can be delayed by 4 to 31 months, making this contraceptive option problematic for women wanting to become pregnant after discontinuation.

Considered as an alternative to Depo-Provera, Lunelle is a new injectable contraceptive agent offering the convenience of once-monthly dosing. Aside from having fewer side effects, the biggest difference is that women can become pregnant within two to four months after discontinuing Lunelle, compared to about ten months after stopping Depo-Provera. When administered every 28 to 30 days, Lunelle has demonstrated to be 99% effective. In a pivotal clinical study, Lunelle was compared with Ortho-Novum among 1,103 women. After 15 menstrual cycles, no unplanned pregnancies were reported in the Lunelle group, while two pregnancies occurred in the group using the oral contraceptive.

The combination of the synthetic hormones progestin and estrogen contained in Lunelle are similar to a woman's natural hormones. Lunelle should be administered at intervals not to exceed 33 days. Menstrual cycles occur regularly while using Lunelle. Women who discontinue use experience a rapid return to ovulation within two to four months.

So what's the downside? Lunelle requires a trip to the doctor's office or clinic every 28 days to receive the shot. However, to improve patient access to the drug, the manufacturers are aiming to make Lunelle available in pharmacies, where pharmacists can administer the injections.

At the cost of $35 an injection, which is comparable to that of a month's supply of oral contraceptives with the option for a quick return to fertility if desired - without the hassle of everyday use - what could be more liberating?

Alternatives to progesterone injectables are progesterone-only pills (POPs), also referred to as "mini-pills." The mini-pills provide a low-dose-alternative to the progesterone injectables, and also reduce progesterone-associated side effects. They are also quite effective. An important disadvantage of the POPs is that much stricter compliance with the dosing regimen is required for maintaining efficacy.

The mechanism of action of the POCs is different from the COCs. Ovulation is suppressed regularly only about 50 percent of the time, and their high efficacy is attributed in addition to the resulting changes in the cervical mucus, making it thicker and more viscous and hence a very effective barrier to sperm penetration.

Non-oral delivery

A desire to simplify contraceptive use and to eliminate gastro-intestinal and liver disturbances associated with the oral contraceptives has led to the development of several non-oral delivery systems, all of which rival the COCs in efficacy, and in many cases reduce the severity of the side effects. A comparison of these new methods is given in Appendix 2 (Table 1).

Implants

One of the first of these alternative methods was the subdermal implant introduced first in Finland in 1983. Since then their use has spread to most countries where contraceptives are available. They are particularly popular in Europe. They require surgical implantation, just below the skin, usually in the underarm. The first approved implant (Norplant I) consisted of six capsules containing the synthetic progesterone analog levonorgestrel; the capsules release the hormone slowly over a period that can be as long as 5 years. Norplant must be inserted within the first seven days after the normal menstrual cycle begins, and protection against pregnancy begins within 24 hours. The practical advantage of an implant is that it avoids the necessity of having to take a pill every day. The slow, constant release of the hormone avoids large daily fluctuations. Clinical trials indicate that Norplant is 99.9 percent effective at preventing pregnancy, of every 10,000 women who use Norplant for five years, fewer than five will become pregnant. The implants have been approved in many countries, including the United States, on the basis of comprehensive, clinical trials.

The most recent addition to the implant arsenal is Implanon, a single rod implant releasing etongestrel, a different progesterone analog. Implanon provides protection for 3 years, and no pregnancies have been reported in over 70,000 cycles. Its ease of insertion and removal have made it more acceptable than Norplant to many women. Major side effects reported are weight gain (20%), irregular infrequent bleeding (30%), breast pain (16%), acne (12.6%), and vaginitis (12%).

The vaginal ring (NuvaRing

These small (2 inches in diameter), flexible, transparent polymer rings are inserted into the vagina and remains in place for 3 weeks, removed for one week, and then another ring is inserted for another three weeks, and so on. It has been available in the U.S. since the summer of 2002. The ring releases low doses of an estrogen / progestin combination which are absorbed through the vaginal wall. This delivery method eliminates the gastro-intestinal problems associated with the oral COC, and because the hormones are taken up very readily, lower doses are required to maintain the same efficacy as the oral COCs. The ring does not interfere with intercourse, and if desired can be removed for short periods of time. The most commonly reported side effects include headaches, vaginal discharge, foreign body sensation, vaginitis, coital problems and ring expulsion. In general, however, the incidence of these effects is low, and NuvaRing appears to be well tolerated by women who use it.

The transdermal patch (Ortho Evra)

Transdermal patches for medication delivery are well known for their use in nicotine withdrawal and prevention of motion sickness. The Ortho Evra patch is the first contraceptive patch available that matches the efficacy of the oral COCs. It can be applied to any of four sites – lower abdomen, upper outer arm, buttock, or upper torso, including the breast. The patch uses the same estrogen / progestin analogs found in the oral COCs, Ortho Cyclen and Ortho Tri-Cyclen, and is applied once a week for three weeks followed by one patch-free week. Compliance with Ortho Evra is better than with COCs, while the efficacy is the same. The most commonly reported side effects include breast tenderness, headache, application site reactions, nausea, and irregular bleeding.

Intraterine Devices (IUDs)

The first IUD for human use was developed about a century ago, and since then a number of types have been marketed. The idea, however, is a very old one, originating according to tradition in the ancient Middle East. In order to keep their camels from becoming pregnant during the long caravan trips between the Middle East and the Far East, the camel drivers put small, smooth pebbles in the camel's uterus. The development of the modern generation of IUDs began in 1963 with a comprehensive study of IUDs initiated by the Population Council of New York. One important outcome of this study was the introduction of plastic IUDs in the shape of a T in 1967, and in 1968, plastic IUDs containing copper.

In the U. S. IUDs had a terrible reputation because of significant risks of pelvic inflammatory disease and uterine perforations with the IUD known as the Dalkon shield. The problems associated with this IUD were the result of a design flaw. The first copper IUD was introduced in 1976, and an improved version, the Copper T 380A, was approved for marketing in the United States in 1984. Since then more than 25 million have been distributed in over 70 countries. It is considered to be one of the most effective, long-acting reversible contraceptives available. The latest versions provide protection for up to 10 years.

Variations of this basic design are being marketed in many countries. Generally a 4–5- month period of adjustment is required. Bleeding during the first few months is common, but will disappear afterwards. The newer IUD models have significantly reduced the risk associated with their use, and on a worldwide basis, IUDs are the most commonly used birth control method, even in many developed countries. In Sweden about 30 percent of women use the IUD, since it is cheaper than, and just as effective as, the COCs.

Some of the newer models (Mirena) have a progesterone-releasing capability, in which the progesterone analog levonorgestrel is delivered continuously in small doses. The data available indicates that these new IUDs significantly reduce the initial blood loss, making them equivalent to the low-dose, progestin-releasing subdermal implants. The current models are effective for 5 years. The risk of ectopic pregnancies with the Mirena IUD is less than that of the copper IUDs, as are the risks of pelvic inflammatory disease.

The mechanism of action of IUDs is complex. The early hypothesis proposed that an IUD interfered with implantation by producing changes in the endometrium, the outer layer of the uterus where the embryo implants. More recent studies suggest multiple effects – inhibition of sperm migration, altering sperm-egg binding, generation of a uterine inflammatory response, and in the case of the progestin-releasing IUDs, thickening the cervical mucus and changes in the endometrium. The copper in the copper-containing IUDs may enhance the contraceptive effect, but the precise mechanism of action is not yet clear. The efficacy of the IUDs depends on combining strategies (1) and (2).

Side effects tend to peak after the first few months and generally seem to reduce over time. A number of side effects do remain and account for discontinuation of IUD use – irregular bleeding, depression, headache, acne, weight changes, and breast tenderness.

Emergency contraception

Yuzpe regimen

When forgetfulness strikes in the heat of the moment - when a condom breaks - or in the case of a sexual assault, emergency contraception is available to prevent unintended pregnancies. The chance of pregnancy among women 19-26 years of age is quite high – close to 50% - when unprotected intercourse occurs during the one to two days before ovulation, but the chance decreases to about 8% for women over 30. The risk of pregnancy is typically reduced to one to two percent by immediate use of emergency contraception. The post-coital or "morning-after" pill is the way the popular media typically refers to emergency contraception. Four types of emergency contraception are available, only three of which are available in the United States.

The first approved in the U. S. is known as the Yuzpe regimen developed in the early 1970s (marketed as Preven or Ovral). These pills provide a high dose of estrogen or a mixture of estrogen and progesterone and are taken in two doses 12 hours apart within 72 hours after intercourse. Although the mechanism of action is not certain, the net effect is that implantation is prevented. The Yuzpe pill can be quite effective (reduces the risk or pregnancy to 2%), but it is not recommended for long-term use, and it is generally not recommended for women who are especially sensitive to estrogen. Postcoital pills have been available in most European countries for more than a decade, where they generally available without a prescription. In the United States, the Yuzpe pills were endorsed by the FDA only in 1997, and approved for distribution in 1998, but can be dispensed only with a prescription.

Plan B

Another product marketed specifically as a morning-after pill is Plan B, which contains progestin exclusively. Considered more effective than Yuzpe in reducing the risk of pregnancy (1%) within a window of 72-120 hours after intercourse, Plan B also has a lower incidence of nausea and vomiting (from 22% (Yuzpe) to 8%). Although a prescription for Plan B was initially required, proposals by the American Medical Association, the American College of Obstetricians and Gynecologists, the American Society of Health-Systems Pharmacists and the FDA's scientific advisors argued that Plan B should be made available over-the-counter without age restrictions. Although it became available for women older than 17, upon insistence by the administration, the FDA maintained the requirement for a prescription for those younger than 17. In April 2013, a federal judge in New York called the administration's action "politically motivated and scientifically unjustified", and ordered the FDA to make the morning-after pill available to women of all ages without prescription.

Historically, access to emergency contraception was problematic for many women. Obtaining an appointment or simply contacting a physician for a prescription was difficult and not always feasible during the narrow window of opportunity for which emergency contraception is most effective. Non-prescription status of agents like Plan B would make it easier to obtain emergency contraception within the recommended 72-hour time frame, especially on weekends or evenings.

A study by Princeton University's Office of Population Research concluded that the number of unintended pregnancies and abortions among U. S. women, ages 15-44, would be reduced by half if emergency contraception were easily available. Although there is no evidence supporting their claims, critics contend that access to morning after pills would make women more careless about regular birth control. Opponents also counter with fears that easy accessibility would foment more teen sex, although the one study that has examined this issue found that teens that had emergency contraception available were not more likely to have unprotected sex. Others, such as the Vatican, condemn emergency contraception with the contention that it is early abortion because the pills interfere with implantation, and not with fertilization. Pro-life groups believe that women will abandon their regular contraception method in favor of emergency contraception. Lastly, insurance companies and state Medicaid systems will no longer cover these agents once they become over-the-counter.

Mifepristone (RU-486)

The use of mifepristone, commonly referred to in the media in the United States as the "abortion pill," has been fraught with almost overwhelming negative publicity. It was finally approved for medical abortion in the U. S. in 2000, but only to physicians who establish an account with the distributor, which severely restricts its access. Clinical trials have shown that a single low dose (10 mg) of mifepristone is as effective as Plan B, with even lower incidence of vomiting and nausea. However, for reasons that remain difficult to understand, this regimen is not available in the U. S., even though medical abortion requires much higher doses (200 mg). In Europe, where use of mifepristone is most widespread, it is used not only for emergency contraception, but also for general contraception. Taking one pill per month is common particularly among older women. The advantages are obvious. Daily pill taking can be dispensed with.

Copper IUD

Several studies have shown that a copper IUD inserted up to 5 days after intercourse is as effective in reducing the risk of pregnancy as hormonally based regimens. One important advantage is that once inserted the IUD can continue providing protection. The initial cost is higher than the hormonal regimens but may be more cost effective in the long run.

Non-hormonal contraception

Prevention of fertilization is probably the oldest form of birth control. The methods that employ this strategy use surgical, physical, or chemical means to prevent the sperm from reaching the egg. For males in fact, these are the only contraceptive methods available.

Barrier methods

As the name indicates, these methods involve a barrier that prevents the passage of spermatozoa. The barrier can be physical or chemical. Physical and chemical barrier methods are probably the oldest birth control methods. There have been significant improvements in their effectiveness, but in general they are considered to be poor substitutes for the hormonal contraceptives because of their high failure rates. Nevertheless, they are still widely used around the world.

In males, the condom is the principal barrier method. In terms of limiting fertility, the effectiveness of condoms in actual use is considerably less than in theory because of slippage or breakage, particularly if stored improperly or used with oil-based lubricants. Most condoms sold in the U. S. are made from latex rubber, although condoms are also made from lamb intestines and newer types of materials, including polyurethane and hypoallergenic latex are also available. While lamb condoms are known to provide the most pleasure and comfort, they do not protect against HIV infection. The polyurethane condom is said to provide greater sensitivity, but has the disadvantage that the slippage and breakage rates are higher than with the latex condoms.

One important advantage of the condom is that it reduces the risk of contracting a sexually transmitted disease (STD), and historically this may have been the principal reason for it usage. To increase their anti-STD effectiveness many condoms are coated with microbiocides, compounds that had anti-bacterial or anti-viral activity. Perhaps the most commonly used microbiocide is a detergent known as nonoxynol-9 or N9, which is known to disrupt bacteria and viruses. However, studies to date have not yet shown convincingly that N9 increases the anti-STD effectives of condoms.

In females, a number of barrier devices are used singly or in combination. These include spermicides, diaphragms, cervical caps, and the recently introduced female condom. These act as both physical and chemical barriers. Spermicides, as the name implies, contain substances that kill or inactivate sperm. Many such compounds have been used. Lactic acid has been a common component of many spermicides. More recently, compounds known as surfactants have been introduced. Surfactants disrupt or dissolve the sperm surface membrane. Spermicides, such as N9, are available in a variety of dosage forms: foams, gels, sponges, and creams. Although also available as suppositories, films and tablets, these forms require sufficient time to dissolve in order to be effective. They are deposited high in the vagina at the vaginal-cervical boundary one hour or less before coitus. While early studies appeared to suggest that N9 could prevent STDs, a protective effect has not been demonstrated. It also appears that frequent use of N9 can cause excessive vaginal irritation and hypersensitivity, actually increasing the risk of HIV transmission.

Contraceptive sponges are designed to be a depository for semen. The Today Sponge is an over-the counter barrier contraceptive impregnated with a spermicide, which entraps and inactivates sperm. It is moistened in water and placed over the cervix as long as 6 hours before intercourse and continues to be effective for 24 hours, even after repeated intercourse. Due to the risk of toxic shock syndrome, it should be removed after 24 hours. Its failure rate is relatively high also. The failure rate of spermicides is highly variable, as might be expected, given the fact that the positioning of the spermicide is critical for its effectiveness. Although relatively inexpensive, spermicides cannot be considered to be very effective.

The diaphragm is a thin rubber cup stretched over a thin wire ring. It is placed in the upper vagina so that it covers the external part of the cervix. It is fitted by a physician and is generally used with a spermicide. It is relatively safe, but not terribly effective, in large part because of the difficulty of insertion. The cervical cap is a variation of the diaphragm, but it is held in place by suction rather than by the wire ring. Its failure rate is similar to that of the diaphragm, butit is considered to be more difficult to insert than the diaphragm.

Sterilization

Sterilization in the female is generally referred to as a tubal sterilization, or colloquially as tying the tubes, and in the male as a vasectomy. In both cases, the passage of spermatozoa is prevented - in females, the sperm will not reach the site in the oviduct to fertilize the egg, and in males, by cutting the vas deferens, the sperm will not be ejaculated. Both are highly effective, and together they constitute the major contraceptive method in the U. S. for those over 35. Because both can be considered effectively irreversible, these procedures are carried out on individuals who are no longer interested in having children. Some more recently developed sterilization procedures are touted as being more reversible, but in the absence of large-scale studies, optimism about the reversibility is probably unwarranted.

In the female

Three major types of procedures are available for tubal sterilization - obstetric sterilization carried out following a vaginal or cesarean delivery, laparoscopic sterilization in which the uterine tubes are approached through a small incision in the abdomen, and hysteroscopic sterilization in which the fallopian tubes are reached through the vagina and uterus. In the first two, sterilization is accomplished by ligation, clamping with clips or rings, or electrocoagulation.

In the U. S. the great majority of obstetric sterilizations (more than 350,000 per year) use the Pomeroy technique, a procedure that has remained essentially the same since it was developed in 1930. It involves placing a plain catgut suture around a loop of tube and cutting the knuckled portion of the tube.

A fairly recent modification of the Pomeroy technique is the use of the Filshie clip, invented by the British obstetrician-gynecologist, Marcus Filshie, and available in the U. S. since 1996. Instead of a ligation the fallopian tubes are clipped. Advertised advantages of the Filshie clip include minimum damage to the tube and surrounding structures, as well as ease and speed of operation. Successful reversal of the sterilization may be greater following Filshie clip placement than following Pomeroy sterilization.

Laparoscopic sterilization, introduced during the 1970s, has become the most widely used sterilization procedure. Reduced morbidity and mortality, a quicker recovery time and reduced hospital costs are the main advantages over obstetric sterilization. The Filshie clip technique is well suited to laparascopic sterilization, and its use has spread to Asia and Latin America. Although laparoscopic sterilization is considered a safe and effective procedure, complications such as bowel damage and hemorrhage occur in about 1-2% of cases depending on the procedure used. The overall risk of pregnancy in terms of 10-year cumulative probability can vary between 3 and 5 per 1,000, depending on the technique used. In addition, a general anesthetic is usually required.

Since the mid-1970s, a number of methods that rely on tubal occlusion, rather than tubal ligation, clipping, or cauterizing have been introduced. That is, the procedures involve introducing obstructions in the fallopian tubes. The approach to the fallopian tubes is through the vagina and uterus, and these different methods are known as hysteroscopic sterilization. Hysteroscopic sterilization, in contrast to laparoscopic sterilization, can be performed in an outpatient setting without general anesthesia. Many attempts have been made to develop a safe and effective method, but until recently, without success. The latest of these is known as the Essure system, and a number of recent studies suggest that it may turn out to be a realistic alternative to laparoscopic sterilization. The Essure device is titanium, stainless steel coil introduced into the fallopian tube. The coil can be inserted quickly, generally less than 11 minutes. The patient can even watch the insertion and is able to go home a few minutes after the insertion. The coil induces an inflammatory response over a period of about three months, and the growth of fibrous tissues leads to the occlusion of the tubes. This also means that the sterilization is irreversible. No long-term follow up studies are available yet, but contraceptive failure over a two year span is very low.

Despite its advantages it is not clear at this stage whether the Essure method will replace the laparoscopic procedures. Only more long-term studies regarding safety, efficacy, and patient acceptability will tell us.

In the male

Vasectomy, or ligation and/or occlusion of the vas deferens, is one of two existing methods of contraception available to men. It is more effective than the condom and has the advantage that compliance by the male is not required. However, it provides no protection against STDs, and reversal is expensive and generally only partially successful. The incidence of vasectomy, as we might expect, increases with the age of the male. For example, in U. S. it varies from 1% in men aged 20–24 yr to greater than 20% in men over 40 yr. It's also interesting that the popularity of vasectomy varies significantly and within each country by ethnic origin, socioeconomic status, and marital status. It is more popular in men who are better educated, more affluent, and who are currently married. Cultural factors also influence the popularity of vasectomy: in Europe, less than 1% of French men choose vasectomies, whereas it is particularly common in New Zealand.

Vasectomies are normally done with a local anesthetic in an outpatient setting, and the patients usually go home within an hour of the procedure. A vasectomy always has two components - accessing the vas deferens, the duct through which the sperm travel to the outside during an ejaculation, which is then followed by occlusion of the vas. The vas is accessed traditionally by a surgical incision or by the "no-scalpel" technique, developed in China, using a specially designed sharp, pointed forceps. The no-scalpel technique has been shown to have fewer complications and is therefore recommended. The traditional occlusion procedure, known as suture ligation and excision, still very popular in countries with scarce medical resources, involves cutting out a short segment of the vas, and tying the two ends of the divided vas with sutures. More effective and recommended methods of occlusion of the ends of the vas include cauterization, followed by fascial interposition, whereby the sheath surround the vas is pulled over one of the cut ends of the vas.

A vasectomy in general is considered to be highly efficacious, with failure rates around 1% with the suture and ligation technique, and probably less with the improvements, but proper assessment of efficacy has been difficult because in practice, a significant proportion of men fail to provide post-vasectomy ejaculates for examination. Short-term failure is usually defined as the presence of sperm in the ejaculate at some arbitrary time after operation (3–6 months) or after 23–25 ejaculates. There are always some sperm present in the initial ejaculates, although after 4 weeks the number and quality in the majority of men is probably insufficient to achieve fertilization.

Failures tend to be identified only after an unexpected pregnancy in the partner. Late failure can occur at any time after vasectomy and is thought to be due to recanalization, or rejoining of the two ends of the severed vas. Reversal is difficult and requires specially trained surgeons, and successful reversal rates depend on the occlusion method used.

Vasectomies, when performed by an experienced surgeon, have few serious side effects. Transient complications include bleeding, pain, epididymitis (inflammation of the epididymis) and hematoma. Incisional vasectomy is associated with a higher complication rate than no-scalpel techniques. The majority of men develop anti-sperm antibodies that persist in the circulation for several years and may lead to continuing infertility even when surgical reversal is successful. There is also some evidence that occlusion of the vas deferens leads in suppression of spermatogenesis over time. Reversal depends not only on the vasectomy technique, but also on the interval the vasectomy and the attempted reversal.

Male contraception – not quite there yet

Two technical developments – the introduction of vulcanized rubber in the 1880s and the development of latex in the 1930s – are important landmarks in male contraception, for they made possible the mass production of fairly reliable and inexpensive condoms. Important as these advances were, they also reveal the sorry state of male contraceptives because aside from vasectomy no other methods of efficacious contraception for males are available. Compared to the variety of female contraceptives currently available, the male contraceptive cupboard is quite bare. There are two main reasons for this circumstance. The first has been that females have a much greater stake in the prevention of an unwanted pregnancy than males. Females played a crucial role not only in the development of the Pill and other types of contraceptives, but they were also instrumental in promoting their usage. Once effective female contraceptives became available the pressure for developing male contraceptives was relaxed.

The second, perhaps even more important, is that suppression of sperm production is not as straightforward as suppression of egg production because suppression of testicular function leads to loss of testosterone, and therefore, the loss of erectile function and sexual drive. In females, suppression of ovarian function does not interfere with the female sexual drive. Hence, what would be needed in males is a way of suppressing sperm production while at the same time maintaining the testosterone-dependent functions. Since testosterone has a negative feedback effect on pituitary function, the rationale for using exogenous testosterone to suppress pituitary production of LH and FSH, both required for spermatogenesis, seemed obvious. And, if fact, it has been known for about 60 years that exogenous testosterone administration is capable of suppressing sperm production.

However, studies have shown that administration of testosterone alone did not lead to complete suppression of sperm production (interestingly, sperm production was suppressed more effectively in about 80% of Chinese males, but only about 66% in Caucasian males). We don't really understand yet how to account for the differences in individual or ethnic responses, but it seems likely that as yet unknown genetic or environmental differences hold the clue. What this means is that other strategies to inhibit sperm production without interfering with the sexual drive, erectile function, and other important androgen functions need to be developed.

Contraception – quo vadis?

The first contraceptive revolution is now about 50 years old. In many ways it is old hat, at least scientifically, since the methods are based on old principles. There have been technical improvements, but no new conceptual advances. Immunocontraception, which represented a new approach, seems to spinning its wheels. Despite frequent articles calling for renewed commitment of research funds for contraceptive research, the outlook for the future looks fairly grim. The big pharmaceutical companies that took the leading role in developing the existing methods have more or less withdrawn from the game. Only two of the twenty largest pharmaceutical companies in the world market female contraceptives and carry out some research and development to improve the existing hormonal contraceptives. None of them has yet taken on the challenge of a male contraceptive, and none is willing to explore contraceptive-vaccine research. In the U. S. in particular, contraceptive research, limited as it is, is increasingly being carried out in a hostile environment driven by opposition from religious conservatives. Moreover, given the hundreds of millions of dollars required to test any new method or product, and the length of time required to demonstrate safety, it seems unlikely that we can expect a second contraceptive revolution any time in the foreseeable future.

What can we expect then, aside from a continuation of the status quo? Carl Djerassi, one of the early pioneers in the first contraceptive revolution, has argued that the emerging field of assisted reproduction technologies (ARTs) (see next chapter) will render contraception, at least as we understand it now, superfluous. Ironically, it may turn out that ARTs, which developed as a way to address the needs of infertile couples, may in the end turn out to be the preferred birth control method. (For a review of ARTs see Chapter 13). Perhaps the most important lesson for the future is that the almost revolutionary ARTs advances have taken place outside of the pharmaceutical industry. ARTs are small-scale research and development, and the rapid pace of advances bode well for the future.

The Pill and other forms of contraception separated sex from reproduction. ARTs take the next step – they separate sex from fertilization.

We can imagine two scenarios. The first is already feasible: cryopreservation of sperm (preservation of sperm by deep freezing) from men whey they are young, and followed by a vasectomy. Then later when the man is ready to start a family, he can do so by artificial insemination. The second scenario could be the extension of ovarian tissue cryopreservation now being developed for women with ovarian cancer and extension of a woman's fertile lifetime (see Topic 11). This technology may be available in the very near future. Both scenarios require early sterilization, but with the difference that the couple at some future date will be able to have the children they would like.

Does this seem farfetched? Will this be acceptable? The best answer may be to remember that the first contraceptive revolution came about not simply because the Pill was available, but because of the desire of women and men to limit births. The social and cultural changes that fed the widespread use of contraceptives and the phenomenal growth and acceptance of ARTs suggest the use of ARTs as birth control may not be as far out as it may appear.

Abortion

In early 2003 the North Dakota legislature considered legislation that would have made it a felony to kill a "preborn child." The proposed law applied both to the physician performing an abortion and to the woman having the abortion. The Catholic bishop of the Bismarck Diocese, Paul Zipfel, testified against the bill, stating that the church "for pastoral, moral and prudential reasons" opposed abortion laws that made women criminals. Abortion is a "grave moral wrong," he said, but "not every moral wrong . . . demands a corresponding penalty in civil law." (5, Alexander Sanger Beyond Choice Reproductive freedom in the 21st century)

A perspective

Induced abortion, or termination of a pregnancy by artificial means, is as old as history. All human societies, as far as we know, have practiced abortion, whether sanctioned by law or not. Despite its ubiquity, abortion remains a contentious, and often bitterly divisive issue in many countries. The conflation of religious, social, moral, ethical, legal, and medical questions often makes it near impossible for a general consensus to be reached. This book is not the place to consider the almost overwhelming complexity of the issues that the abortion debate raises, nor am I equipped to do so. The abortion debate has generated hundreds of articles and many books that argue the pros and cons. *Ronald Dworkin's Life's Dominion*. An Argument about Abortion, Euthanasia, and Individual Freedom, published in 1993 provides one of the most balanced, judicious, and thorough discussion of the abortion dilemma, along with a historical perspective and free of the inflammatory rhetoric that often characterizes the abortion debate, is. The author provides an extensive bibliography that the interested reader can consult.

Our purpose here is to review modern abortion methods, both surgical and pharmacological, all of which have been developed and perfected only in the last 20 years or so. In fact, it has been the liberalization of abortion laws in the developed countries that have been the spur for the development of safe and efficacious abortion methods. Before we embark on that we think it is worthwhile considering briefly the connection between abortion and broader public health policy issues. For abortion is not simply a private matter, but the regulations that determine when and where, or whether, an abortion can be carried out also have widespread repercussions in the public health arena.

Unsafe and illegal abortion

Unsafe and illegal abortions are not synonymous, but the result is usually the same – high maternal mortality. The World Health Organization estimates that about 70,000 women die each year from the complications of unsafe or illegal abortions. Those who survive are left permanently scarred – including chronic pelvic pain, genital trauma, and infertile. Unsafe abortion is an endemic problem in many developing countries where even if abortion is legal, the lack of skilled physicians, poorly funded hospitals or clinics, broken equipment, lack of water and electricity, poor stock of drugs and medications, and difficult access, make it one of the five leading causes of maternal death. It has correctly been pointed out that the tragedy of unsafe abortion continues in part because the victims are mainly in developing countries.

The connection between maternal mortality and illegal abortions has been well known for sometime. In the U.S. the legalization of abortion eliminated the septic abortion wards in the major city hospitals, and

207

maternal deaths from illegal abortions dropped precipitously a few years after nationwide legalization. In Romania maternal mortality rates soared to the highest in Europe after the dictator Ceaucescu decreed abortions illegal. After Ceaucescu's fall, abortion again became legal, and maternal mortality rates plummeted. Poland, like Romania, after decades of easy access, has made abortion illegal, and the result has been a large increase in the number of illegal abortions, women seeking aid in other countries, increase in maternal mortality and morbidity. One thing that is clear from these and other studies - restriction of legal abortion leads invariably to an increase in illegal abortion with its concomitant maternal mortality, health complications, permanent injuries, and deterioration of public health.

These historical examples may be critically relevant if it turns out that as many observers predict that the U. S. Supreme Court will at some point reverse the Roe v. Wade 1973 ruling. It is already the case that although the anti-abortion partisans have not yet succeeded in banning all abortions, they have succeeded, through more than 335 anti-choice laws passed in different states, in making it more and more difficult for women to access and clinicians to provide abortion care. Significant restrictions on where abortions can be performed and widespread intimidation of clinicians has led hospitals to routinely refuse to perform abortions. Fewer than 2,000 abortion clinics now function in an atmosphere of fear and violence directed against the clinicians and women who have abortions. In 2005 only one abortion clinic was functioning in the state of Mississippi.

The consequence of banning abortion will be to drive abortion underground. Abortion as a criminal activity will be controlled by criminal organizations. The cost will be driven up and the dangers to women of unsupervised abortions will skyrocket. And, of course, the women who will suffer the most will come from the lower economic and social strata of our society. The public health consequences of banning abortions will be enormous.

Contraception and abortion

Throughout human history, and especially before modern contraceptive methods became available, induced abortion was widely used as a birth control method. Even in the latter part of the 20th century abortion was the primary method of birth control in countries where modern contraceptive methods were not available. The two primary examples are Japan, which only made hormonal contraceptives available in 1999, and the countries of the former Soviet Union. Both countries had the highest rates of abortion in the world, close to 200 abortions per 1000 women aged 15-44. The mean number of abortions undergone by the average woman during her reproductive lifetime in the countries of the former Soviet Union was, officially, about 4, but it was not uncommon for a woman to have 10 or more abortions. In contrast, the abortion rate in the Netherlands is one of the lowest (5 per 1000). In the U. S. the rate is about 30 per 1000, while the worldwide average is between 32 and 46 abortions per 1000 women aged 15–44.

One of the important conclusions from these demographic studies is that the abortion rate is a function not only of the effectiveness of contraceptives, but also their cost and availability. It is estimated that the average woman would undergo 10 abortions during her lifetime in a society that does not provide accessible alternatives to abortion to control fertility. On the other hand, about 0.7 abortions per lifetime would be expected in a society that does provide highly effective and ineffective contraceptive alternatives. The critically important lesson is that abortion rates are lowest where the latest and most effective contraceptive options are available free or at low cost, where counseling and sex education is widespread, easily available, and informative, where the society promotes reproductive responsibility in a positive and open manner. Ironically, the groups who favor limiting abortion are also the groups who if not against contraception, work to limiting access and information to contraception.

Abortion rates will never drop to zero for two main reasons. First, no contraceptive regimen is 100 percent effective. Despite the high theoretical efficacy of modern regimens, faulty compliance means that the actual failure rates will be considerably higher. The failure rates for different birth control methods vary considerably. Second, some couples, even if contraceptives are easily available, do not use any form of contraception. Perhaps the main reasons are ignorance, immaturity, and/or fear or reticence in asking for information. In the United States, it is estimated that about 10 percent of the couples who use no contraceptive method contribute over 50 percent of the unintended pregnancies, while the other 50 percent is contributed by contraceptive failures in the 90 percent of couples who do use some type of birth control regimen. About half of these pregnancies were terminated by abortion. It is estimated that unintended pregnancies account for more than half of the total number of pregnancies in this country. Most of the unintended pregnancies occur in women younger than 25. Hence, the availability and adoption of more effective contraceptive methods by young couples would substantially reduce both unplanned pregnancies and the abortion rate.

Abortion methods

Before the introduction of modern abortion techniques, many procedures were used to induce abortions, but they generally involved physical trauma to the uterus (for example, by sharp blows to the abdomen) or the introduction of sharp objects or toxic substances into the uterus. All of these procedures posed grave risks to the mother, and hence, maternal mortality rates were quite high. With the introduction of modern surgical techniques mortality rates have dropped significantly. The introduction of pharmacological abortion techniques (often referred to also as medical abortion), interventions that do not require mechanical removal of the fetus, has provided, at least in the view of some, more acceptable alternatives to surgical abortions. Despite the relative efficacy of the newer pharmacological alternatives, surgical abortions are still considered a last resort, something to try when all else has failed.

The risk to the mother associated with an abortion varies significantly with gestation time. Abortions during the first trimester (up to 12 weeks), performed according to current standards, carry a small risk. The abortion maternal mortality rate is lower than that of normal childbirth. For example, during the period 1979 to 1986, the mortality rate from pregnancy or childbirth (9.1 per 100,000 live births) was 15 times higher than the mortality rate from legal first trimester abortions (0.4–0.6 deaths per 100,000 procedures). The mortality risk for pregnancy for a woman 35-39 years of age is even higher (21 per 100,000, or 35 times higher than the abortion risk. Abortions during the second (12 to 24 weeks) and third trimester (after 24 weeks) carry a higher risk, and in many cases, the mortality rate is higher than that for normal childbirth.

First trimester abortions

In the United States close to 94% of all abortions are carried out during the first trimester. A number of different surgical or pharmacological methods are available for inducing abortions during the first trimester

210

(Table 3). The frequency with which they are used differs from country to country. The major surgical method, vacuum aspiration (VA), also called suction curettage, was introduced into the United States in 1967, and is now the most widely used method (over 90 percent of abortions are performed by VA). A VA can be performed on an outpatient basis and is considered to be a very effective and safe way of inducing early, first trimester abortions. (The mortality rate is 0.4 per 100,000). A suction tube, whose diameter increases with the weeks of gestation, is connected to a vacuum pump, and inserted into the uterus. The fetus and endometrial tissue are suctioned out. Different methods are used to dilate the cervix to introduce the suction tube into the uterus. Vacuum aspiration can be performed in a physician's office with only a local anesthetic up through about the ninth week.

After the ninth week and up through the fourteenth week, a variant of VA known as dilatation and curettage (D&C), is used. In this case the cervix is dilated and an instrument with a sharp loop at the end is inserted into the uterus and the inside wall of the uterus is scraped and the embryo is removed by suction. A D&C is carried it out in a hospital. Uterine bleeding and severe cramping can often accompany the procedure.

Pharmacological alternatives to surgical methods came into their own with the introduction of mifepristone (RU-486), first marketed in 1988 in France, and now available in Britain, Sweden, other European countries, and China. Its use in the United States has been severely restricted because of religious opposition. Although mifepristone by itself can work, extensive studies indicate that a combination of mifepristone and a synthetic prostaglandin analog misoprostol is more effective and safer. Prostaglandins, which produce uterine contractions, have been used alone effectively up to about week 3. The studies involving mifepristone and misoprostol indicate that the combination is close to 100% percent effective in inducing abortion up through weeks 8 or 9, especially if the misoprostol was administered vaginally. Because mifepristone is expensive and not available in many countries, alternatives are available. One combination is methotrexate (a cytotoxic compound sometimes used for tumor therapy) and misoprostol is also effective in inducing an abortion up through weeks 7 to 8, but not quite as effective as the mifepristone-misoprostol combination. An advantage is that both of these compounds are inexpensive and easily available in most countries.

Table 11.3	Modern Abortion Methods

Method	Time in Gestation
Surgical abortion	
Vacuum aspiration	Through weeks 7 - 8
Dilatation & Curettage	Weeks 7 - 14
Dilation and Evacuation	Weeks 8 - 16
Instillation	Second trimester
Hysterotomy	Third trimester
Pharmacological abortion	
Prostaglandins alone	Through week 3
Mifepristone / misoprostol (vaginal suppository)	Through weeks 7 - 8
Methotrexate / misoprostol	Through week 9
Mifepristone / gemeprost (vaginal route)	Through week 19
Intravenous prostaglandin/ potassium chloride injection/	
Vaginal delivery	Third trimester

Second trimester abortions

Second trimester abortions are considered to be more risky and complicated than first trimester abortions. Dilation and evacuation (D&E) is the most common procedure used in the United States. It is generally performed between 8 and 16 weeks gestation, although some proponents use this method up through 20 weeks. Since the fetus is much larger in the second trimester, surgical crushing instruments are needed and the cervix must be dilated to a greater extent. Among the several methods available for dilating the cervix is the use of laminaria tents, small cylinders of dried and sterilized seaweed. The tent is placed in the cervix. It absorbs water readily and swells to a diameter 3 to 5 times greater than its original size. The second part of the procedure, the evacuation, involves using a metal scraper to remove the fetus and endometrium and more powerful suction pumps to remove the crushed tissue. A D&E carries an eightfold greater risk than a vacuum aspiration, can produce severe discomfort and even pain, and should always be performed in a clinic or hospital.

Pharmacological methods are also available up to about week 20. An effective method developed in Britain is to administer a high dose of mifepristone taken orally and followed 36 hours later with multiple doses of another prostaglandin analog, gemeprost, given vaginally, over a period of 24 hours. It induces expulsion faster and has fewer complications. The maternal death rate is relatively low (7–8 per 100,000), but higher than that of vacuum aspirations.

Third trimester abortions

In the U. S. third trimester or late term abortions account for less than 1% of all abortions. These are the most problematic because at this stage the fetus could in rare cases survive outside the womb. Several methods are in use. The older procedures, referred to as instillation techniques, involved injecting substances toxic to the fetus into the amniotic sac. One standard method used a concentrated saline solution. The high salt concentration kills the fetus and induces expulsion after 24 to 48 hours. Alternatives to salt, such as urea and glucose, have also been used. Injection of prostaglandins, especially up to week 19, has been used in the U. S. Instillation methods can have significant complications, the most serious being severe uterine hemorrhage, failure of the placenta to detach, and the fetus being born alive. (After expulsion, the fetus dies quickly due to respiratory failure.) Another method used only rarely now is a hysterotomy, which can be likened to a cesarean section.

The most commonly used method in the U. S. is the intravenous administration of the prostaglandin PGF2. Expulsion begins in 12-19 hours, but there is a chance the fetus will be born alive. One way of avoiding that happening is to inject potassium chloride into the fetal heart to kill the fetus painlessly.

The procedure that has generated the most controversy in the U. S. is the so-called partial birth abortion, or technically, intact Dilation and Evacuation, in which labor is induced, and the fetus is destroyed as it emerges from the birth canal. This procedure was first described in 1992, but we have no accurate estimates of how many of these procedures have been carried out. One estimate suggested that around 0.1 – 0.2 % of late term abortions used intact D&E. The U. S. Congress banned this procedure in 2003.

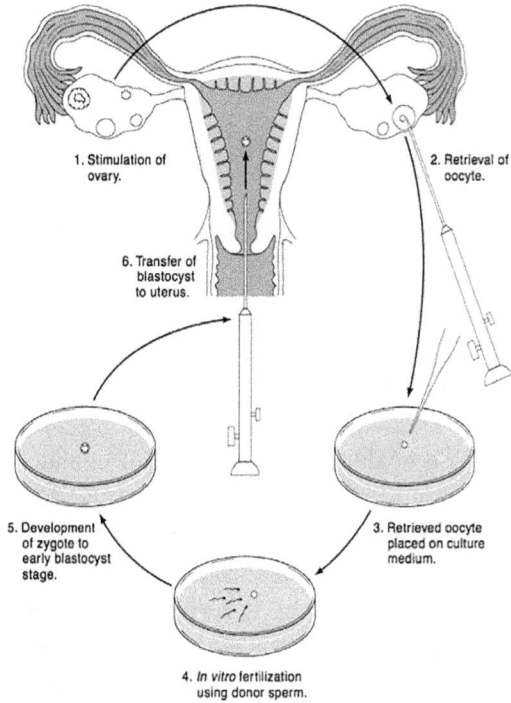

1. Stimulation of ovary.

2. Retrieval of oocyte.

6. Transfer of blastocyst to uterus.

5. Development of zygote to early blastocyst stage.

3. Retrieved oocyte placed on culture medium.

4. *In vitro* fertilization using donor sperm.

Chapter 11

Infertility and Assisted Reproduction

Infertility and its remedies – a brief historical perspective

> *Grief fills the room up of my absent child (1, W. Shakespeare, King John)*

Infertility has been a source of grief and lament probably for as long as human societies have existed, and until very recently it has been a problem about which little could be done. Through most of human history the source of the infertility was attributed to the woman, rarely the man. In many societies an infertile woman – the barren woman – was an object of pity and even ridicule, and most often was unable to keep a husband. Yet, all societies have tried to understand the causes of infertility and devise remedies based on the presumed causes. In the Kahoun papyrus (2200 – 1950 BCE), considered the first known gynecological medical text, the Egyptian physicians thought that infertility was due to the disruption in the continuity between the digestive and reproductive tracts, leading to symptoms such as to flatulence and vomiting. Hippocrates, the 'father of medicine', adopted some of the Egyptian teachings, and added some of his own. For example, one cause was a tight cervix, and the therapy – *"when a cervix is closed too tightly the inner orifice must be opened using a special mixture of red nitre, cumin, resin and honey . . . or it could be dilated by inserting a hollow leaden probe into the uterus enabling emollient substances to be poured in" (2, cited in Stephanie A. Beall and Alan DeCherney History and challenges surrounding ovarian stimulation in the treatment of infertility).*

During the Renaissance significant advances in understanding the anatomy of the reproductive organs took place, particularly with respect to the ovary and follicular function. In the 18th century tubal blockage, ovarian sclerosis, and the absence of follicles in the ovary were recognized as important causes of infertility. The discovery and some understanding of the role of steroid hormones, the gonadotropins, and chorionic gonadotropins (hCG) sparked the birth of reproductive endocrinology in the first half of the 20th century. In the 1930s the first experiments in superovulating immature mice were carried out. These techniques, refined and modified with human gonadotropins, led eventually to the field of assisted reproduction.

We now associate assisted reproduction with in vitro fertilization (IVF). IVF means literally "fertilization in glass" and involves mixing sperm and egg in a small glass container and allowing the sperm to fertilize the egg. The groundwork for IVF was laid in animal experiments dating to the 1890s. The first reports of successful IVF in humans appeared in the 1940s and 1950s. But the historical turning point came in 1978, with the success of joining two procedures – IVF and embryo transfer (ET), the transfer of the IVF fertilized egg into the uterus of recipient female, and the birth of what was called in the media the first "test tube baby". Little Louise Brown was not really a test tube baby in the sense that she developed in a test tube, but she was the first of many children conceived by IVF. Success had not come easily to the British physicians, Robert Edwards (endocrinologist) and Patrick Steptoe (a pioneer in laparoscopy), responsible for Louse Brown – she was the first successful pregnancy in 70 attempts.

Since the first successful IVF + ET procedure in 1978 thousands of pregnancies have been achieved worldwide by a continual refinement of the original procedures now referred to as assisted reproductive techniques (ARTs), or more simply assisted reproduction. The social acceptance of these revolutionary procedures was so rapid that discussion of the social, ethical, and moral issues that they raised took place after the fact.

During the first two decades many alarmist scenarios about the dangers of assisted reproduction ran rampant: that it was 'unnatural', that it violated the laws of God, that it would cheapen the value of human life, that the babies so conceived would be seriously abnormal, that families would be damaged because the act of sex would now be separated from conception. Louise Brown's parents recall that many of their neighbors were afraid to look at Louise after she was born because they expected to see a deformed baby. Once they saw her, their fears disappeared. Louise's father would tell them "IVF is just helping nature along a bit." The 'unnatural' scenario, at least for most people, was laid to rest after Louise and many other IVF babies grew up and had their own children.

Although some religious denominations persist in condemning IVF and other assisted reproduction procedures, this resistance borders on the perverse because, as many commentators have emphasized, children conceived by assisted reproduction are probably the most wanted in any society. The British journalist, Claire Rayner, captures the strong and poignant sentiments:

The ability to reproduce is valued a great deal more highly than some people I suspect realize. All the emphasis that is being placed these days on the role of pornography, the rights and wrongs of abortion, the ins and outs of contraception may cloud our awareness of how much people want babies, need babies and become frantic with fear, quite literally, at any threat to their ability to have babies. (3, Claire Rayner The meaning of sex: a view from the agony column)

Virginia Woolf, who never had children, struggled with her infertility for more than a decade

". . . and all the devils came out - heavy black ones – to be 29 & unmarried - to be a failure – childless – insane too, no writer" (4, cited in Belle Boggs The art of waiting)

Perhaps because infertility weights so heavily on some couples, the objections and proscriptions by religious organizations have been ignored by a wide segment of the public. For the great majority of the public, assisted reproduction no longer poses any serious moral or ethical problems. The contribution of assisted reproduction has been that we now see infertility as a medical problem, something fixable, rather than a personal tragedy visited upon the parents by the will of some inscrutable power in the universe.

Moreover, the development and refinement of these procedures has greatly increased our knowledge of the mechanisms of fertilization and implantation, and has led to a deeper understanding of the factors or conditions that influence the fertility of couples. Since Louise Brown, a complex battery of ARTs protocols have been developed to enable infertile couples to have children. The principles of the ARTs procedures are relatively easy to understand, but their practical application is technically demanding, requiring tremendous skill on the part of the clinicians carrying them out. The ARTs success rates depend on many factors and remain lower than many couples might desire.

Before describing the essentials of ARTs, let's begin with a short review of how infertility is defined and the main causes of infertility in females and males. We then continue to describe briefly the rapidly developing field of ARTs, which provide hope for many couples for whom no hope was available before. And finally, new protocols that are currently in the experimental stages, but which may be useful in the future.

Infertility today

A large part of the frustration of infertility comes from the feeling that fertility is normal, natural, and healthy, while infertility is rare and unnatural and means something is wrong with you. (4, Belle Boggs The art of waiting)

How is infertility defined?

We can think of infertility in two ways – either as the difficulty in conceiving, or alternatively as the difficulty in having a successful pregnancy. Thus, for example, a couple may conceive, but the pregnancy may be terminated spontaneously before term (miscarriage). These two clinically different measures of infertility can generally be distinguished except in the cases of very early pregnancy loss, where the loss occurs before implantation takes place, that is, before a pregnancy is established.

Typically, the first measure of infertility is used in most clinical settings, and a couple is said to be infertile if they have not achieved a pregnancy after 12 months of unprotected intercourse. This period is somewhat arbitrary but has been accepted as useful for a diagnosis of infertility because the probability of becoming pregnant after one year of unprotected intercourse is 85 percent. For women over the age of 35 a shorter period may be used.

Using this convention, about 10 - 15 percent of all couples in the U.S. are infertile. This percentage translates into about 6 – 7.3 million couples (women aged 15-44) unable to achieve a pregnancy by normal means. Seen in this light, infertility is one of the most prevalent chronic disorders of young adults in the U.S.

While the focus in infertility is always the couple, studies suggest that in about one-third of cases the infertility is due to the woman, another third is due to the man, and the remaining cases the causes are unknown or a mixture of the two. We shouldn't think about this as assigning blame – for neither partner is to blame – but as information that may be useful in trying to understand the cause of the infertility. However, it is important to emphasize that relatively few definitive causes of infertility have been identified. This means that in many cases, and after undergoing many different tests, to the understandable disappointment of the couple, the infertility may remain unexplained, even if one or the other partner is identified as the source of the infertility. In many cases, it may be the result of a combination of factors that vary from couple to couple.

Causes of infertility

First, infertility may be the result of intrinsic endocrinological, physiological, or neurological disturbances that interfere with egg or sperm formation, sexual functioning, or the ability of the female to sustain a pregnancy to term.

Second, infertility can arise from normal, nonpathological processes that are associated with the perimenopause. We have already considered these factors in Chapter 6.

Third, infertility may be a consequence of life style factors and behaviors, such as smoking or drinking, or the use of therapeutic or recreational drugs, extremes of weight or exercise, or exposure to environmental toxicants.

Female infertility

Disorders of fertility

We can group the causes of female factor infertility into three general categories: ovulation disorders, tubal disorders, and miscellaneous disorders.

Ovulatory problems account for most case of female infertility, and they generally manifest themselves by their effects on menstruation. These range from complete cessation of ovulation (anovulation) manifesting itself as amenorrhea, cessation of menstruation, to oligomenorrhea (less than 6 periods per year), or to irregular cycles. Although many conditions are known to contribute to ovulation disorders, one condition, polycystic ovarian syndrome (PCOS) accounts for 50 to 70% of all ovulation disorders. PCOS is a multifaceted disorder with a complex array of symptoms. The name itself comes from the observation that PCOS females have ovaries that are full of large non-ovulated follicles. The precise defect in PCOS remains unknown, but it leads to a disturbance in ovarian function that results in elevated androgen levels, and lower estrogen to androgen ratios. One consequence is that follicular dynamics is disturbed, and ovulation does not take place. The disturbance in estrogen synthesis may account for the observation that large numbers of Graafian stage follicles accumulate in the ovary (the large follicles were originally referred to as cysts, hence, the origin of the name PCOS). Roughly 50 percent of PCOS females are obese and are at a high risk for developing diabetes. The elevated androgen levels associated with PCOS may also lead to the growth of body hair (clinically known as hirsutism).

Tubal disorders arise from defects in the oviducts that affect the ability of the sperm to reach the site of fertilization or that affect the ability of the conceptus to move into the uterus for implantation. Some tubal disorders are congenital (present at birth) and may be characterized by complete or partial blockage of the oviducts. Such defects may be correctable by surgery. In other cases, the tubal failure may be physiological rather than anatomical. Currently, however, the major contributor of tubal infertility is pelvic inflammatory disease (PID), caused primarily by sexually transmitted microorganisms. Chlamydial infections, for example, account for about 75% of cases of tubal infertility. Antibiotics can cure chlamydial and other bacterial infections, but scarring left over from the infection may seriously affect oviduct function, thus leading to infertility.

A variety of other miscellaneous disorders contribute to female infertility. One fairly common one is endometriosis, a condition in which endometrial tissue grows outside the uterus. The condition was first described in the 1800s, but the term itself was not coined until 1927. The cause of endometriosis is not known with any certainty. What is known is that the transplanted endometrial tissue begins to grow at these sites, and once it has done so, undergoes the same changes that would occur in the uterus. Transplantation of endometrial tissue occurs most commonly into the uterine tubes, but endometriosis can occur in the abdominal cavity, and very rarely in distant organs. In these unusual cases, it is presumed that endometrial cells are transported by the circulatory system and deposited at distant sites.

The relationship between endometriosis and infertility is complex. Some studies suggest that 20 to 40 percent of infertile women suffer from endometriosis, and, indeed, endometriosis is suspected in any woman complaining of infertility. On the other hand, 10 percent of fertile women have endometriosis. Endometriosis is an important disorder in women: about 4 per 1000 women in the 15 to 64 age range in the United States are hospitalized with endometriosis each year, slightly more than are hospitalized with breast cancer. Endometriosis in the uterine tubes can certainly compromise fertility, but disappointingly, medical suppression of endometriosis or surgical removal of the tissue may not always improve fertility.

Other conditions that occur much less frequently: unusually viscous cervical mucus acts as a very effective barrier to sperm movement through the cervix and into the uterus. A small fraction of infertile women produce such mucus. Another small fraction of infertile women produces anti-sperm antibodies spontaneously, although the reason for their production remains unknown. The antibodies inactivate the sperm and prevent fertilization. Immunosuppressive drug therapy has been shown to successful in restoring fertility in some cases.

Impaired uterine receptivity can result either in the failure of implantation or in pregnancy loss at a later stage in gestation. Traditionally, lack of appropriate progesterone stimulation was considered to be the main cause of implantation failures, but implantation also depends on many factors other than progesterone. Recurrent spontaneous abortions are often associated with uterine cavity abnormalities that prevent normal completion of gestation. About one-third of women with recurrent abortions also experience difficulties in conceiving, and 40 to 50 percent of these women also suffer from polycystic ovarian syndrome (PCOS).

The perimenopause – normal decline in fertility

Because we spend much of our young lives dramatizing and imagining ourselves as parents, it isn't surprising that even the strongest of us let the body's failure become how we define ourselves. (4, Belle Boggs The art of waiting)

Women greet the decline in their fertility during the perimenopause with mixed emotions - regret, anxiety, relief, sadness, equanimity, a sense that life is going too fast. Some welcome it as the entry into a new phase of their life. For those who postponed having children, the realization that their 'biological clock' will soon 'run out' can be a source of anxiety. This period of time has been written about so often and in so many venues that we would assume every woman in her late 30s or early 40s would be aware of its consequences. Yet, many women continue to believe that they are still fertile if they are menstruating regularly and assume that they can get pregnant up until around 45. Or, the publicity associated with the successful pregnancies achieved in women in their 40s may lull them into thinking that they too will be able to get pregnant. We can get a sense of some of the ways women view their perimenopausal transition from a recent report that summarizes interviews with women who eventually opted for assisted reproduction.

One woman, age 40 at her child's birth, stated: *"I honest to God thought if I was still cycling, life was good." (5)*

Another woman, 44 at the birth of her child, described her first meeting with a reproductive endocrinologist:

I ended up at what now is the [infertility clinic]. Total novice. I purely was thinking that I needed a better kind of thing [treatment]. And that was a rude awakening because I started to see some real statistics on what my chances were. It never occurred to me that age could be an issue because

I was still in my thirties. After all, wasn't that still young? Maybe, but not reproductively it wasn't. (5, Carrie Friese, Gay Becker, and Robert D. Nachtigall Rethinking the biological clock)

Another expressed regret for lost time and lost opportunity:

I walked around with all these little, bubbling eggs inside me, and I didn't give it a thought. I didn't show appreciation. I didn't give thanks for it, didn't think it was something valuable. I just pissed on it, you know. And now, that I want it, it's gone (43 at birth of child). (5, Carrie Friese, Gay Becker, and Robert D. Nachtigall Rethinking the biological clock)

Other women began to see themselves as old and unhealthy. One, 39 at the birth of her child stated:

I felt that my infertility—it felt like I was unhealthy, to me. That's how it felt. And that I was older, and I was trying to get pregnant. So I felt old, a little bit. (5, Carrie Friese, Gay Becker, and Robert D. Nachtigall Rethinking the biological clock)

Many women felt that they did not have enough information in making their reproductive choices. One woman, 35 at the birth of her child, stated:

I tell people, 'don't wait too long.' I wouldn't wish this on anybody. I don't love my daughter any less, and I'm not angry that I had to go through this, but I would never wish this on anybody else. I would not want somebody to have to go through this way of conceiving children. But it doesn't mean that, in the end, it didn't turn out okay for me. (5, Carrie Friese, Gay Becker, and Robert D. Nachtigall Rethinking the biological clock)

The authors conclude their report as follows:

The narratives of these women speak to the profound social changes that engulf them and provide a window into a social life transition that is occurring globally. The resulting social changes are currently being experienced as upheaval, but it is likely they will be seen in the future as commonplace. (5, Carrie Friese, Gay Becker, and Robert D. Nachtigall Rethinking the biological clock)

As discussed in Chapter 6, the decline in egg quality is the most important cause of loss of fertility during the perimenopause. One important consequence of this decline is an increase in preimplantation loss. Preimplantation loss is important at any age, but increases even more as the female ages. This decline in egg quality results in a progressive decline in implantation rates, which drop from around 20% at the age of 30 to less than 4% by the age of 40. The decline in egg quality is also considered to account for the significant increase in the rate of spontaneous abortions (miscarriage) after the age of 35. For a woman over the age of 40 the risk of a miscarriage is over 50 percent.

Some investigators have suggested that uterine factors, for example, a loss in endometrial receptivity, and other changes in uterine anatomy or physiology, may also play a role in the decline in fertility. However, there is no compelling evidence to support this view. In fact, the evidence suggests quite the opposite. For example, the rate of successful pregnancies in perimenopausal women who have been implanted with embryos derived from the eggs of younger women clearly indicates that under most circumstances the important determinant of a successful pregnancy is egg quality.

Can fertility be extended?

Fertility experts are exploring different ways of extending a woman's reproductive life. Let's consider a few.

Transplanting frozen ovarian tissue

Sheep were the first guinea pigs. The experiment was simple in concept – remove the ovaries from a sheep, cut out a strip of the outer layer of the ovary (this is the region of the ovary that contains the follicles), freeze the strip at −196 C (-321 F); then later thaw out the frozen ovarian tissue and transplant it back into the same sheep. The critical question was: could the transplanted ovarian tissue generate functional follicles? Unbelievably perhaps, the grafted tissue not only sustained follicular growth, but the follicles contained mature oocytes (eggs) that were fertilized and restored fertility to the sheep.

At the time – 1994 - this was an amazing experiment, for it showed that primordial follicles (these are the only ones that survive the freezing and thawing) in the ovarian tissue slices are able to develop and release mature oocytes. This experiment also laid the groundwork for the extension of these procedures to humans.

A human experiment was begun in England in 1995. Ovarian tissue was removed from a 3-year-old girl who was to undergo radiation therapy for cancer because the radiation would render her permanently sterile. The radiation therapy was successful in eliminating the cancer, and the young girl is healthy and growing normally. At some future date, if the young woman so desires, her frozen ovarian tissue stored for many years, could be re-implanted into her ovaries.

And in October 2004, the first proof of this possibility came: a research group in Belgium reported that a woman had given birth after the transplantation of ovarian tissue that had been removed prior to her undergoing cancer chemotherapy. In other words, they showed that the sheep experiment could be replicated in humans. Since then 13 live and healthy children are known to have been conceived through the transplantation of ovarian tissue. In 2012 Spanish physicians in Barcelona reported establishment of a pregnancy in a woman (31 years old) whose ovaries had been removed because of bilateral ovarian tumors, using some viable tissue extracted from a non-cancerous region of one of her ovaries. The ovarian tissue was grafted to the broad ligament of the uterus. After some months, hormone activity from the transplanted tissue, and the physicians were able to extract viable oocytes from the graft, which were then fertilized in vitro and transplanted into the patient's uterus. The team leader commented that to the best of his knowledge *"this the first time in which [this procedure] is performed without [the patient] having any traces of ovarian tissue." (6, Aser Garcia Rada (2012)* Spanish women becomes pregnant through ovarian tissue transplantation)

Transplanting ovarian tissue from one person to another would be much more difficult because the normal immune reaction against foreign tissue would have to suppressed. Immunosuppressive methods are available, but they are not completely effective, and they carry their own risk. However, if effective immunosuppressive therapies can be developed, transplantation between different individuals would be possible. Moreover, ovarian tissue could be derived from persons who have just died or even from fetal ovaries. This latter possibility has been carried out in mice, with the fertility of adult mice being restored by transplanted mouse fetal ovarian tissue.

The original justification for these projects was to preserve fertility of children or women who had been rendered completely infertile as a consequence of cancer therapy.

One mother captures the dilemma she faced in a particularly moving and poignant way:

It was an endless series of bad news, good news – an emotional rollercoaster. The day the doctors told me my six year old daughter had cancer was the darkest day of my life. Then they told me her chances of survival were good but she would never have children and she may have other permanent damage like hearing loss and heart problems. I thought about how much having children meant to me, how being a mother was what I had dreamed of when I was a little girl. My little girl seemed to have the same dream. She mothered her dolls, mothered the cat, she liked to dress up in my high heels and purse and say she was going to the store to buy food for her baby dolls. Now she was going to be robbed of this experience.

The good news was she was likely to survive but the bad news was she was never going to have the life we wanted for her and we thought she wanted for herself. I asked her doctor if there was anything we could do to prevent the sterility. He told me there was an experimental procedure we could consider where they froze some tissue from her ovaries. He said there were no guarantees and it was expensive and not likely to be covered by our insurance. I thought about it for a long time and weighed the pros and cons. If I didn't do this procedure for her would she be angry at me when she was older? If I allowed her to have the procedure would the extra time and money be worth it? Would my daughter feel compelled to have a child because I had stored her tissue for her? Would this experimental procedure lead to a baby for her one day?

I had a lot of questions but no answers. I asked the doctors if there was another parent I could talk to who was faced with the same decisions as me. I felt very alone, and even selfish when they told me that most parents were grateful if their child had a good survival prognosis and didn't worry about fertility. I didn't have a lot of time to make a decision either – they wanted to start treatment right away. I did some searching on the Internet and found a national organization. I started to read about how other parents were in the same quandary as me – I was not alone but most parents didn't express their concerns to their child's oncology team because they were waiting for the team to bring it up. In the end I decided to have my daughter's ovarian tissue frozen. Was it the right thing to do? I don't know and won't know for a long time. But I thought about how we saved for college for her, so she would have that option. This seemed like another type of savings plan. Time will tell if I made the right decision. Emma, Mother of Pediatric Cancer Survivor G.P. (7, Bethanne Power and Gwendolyn P. Wuinn Fertility prevention in cancer patients)

It seems likely, however, that these protocols will almost inevitably become available for women who simply want to delay having children until they are ready to start a family later. Such women will have a section of their ovary removed and frozen, and later when she is ready to start a family, the ovarian tissue will be thawed, and grafted back into the woman. Appropriate hormonal stimulation will be needed to elicit sustainable follicular growth. We are not at this stage yet, but it is not too difficult to imagine that within the next 20 years or so this technology will have been perfected.

Slowing the follicular clock

The rate of follicular atresia is a critical factor in determining the age of menopause. Could menopause be delayed, and therefore, fertility extended if the rate of follicular atresia could be slowed down? The answer, at least in mice, is yes. By knocking out a gene, Bax, one of several genes that regulate the genetically programmed cell death that regulates follicular atresia, the mouse ovaries kept producing eggs up through the mouse equivalent of 100 years old. Such older mice did not get pregnant normally, but the eggs recovered from the very old ovaries could be fertilized and normal offspring born.

Knocking out genes cannot be carried out in humans, but investigators are searching for ways to inactivate the BAX gene or the BAX protein in humans. To be useful the inactivation has to be ovary-specific because the BAX gene works in many other human tissues. Other proteins that are also involved in regulating follicular atresia are being targeted for inactivation.

Even if slowing the follicular clock is feasible in humans, there is still the question of whether the oocytes retrieved from slowed down ovaries will be quality oocytes. The quality of oocytes declines with maternal age, and does not depend on the rate of follicular atresia. Hence, extending the age of menopause may mean that the oocytes recovered will be aged oocytes, and therefore unlikely to support a successful pregnancy.

Generating eggs in vitro – an artificial ovary?

This scenario has a science fiction quality to it: develop an artificial ovary, so that primordial follicles can be developed into mature ones in a test tube. This is clearly a formidable challenge, but some initial steps are being taken in exploratory studies in the mouse. The most difficult problem is finding incubation conditions that will keep the artificial ovary functional long enough for the follicles to develop. Recall that follicular development is a long drawn out process in humans. The signals that guide follicular development are poorly understood, and we don't know if follicular development can be accelerated even if we knew which molecular signals are required.

Despite these formidable obstacles, optimistic reproductive biologists suggest that within 20 - 30 years it may be possible to generate eggs in vitro from human primordial follicles. The possibilities that can be imagined are so far-reaching that we may find them repellent. For example, an aborted female fetus with its millions of primordial follicles could be the source of eggs for many pregnancies, thereby becoming the biological mother of literally thousands of children. This capability would be useful in preserving a species that was on the brink of extinction, but it is much more difficult to imagine acceptable applications for humans.

Continual generation of oocytes from adult ovaries

The question: would it be possible to generate oocytes in a normal ovary continuously? You may recall that the stock of oocytes is generated only once in the female's life. This has been perhaps the only dogma in female reproductive biology for over 60 years. However, a few recent publications are suggesting that a possibility that this standard view may be wrong. The first report appeared in 2004. Briefly, the finding reported is that adult mouse ovaries contain stem cells that continue to produce new ovarian follicles. The rate of production diminishes with age but even in old mice the ovaries are said to contain a few young follicles. If true, this is a revolutionary finding. Since then a couple of other reports have been published. The latest publication comes from a group at Massachusetts General Hospital in Boston who report that they have isolated a group of human cells, referred to as oogonial stem cells (OSCs), which appear to have some of the properties of oocyte precursor cells. Whether the oocytes produced by these cells are functional and can be fertilized remains unknown. The authors of this report are properly cautiously optimistic:

"There's no confirmation that we have baby-making eggs yet, but every other indication is that these cells are the real deal — bona fide oocyte precursor cells" (8, Kendall Powell Egg-making stem cells found in adult ovaries)

A much more complex world may be just around the corner. Our problem is that we have not yet fully assimilated the current assisted reproduction methods, and soon we may be asked to think about developments that may stretch our views about human reproduction in ways that we cannot imagine now.

Is extending fertility desirable?

What will be the consequences of extending a woman's reproductive lifespan? It's a new question, and one that few people have considered carefully. Is this an issue only for individuals, the way having children normally is, or is this an issue in which society at large should take part? Some fertility experts, as one might expect, argue that it should be an individual choice. After all, why should only young women be able to have children? If a woman decides to delay reproduction for the sake of her professional career, why should she be denied the privilege when she is older? But perhaps, as some critics suggest, the focus should not be on a biological solution, but instead on finding ways of permitting women to have children early without compromising their career choices. But the train has already left the station – the drive to find ways of extending fertility is at least motivated as much by scientific curiosity as it is to find ways to help older women have children.

Male infertility

The true extent of male infertility remains somewhat controversial. Over the past 50 years the perception of the degree to which males were involved in the infertility of the couple has oscillated. Initially, infertility was seen as primarily a female problem; later the pendulum swung to the other side, and some studies in the United States indicated that 40 percent of all infertility was due to the male. More recently, a downward trend in the male contribution has been noted, but precise and reliable numbers are very difficult to obtain. Due to the redefinition of the lower limit of the "normal" sperm count, many men who would previously have been characterized as infertile or subfertile are now being considered normal.

Male infertility falls into three treatment categories: untreatable sterility (12.5 percent); potentially treatable conditions (12.5 percent); and untreatable subfertility (75 percent). These statistics are discouraging in that they indicate that most cases of male infertility are untreatable by methods that do not involve ARTs.

The untreatable sterility category encompasses severe and persistent impairment in the ability to produce sperm. This condition can come about in a number of different ways. Primary seminiferous tubule failure refers to a complex of disorders that profoundly disturb seminiferous tubule function, for example, to Sertoli cell failure. Sertoli cells are absolutely essential in sperm production. Recent studies of azoospermic (no sperm production) males have shown that some of them show small deletions in the Y-chromosome that result in a severe impairment in the production of sperm, clearly indicating that the missing genes are necessary to produce sperm. Sperm production also ceases as a consequence of trauma or disease of the testis, or from radiation therapy.

A number of potentially treatable conditions are recognized. Genital tract obstructions in the vas deferens, the epididymis, or the prostatic urethra can be congenital or they can develop as a consequence of sexually transmitted infections (STIs), tuberculosis, trauma, or from a number of other conditions. (refer to Chapter 5 for the importance of these tissues in the testis) Many are potentially treatable by surgical intervention to remove the blockage, or in congenital cases, reconstructive surgery to repair the malformation. For example, intervention to remove blockages in the epididymis and vas deferens, the ducts through which the sperm are ejaculated to the outside, are moderately successful, with about 70 percent of men achieving substantial sperm output within a year after the surgery. The success rate in other types of treatments varies considerably.

An autoimmune attack (the generation of anti-sperm antibodies) on sperm is another type of condition affecting sperm function, and it is also perhaps the most common medically treatable condition seen in men. The causes that lead to the production of sperm antibodies are not usually known. Most cases arise spontaneously; others are due to trauma to the testis or to obstructions that result in breakage of the Sertoli cell barrier. The condition is characterized by the presence of antibodies to sperm in seminal fluid or even in the circulatory system, or by proteins of the immune system (immunoglobulins) coating the sperm. Sperm antibodies are often found in fertile men, but presumably the concentration is too low to impair fertility. Therapy involves the use of immunosuppressive drugs taken over a period of 4 to 6 months. About 25 percent of couples are able to establish a pregnancy during such a regimen.

Organic defects that result in erectile dysfunction, ejaculatory failure, or retrograde ejaculation (ejaculation of the sperm into the bladder rather than into the urethra) are generally infrequent in the industrialized countries. Some types of organic defects can be treated surgically. Short periods of psychogenic erectile dysfunction are seen, but these cases can usually be treated with psychotherapy.

Most cases of male infertility (untreatable subfertility) are due to poor semen quality. Semen quality includes a broad category of characteristics, such as sperm count, sperm morphology, sperm motility, ejaculate volume, and composition of the seminal fluid. Sperm counts that are lower than normal, or that contain a substantial fraction of abnormal or dysfunctional sperm compromise fertility significantly. Many treatments have been tried over many years to improve semen quality, but none has been consistently or uniformly effective. No therapy is available, for example, to increase the sperm count or to increase the fraction of motile sperm. If the sperm count is not too low, continual attempts to conceive over several years has been successful in some cases.

Infertility and life-style

Infertility in the female athlete – energy availability is the key

Other women [athletes] acquire their menstrual disorders by following bad advice about diet and exercise, and their treatment is to be found within athletics in the form of better advice. (9, Leanne M. Redman and Anne B. Loucks Menstrual disorder in athletes)

Numerous factors, such as strenuous exercise (running, ballet dancing, figure skating, gymnastics), low body weight or low fat, and weight loss, as well as emotional trauma, and psychological disturbances have long been associated with menstrual disorders and associated with reduced fertility in females. At one extreme complete cessation of menstruation (and ovulation) occurs, known clinically as amenorrhea. Amenorrhea is divided into two types: primary amenorrhea has been redefined recently as "absence of menstrual cycles in a girl who has not menstruated by 15 years of age, even though she has undergone other normal puberty changes". The incidence of primary amenorrhea in the general population in the U. S. is less than 1%. Secondary amenorrhea refers to the development of amenorrhea after menarche, that is, after the first menstruation, and its incidence in the general population is 2 – 5 %.

Other disorders span a wide spectrum of reproductive deficits. Two of the most common are anovulation (failure to ovulate) but with continued menstruation, and luteal phase deficiency, also known as luteal suppression. In the anovulatory condition, estrogen levels are too low to support ovulation, but high enough to stimulate some endometrial development, and consequently menstruation continues. Luteal suppression is characterized by decreased progesterone secretion during the luteal phase and a shortened luteal phase. Ovulation continues in luteal suppression, and fertilization can take place, but the low progesterone levels prevent successful implantation. Precise estimates of the incidence of these two conditions are difficult to obtain, but generally range around 10%. All of these disturbances lead to impaired fertility, in some cases because of failure to ovulate, and in others because implantation is inhibited.

The incidence of these disorders is much higher in athletes, for example, 7-8 % primary amenorrhea, 60-80 % luteal suppression in college athletes, with the incidence often related to the type of athletic activity and the intensity of the training.

The good news about these menstrual disturbances is that they are reversible. As soon as the activity that precipitated the menstrual dysfunction is removed, ovarian function returns. This reversibility clearly indicates that the dysfunction is not due to an organic lesion, but that it is due to some type of metabolic disturbance that is not permanent.

The menstrual dysfunction is important clinically because it can have long term, and sometimes, irreversible consequences, even if ovarian function returns. These are due to the low estrogen levels that result from the inhibition of ovarian function. The loss of estrogen has several effects. Perhaps the most well known is the reduction in bone density, which occurs because the rate of bone formation and the levels of a number of other hormones that promote bone formation are reduced if estrogen levels are too low. The low estrogen levels also impair both cardiac and skeletal muscle function, thereby increasing the risk of cardiovascular disease and skeletal problems later in life. Especially vulnerable are adolescent athletes. Impairment of bone formation prevents their achieving their genetic potential for peak bone mass. This may lead to an early development of osteoporosis.

What causes the increase in the incidence of menstrual disorders in athletes? What complicates the question is that athletes are not all the same – they present a wide spectrum of different characteristics – in the type of physical activity (running, ballet dancing, figure skating, gymnastics), low body weight, low percentage of fat, or extremes of weight loss. Certain features that occur together are seen quite frequently and these have defined the clinical condition known as the "female athlete triad", characterized by menstrual dysfunction, disordered eating, and bone loss.

What is it about athletic activity that precipitates the menstrual disturbance? A significant advance in understanding came with discovery In the 1980s that these exercise-associated menstrual disorders are characterized by the suppression of the GnRH pacemaker from the hypothalamus. Recall that the GnRH pacemaker (refer to Appendix 2) controls pituitary function and in turn ovarian function. Hence, suppression of the GnRH pacemaker would lead to loss of ovarian function, and the different types of menstrual disorders depend on the severity of inhibition of ovarian function.

This discovery demonstrated that the menstrual dysfunction associated with athletic activity is of hypothalamic origin, that is, it arises from suppression of GnRH from the hypothalamus. The focus of research now shifted to trying to understand what characteristics of athletes resulted in the suppression of GnRH release by the hypothalamus. One proposal, formulated early on, and based on animal studies, was referred to as the stress hypothesis – which proposed that athletes were under two types of stress – physical stress because of the demands of the physical activity itself, and metabolic stress due to disordered eating habits, dietary deficiencies, low body weight, or low body fat. The basic idea was that the response of the body to the physical and metabolic stress was the trigger inhibited GnRH release.

One important question was whether physical and metabolic stress have differential effects. Can physical stress (intense physical activity) be distinguished from metabolic stress (reduced food intake, low weight, low fat, etc)? The distinction between the two is important because physical stress is often accompanied by metabolic stress as well. Studies in animals as well as detailed comparisons of amenorrheic and non-amenorrheic athletes have shown that physical activity (i.e., physical stress) by itself was not the cause of the menstrual dysfunction. This was an unexpected conclusion for many scientists.

What appears to be the critical parameter is energy availability, which is defined as the dietary energy intake minus exercise energy expenditure. The basic idea implies that the body is monitoring its energy availability continuously, and that whenever it falls below a certain threshold a signal is sent to the hypothalamus to begin suppressing GnRH pacemaker activity. Menstrual dysfunction is triggered in athletes because their daily caloric intake is too low to maintain their energy availability above the required threshold.

The energy availability idea makes it easy to understand the severe consequences of eating disorders, such as anorexia nervosa, in which the anorectic limits their food intake severely. In these cases, the GnRH pacemaker is completely suppressed, leading to amenorrhea, the cessation of menstruation. The energy availability threshold varies from one woman to another, and this explains the variability in responses to strenuous physical activity (from athletic training or from basic training in the armed services) from one woman to another. This is very important to know because steps can be taken to minimize the long-term effects of the suppression of ovarian function. In many cases, it may be as simple as increasing the daily food intake.

In the male

What about males? The general view has been that males are much less sensitive to the demands of athletic activity than females. But there have been relatively few studies that have examined the question carefully. The information we have is sparse –some studies report lower sperm counts and testosterone levels in wrestlers and weight lifters. The decrease has also been observed in long distance has been observed. It does seem clear, however, that the severe suppression of testicular function associated with athletic activity is rarely seen in male athletes. The energy availability hypothesis provides a straightforward way of understanding the lowered sensitivity of males.

This was clearly shown in 12 week study of U. S. Army Ranger recruits who were subjected to a constant level of physical stress – forced marches with heavy back packs, strenuous basic training exercises, etc. – and different levels of caloric intake (2000 and 5000 calories per day) in alternate weeks. In essence, the physical stress was kept constant, but the metabolic stress was varied from week to week. During the 2000 calorie per day weeks, testicular function diminished as shown by a decrease in testosterone levels and sperm count. During the 5000 calorie per day weeks, testicular activity returned to its former levels.

The conclusion was quite clear: the transient disruption of testicular activity was due to the decrease in energy availability below the critical threshold necessary to maintain adequate GnRH release. The reason males normally appear less sensitive to the demands of athletic activity is that their caloric intake is generally significantly greater than that of females.

The important general conclusion from these studies is that exercise itself (i.e., physical stress) does not have a deleterious effect on menstrual or reproductive function, and when it appears to do so it is because of its impact on energy availability. Metabolic stress really means reduction in energy availability.

The 64,000 dollar question now is: how does the body measure energy availability? What is the signal, and how does it lead to the inhibition of the GnRH pacemaker? These turn out to be difficult questions. We don't have the answer yet, but recent studies suggest that there are probably several signals, markers of metabolic activity, localized perhaps in different regions of the central nervous system. It will be exciting to identify them and learn how they work.

Psychogenic infertility – poorly understood

Ovarian function can also be inhibited by emotional trauma or psychological disturbances. This was first clearly documented during World War II in many of the women who served in the armed services in the battle zones, and was given the name of psychogenic amenorrhea, for those cases in which the trauma led to complete suppression of menstruation. As in exercise-associated infertility, psychogenic infertility also presents a spectrum of different degrees of inhibition of ovarian function, and the sensitivity to emotional trauma varies among women. A very important difference, however, is that the inhibition of ovarian function is not uniformly correlated with the inhibition of GnRH release. Low energy availability, for example, is not a common feature of women who suffer from psychogenic infertility. This latter observation indicates that a different set of factors are involved in the response to emotional trauma.

The psychogenically infertile women present a much more complex set of features. They report more depressive symptoms and dysfunctional attitudes, and significantly more symptoms of disordered eating. Numerous recent studies suggest that psychogenic infertility is precipitated by a combination of metabolic challenge (subtle eating disorders - fear of weight gain, tendencies to engage in binge eating, concern about body image, etc.) and mild psychosocial stressors (vulnerable to depression, feelings of inadequacy, insecurity, lack of control over life, etc.) The reality of these types of factors has been shown by the efficacy of both hypnotherapy and cognitive behavior therapy in restoring ovarian function.

Although it is difficult to define the important precipitating factors in any given individual, the general inference from these studies is that women predisposed to psychogenic infertility are those with certain personality characteristics that result in subtle nutritional / metabolic deficits, that may include energy availability, but also others that remain to be defined.

Recreational drugs and fertility

For most illicit recreational drugs we have little reliable information about their effects on fertility. The information available is anecdotal and difficult to interpret because most users of illicit drugs use drugs in combination and have many other health problems, and it is essentially impossible to separate out the specific effects of any specific drug. We have much more information of the two most commonly used licit recreational drugs – alcohol and tobacco.

Alcohol

Alcohol has a wide variety of effects in women – amenorrhea, anovulation, luteal suppression, ovarian pathology, and hyperprolactinemia (high levels of the pituitary hormone prolactin). The effects vary with the amount of alcohol consumed, alcohol tolerance, and acute versus chronic use. There is also great individual variation in severity of alcohol effects: some women appear to be highly resistant to the effects of alcohol, and there are many examples of heavy alcohol users who get pregnant; other women seem to be very sensitive, and small doses have major effects on ovarian function. The differences in the sensitivity remain unexplained.

In males, the primary effect is quite localized; its main target is the testis. Typical responses include suppression of testosterone synthesis, decreased sperm count, larger fraction of morphologically abnormal sperm, and concomitant reduced fertility. In chronic alcohol use, there is increased conversion in liver of testosterone to estrogen, leading to hypogonadism (shrinkage of the testis) and gynecomastia (breast development), decreased sexual drive, erectile dysfunction.

Tobacco

The effects of tobacco smoking on females have been studied extensively. Menstrual irregularities, reduced fertility, earlier menopause have been consistently found in the published studies. Recent studies indicate that these effects are due to (a) accelerated depletion of follicular reserve by increasing atretic follicular loss (hence, the earlier menopause), and (b) interference with follicular development (leading to menstrual irregularities and reduced fertility).

In males, tobacco, like alcohol, has the testis as its primary target. Generally findings include suppression of testosterone synthesis, lower sperm count, smaller ejaculate volumes, increased fraction of morphologically abnormal sperm.

Assisted Reproduction – a growth industry

Since the first successful IVF case in England in1978, thousands of babies conceived by assisted reproduction have been born around the world. Assisted reproduction is technology driven and has become one of the main growth industries in human reproductive biology. The technology has seen the birth of hundreds of fertility clinics, led to the development of a medical specialty, and has resulted in the founding of dozens of medical societies and scientific journals dedicated to research and the formulation of protocols and guidelines that establish standards for all fertility clinics. Today assisted reproduction is the only option for many cases of infertility in males and females. With so much fervent, it is difficult to predict what the future will bring.

IVF and embryo transfer (ET) – the goal is one

In vitro fertilization (IVF) was originally developed for patients with tubal infertility that could not be corrected surgically. The goal was simply to bypass the uterine tube. To work, fertilization had to take place outside the tube, the fertilized egg then had to be returned (transferred) at the appropriate stage to the uterus and hope that it would implant Conceptually, IVF and ET is simple, but as in most other things, the devil is in the details.

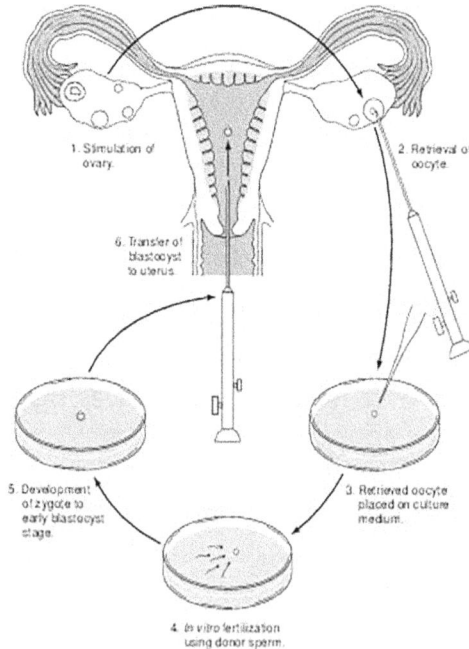

1. Stimulation of ovary.

2. Retrieval of oocyte.

6. Transfer of blastocyst to uterus.

5. Development of zygote to early blastocyst stage.

3. Retrieved oocyte placed on culture medium.

4. In vitro fertilization using donor sperm.

Figure 11.1

The steps include the following (Fig 12.1):

1. Collect follicles from the woman after the ovary has been stimulated to produce several large follicles.

2. Remove the largest follicles from the ovary, then remove oocyte from each follicle; mix each oocyte with sperm collected from the husband or a donor and allow the oocyte to be fertilized.

   - If fertilization takes place, culture the fertilized egg and let it develop into the early blastocyst stage at which point it is ready to implant (refer to Chapter 7 for a discussion of the blastocyst embryo)

   - Transplant the blastocyst embryo (this is the ET part of the procedure) into the uterus of the recipient female (usually the donor of the oocytes), whose endometrium had been primed with estrogen and progesterone to prepare it for implantation.

The first step, ovarian stimulation, is critically important because if not controlled properly, the eggs obtained may be too immature and not be able to support a full pregnancy. The stimulation protocols have become quite complex, but fundamentally they involve the use of FSH and LH, or human chorionic gonadotropin (hCG) (see Chapter 7). The newer methods of ovarian stimulation generally include methods that more or less shut down ovarian function, and afterwards, function is restored and carefully controlled by human FSH and LH. Typically, ovarian stimulation yields several oocytes (5 – 8 or more).

It has generally been the case that more embryos are generated than are implanted. Freezing them at very low temperatures saves the embryos not transferred. Until recently, clinicians had hesitated to use the frozen embryos for fear that the freezing or thawing might produce serious defects in the embryos. However, the first successful pregnancy generated from a thawed out embryo has now been reported. It is not yet clear whether this procedure will have general applicability, but it is a measure of how far the technology of freezing and thawing embryos has improved.

Egg donation and surrogacy

Although initially the woman who wanted to get pregnant was the egg donor, very quickly it became apparent that in many cases either she couldn't be, because the ovarian stimulation protocol did not work, or didn't want to be because she was afraid that she might transmit a serious genetic defect to her child. These different circumstances have generated a huge demand for donated eggs. Unlike sperm, which are available in dozens of sperm banks around the country and for which there is an essentially limitless supply, a human egg is an extremely rare commodity. Indeed, the human egg is the rarest cell in the body. Egg scarcity has generated another growth industry – egg donation. Newspapers today are full of advertisements calling for egg donors with financial rewards ranging from a few thousand dollars to as much as $80,000 for the woman with the proper qualifications. This last figure comes from an advertisement in a university newspaper calling for an egg donor with the following qualifications: Caucasian, 5'6" or taller, a high SAT score, college student or graduate under 30 years of age, and with no genetic medical issues. Extra compensation would be available for a donor gifted in athletics, science/mathematics, or music.

While the financial benefits may be attractive, the selected donors must also submit themselves to demanding ovarian hormone stimulation protocols lasting 1 to 4 months. The protocols are not entirely without risk. Problems reported are nausea, headaches, bloating, production of ovarian cysts, and possibly even increase the risk of ovarian cancer.

More recently an increasing number of perimenopausal women who wish to have children have chosen to rely on donated eggs. The good news is that egg donation has been successful in both perimenopausal and postmenopausal women. In the U. S. more than 70% of all assisted reproduction protocols are carried out at the age of 46 and older rely on donated eggs. Success rates very similar to those obtained for normal assisted reproduction in younger women. Hence, egg donation is the most reliable option for the older woman.

Egg donation for the recipient, however, is not problem free. A number of serious obstetric complications have been seen in egg donation pregnancies. Examples include vaginal bleeding, hypertension, and premature rupture of the membranes, premature labor, and intrauterine growth retardation. These problems appear to arise from the immunological incompatibility between the fetus and the mother, that is, the fetus is seen as a foreign object by the immune system of the mother (the recipient). Close medical supervision is absolutely necessary to increase the chances of a successful pregnancy.

Variations on the original theme

Modifications of the original in vitro fertilization (IVF) and embryo transfer (ET) protocols have been introduced in attempts to simplify the procedure, to improve the success rate, and to extend it to patients for whom standard IVF procedures were inadequate. One of the earliest successful modifications of IVF was gamete intrafallopian transfer (GIFT). GIFT uses IVF protocols for ovarian stimulation and oocyte retrieval, but it differs in that fertilization is accomplished by transferring both the oocytes and spermatozoa directly into the uterine tubes. A potential advantage is that fertilization takes place in a more "normal" environment, that is, in the oviduct, rather than in a laboratory dish. However, uterine tube function is required. Hence, GIFT is not indicated in cases of tubal absence or tubal defects. In general, greater skill on the part of the clinician is required also.

Zygote intrafallopian transfer (ZIFT) differs from standard IVF and ET protocols in that embryo transfer is carried out shortly after fertilization. The newly formed fertilized egg is transferred to the fallopian tube so that the very early development of the embryo take place in the tube, as happens normally.

Both GIFT and ZIFT protocols in the 1990s represented about 10% of assisted reproduction efforts, but are only occasionally performed currently.

The modification that has continued to be performed since its introduction is known as intracytoplasmic sperm injection (ICSI), first applied to humans in 1992, after first being tested in animals since 1966. The three procedures described above require that sperm be able to penetrate the zona pellucida in order to fertilize the oocyte. Perhaps for this reason they have not been very successful in cases where the sperm count was extremely low or when sperm were unable to fertilize. In the ICSI procedure, the sperm tail is removed from an individual sperm, the sperm head is absorbed to the tip if an extremely fine glass needle, and then by puncturing the egg membrane, the sperm head is introduced directly into the egg. ICSI, therefore, dispenses with the normal route of fertilization. The major advantage of ICSI is that it provides a relatively successful treatment alternative for the types of male infertility that constitute the majority and for which no other therapy was available.

Outcomes and risks

Success rate The success rate has improved from the early years. For parents the most important measure of success is not the clinical pregnancy rate but the live birth rate. In the 1980s this was 12 to 14 percent using fresh, non-frozen embryos. In the period between 1997 and 2009 the overall live birth rate improved from 24% in 1997 to 30% in 2009. Rate of live births using frozen embryos is lower than with fresh embryos.

The live birth decreases with maternal age: in women younger than 34 the success rate is about 45%; after that the success rate drops 2-6% per year, so that at age 43, success rate falls to 5%. Overall 50% of pregnancies conceived with in vitro fertilization result in miscarriage. Intracytoplasmic sperm injection use, because it provides the only therapy for many cases of male infertility, has increased greatly since its introduction. Its success rates are comparable to standard IVF and ET.

Risks: There are two categories of risks with IVF/ICSI – obstetric and fetal complications, and multiple pregnancies.

Obstetric and fetal risks: A comprehensive analysis of 30 studies of IVF/ICSI outcomes published in 2012 reported a higher risk of obstetric and perinatal complication compared to spontaneous conceptions: ante-partum hemorrhage – 2.49; congenital abnormalities – 1.67; hypertensive disorder of pregnancy – 1.49; premature membrane rupture – 1.16; Caesarian section – 1.56; low birth weight – 1.65; perinatal mortality – 1.87; preterm delivery – 1.54; gestational diabetes – 1.48; induction of labor – 1.18; small for gestational age – 1.39. These numbers, while not huge, are still sobering because of the increased risks for both the mother and the baby.

Multiple gestations: The birth of octuplets to Nadya Suleiman in 2009 after she underwent assisted reproduction and the publicity surrounding her life and doctor made the public at large much more aware of the impact and cost of multiple pregnancies. It also raised many questions about ways to reduce the incidence of multiple gestations in assisted reproduction. During the formative years of in vitro fertilization (IVF) and embryo transfer (ET), it was customary to transfer several embryos into the uterus because the probability of establishing a successful pregnancy increased with the number of embryos transferred - for example, about 9 percent with one embryo, 18 percent for two, 29 percent for three, and 32 percent for four. It was clear to physicians at the time that the most serious drawback of transferring more than one embryo is that the likelihood of multiple pregnancies increases. Multiple gestations carry greater risk for mothers and infants: gestational diabetes, pre-eclampsia, hypertension, postpartum hemorrhage, cesarean delivery, pre-term delivery, pulmonary and neurological disorders for the infant, and not least, very high hospital costs. Although multiple gestations account for 3% of live births nationally, they are associated with 23% of births before 32 weeks, and 26% of very low birth weights (< 1500 grams).

A 1995 summary of assisted reproduction outcomes in clinics in the U.S. and Canada reported 63.7 percent were single births, 28.3 percent were twins, 5.9 percent were triplets, and 0.6 percent was higher order births. In 2003, 31% twin gestations and 3% triplet or higher resulted from IVF. Improvements in assisted reproduction techniques between 1997 and 2009 led to a decrease in the number of embryos transferred from 3.8 to 2.4, and this change resulted in a 62% decrease in higher-order (greater than two) gestations), but no decrease in the incidence of twin pregnancies which has remained in the 25- 30% range.

Transferring only one embryo could reduce incidence of multiple gestations, but better methods of choosing the best embryos still need to be developed. The main reason for not limiting the number is the lower success rate. The number of embryo transfers is controlled more stringently in countries where governments cover many of the assisted reproduction costs. Sweden and Belgium permit only one embryo transfer; England limits the number to two, but three is permitted if woman is over 40. Italy and Germany two or three. Current guidelines in the U.S. (not government guidelines, but recommendations by American Fertility Association) permit up to five transfers, especially if woman is over 40.

Dilemmas – sparse agreement

Assisted reproduction has been a real success story, and has enjoyed wide acceptance among the public at large, often despite the disapproval and even proscription by religious groups. Still many thoughtful observers have noted that like other advances in the sciences it is not free of ethical dilemmas. Debate on these issues continues, but no general consensus exists yet about most of issues raised. The following is a list of some of the concerns and questions most commonly mentioned.

Frozen embryos: current estimates indicate that there are over half a million frozen embryos kept in storage. What should be done with them? How long should they be kept in storage? Who should pay for the custody? Can couples generate more embryos than they need, and then sell off the ones they don't want? Can couples sell off their unused embryos for research? Some countries, Italy and Germany, for example, forbid embryo storage.

Preimplantation genetic diagnosis: The understandable desire of couples to have children without birth defects has triggered another growth industry – preimplantation genetic diagnosis (PGD). The objective is the identification of normal embryos (elimination of those embryos carrying chromosomal abnormalities or harmful genetic mutations) to improve success rates of healthy children. New techniques permit chromosome or genetic analysis of one or two blastomeres from 3 - day old embryo, or in some cases of polar body. Chromosome analysis is limited because only a few chromosomes can be assessed, and not very accurate (false positives and false negatives). Genetic analysis is limited because only a few mutations can be identified using a single cell. In addition, removal of blastomere (embryo biopsy) can damage the embryo, impairing its ability to implant and survive.

Should couples be free to discard embryos that don't carry the genetic markers they desire? Can they discard embryos on the basis of sex, hair color, etc?

Should these decisions be left to individual couples, or should legislation regulate what can and cannot be done?

CITATIONS AND READINGS

1. I. A. Hughes (2010) The quiet revolution *Best Practice & Research Clinical Endocrinology & Metabolism* 24, 159 -162
2. Elizabeth Reis (2007) Divergence or Disorder, the politics of naming intersex *Perspectives in Biology and Medicine* 50(4), 535-41

J. Colapinto (2000) *As Nature Made Him* HarperCollins: New York, 2000

Anne Fausto-Sterling. (2000) *Sexing the Body: Gender Politics and the Construction of Sexuality* Basic Books, New York

I.A. Hughes *et al.* (2006) Consensus Group Consensus statement on management of intersex disorders. *Arch Child Dis* 91, 554-563

P.D.E. Mouriquand (2004) Possible determinants of sexual identity: how to make the least bad choice in children with ambiguous genitalia. *BJU International* 93, supplement 3, 1-2

V. Pasterski et al (2010) Impact of the consensus statement and the new DSD classification system *Best Practice & Research Clinical Endocrinology & Metabolism* 24, 187-195

W.G. Reiner (2004) Psychosexual development in genetic males assigned female: the cloacal exstrophy experience. *Child Adolesc Psychiatr Clin N Am.***13(3):**657-74

Joan Roughgarden (2004) *Evolution's Rainbow: Diversity, Gender, and Sexuality in Nature and People.* University of California Press, Berkeley

D.F.M. Thomas (2004) Gender assignment: background and current controversies. *BJU International* 93, supplement 3, 47-50

A. Vilain (2002) Anomalies of human sexual development: clinical aspects and genetic analysis. In: Chadwick, D., Goode, J. (Eds.) *The Genetics and Biology of Sex Determination.* Novartis Symposium, Vol. 244. Wiley: Chichester

Chapter 1

(1) A.M. Leroi (2003) *Mutants On genetic variety and the human body* Viking: New York, p. 217

(2) Plato. *Symposium. The Dialogues of Plato* Tr. Benjamin Jowett Encyclopedia Britannica, Inc.: Chicago, 1952

(3) D. Crews (1994) Animal Sexuality. Scientific American. 270(1), 108-114

Stefanie Eggers and Andrew Sinclair (2012) Mammalian sex determination – insights from humans and mice Chromosome Research 20, 215-238

R. Piñon, Jr. (2002) Biology of Human Reproduction University Science Books: Sausalito, CA

E. K. Ungewitter and H. H-C Yao (2012) How to make a gonad: cellular mechanism governing formation of the testes and ovaries Sex Development DOI: 10.1159/000338612

Chapter 2

(1) Shelly Jackson (2002) *The melancholy of anatomy.* Anchor Books: New York

(2) Regnier de Graaf On the human reproductive organs (1972) *Journal of Reproduction and Fertility* **5, Suppl. 17**

(3) Pott,W (1775) *Chirurgical Observations.* London, UK. Cited in R. V. Short (1977) The Discovery of the Ovaries. In *The Ovary,* 2nd edition, Vol.1 Lord Zuckerman and B.J. Weir, (Eds). Academic Press: New York

(4) Galen *On the Natural Faculties* Book One Tr. Arthur J. Brock. (Encyclopedia Britannica: Chicago, 1952)

(5) Cited in E. Grant, editor (1964) A Source Book in Medieval Science. Harvard University Press: Cambridge, MA

(6) Hippocrates. *Aphorisms The Hippocratic Writings* Tr. Francis Adams. (Encyclopedia Britannica: Chicago, 1952)

Ovarian and Menstrual Cycle

G.W. Corner (1933) The Discovery of the Mammalian Ovum. In *Lectures on the History of Medicine,* Mayo Foundation Lecture Series, 1926-1932 W.B. Saunders, Co.: Philadelphia, PA

Colin A. Finn (1996) Why do women menstruate? Historical and evolutionary review *Eur. J. Obst. Gyncol. & Reprod. Biol.* **70***, 3-8*

J. E. Markee (1940) Menstruation in intraocular endometrial transplants in the Rhesus monkey *Contributions to Embryology* **28,** 219-308

N. Oudshoorn (1994) *Beyond the Natural Body. An Archeology of the Sex Hormones* Routledge: London, UK

R. Piñon, Jr. (2002) *Biology of Human Reproduction University* Science Books: Sausalito, CA

P. Vanezis (1991) Women, violent crime, and the menstrual cycle: *a review Medicine, Science, and the Law* **31(1),** 11-14

S.S.C. Yen (1999) The Human Menstrual Cycle In *Reproductive Endocrinology Physiology, Pathophysiology, and Clinical Management,* 4th edition. S. S. C. Yen, R. B. Jaffe, R. L. Barbieri, Eds., W. B. Saunders Co: Philadelphia

PMS

T. Bäckstrom et al. (2003) Pathogenesis in Menstrual Cycle-Linked CNS Disorders. *Annals N.Y. Academy of Sciences 1007:* 42-53

C.L.Domoney, A. Vashisht, and J.W. Studd (2003) Premenstrual Syndrome and the use of alternative therapies *Annals N.Y. Academy Sciences* **997,** 330-340

Ellen Freeman (2010) Therapeutic management of PMS *Expert Opinion Pharmacotherapy* 11(17), 2879-2889

Treating Premenstrual Dysphoric Disorder (2009, October) *Harvard Mental Health Letter*

Chapter 3

(1) R. J. Aitken and J. A. M. Graves (2002) The future of sex *Nature* **415,** 963-65

Mythology of the Witness

W.J.Bremner (1981) *Historical aspects of the study of the testis In The Testis,* H. Burger and D. de Kretser (Eds) Raven Press, New York

J. P. van Basten *et al.* (1996) Fantasies and facts of the testes *British Journal of Urology* **78,** 756-762

The post-pubertal testis

D.L. Garner (2009) Hoechst 33342: the dye that enabled differentiation of living X-and Y-chromosome bearing mammalian sperm *Theriogenology* 71, 11-23.

Glass, A. R. Gynecomastia (1994) *Endocrinology and Metabolism Clinics of North America* **23(4)**, 825-839.

D.S. Karabinus (2009) Flowcytometric sorting of human sperm *Theriogenology* 71, 74-7

A.M. Matsumoto (1996) Spermatogenesis In *Reproductive Endocrinology, Surgery, and Technology*, E. Y. Adashi, J. A. Rock, and Z. Rosenwaks, Eds. Lippincott-Raven Publishers: Philadelphia

R. Piñon, Jr. (2002) *Biology of Human Reproduction* University Science Books: Sausalito, CA

G. E. Seidel Jr. and D. L. Garner (2002) Current status of sexing mammalian spermatozoa *Reproduction* **124,** 733-743

Sharpe, R. M. (1998) The roles of estrogen in the male *Trends in Endocrinology and Metabolism* **9(9),** 371-377

Plight of sperm

(2) R. J. Aitken, P. Koopman, and S.E.M. Lewis (2004) Seeds of concern *Nature* 432, 48-52

(3) Loa Nordkap et al (2012) Regional differences and temporal trends in male reproductive health disorder: semen quality may be a sensitive marker of environmental exposure *Molecular & Cellular Endocrinology* 355, 221-230

A.A. Pacey (2010) Environmental and lifestyle factors associated with sperm DNA damage *Human Fertility* 13(4), 19-193

Hiltrud Merzenich, Hajo Zeeb, and Maria Blettner (2010) *Biomed Central* 10, 24-29.

Performance-enhancing drugs

(4) Diotima's dialogue in Plato *Symposium The Dialogues of Plato.* Tr. Benjamin Jowett. Encyclopedia Britannica: Chicago, 1952

(5) J.M. Hoberman and C. E Yesalis (1995, February) The history of synthetic testosterone *Scientific American*

(6) A sporting chance (2007) Nature 448, 2 August, p. 512

Daniel G. MacArthur and Kathryn N. North (2005) Genes and human elite athletic performance *Human Genetics* **116,** 331-339

Ramez Naam (2005) *More than human: embracing the promise of biological enhancemen*t Broadway Books: New York

Stephen Pincock (2005) Feature: Gene doping *Lancet* 366, 518-19

J. Savulescu et al. (2004) Why we should allow performance enhancing drugs in sport. *British Journal of Sports Medicine* 38, 666-670

Markus Schuekle *et al.* (2004) Myostatin mutation associated with gross muscle hypertrophy in a child *New England Journal of Medicine* **350,** 2682-2688

H. Lee Sweeney (2004) Gene Doping *Scientific American* **291(8),** 62-70

J. M. Tokish *et al.* (2004) Ergogenic aids: a review of basic science, performance, side effects, and status in sports *Am. J. Sports Med.* **32(6),**

1543-1553

Chapter 4

(1) Peter T. Ellison (2001) *On Fertile Ground* Harvard University Press: Cambridge

(2) Ayse K. Uskul (2004) Women's menarche stories from a multicultural sample *Social Science & Medicine* **59,** 667-679

(3) Alan Soldofsky (1994) *Thirteen In The Male Body* L. Goldstein, ed. , University of Michigan Press: Ann Arbor

(4) Dale F. Bloom (2004) Is acne really a disease?: a theory of acne as an evolutionarily significant, high-order psychoneuroimmune interaction timed to cortical development with a crucial role in mate choice. *Medical Hypotheses* **62,** 462–469

(5) Till Roenneberger *et al.* (2004) A marker for the end of adolescence. *Current Biology* **14,** R1038-1039

Puberty and its timing

I. Banerjee and P. Clayton (2007) The genetic basis for the timing of human puberty *Journal of Endocrinology* 19, 831-838

Judy L. Cameron (2004) Interrelationships between hormones, behavior, and affect during adolescence *Ann. N. Y. Acad. Sci.* **1021,** 110-123

Deborah Christie and Russell Viner (2005) Adolescent development *Brit.Med. J.* **330,** 301-304

Lorah D. Dorn and Deborah Rotenstein (2004) Early puberty in girls: the case of premature adrenarche *Women's Health Issues* **14,** 177-183

Marcia E. Herman-Giddens, Paul B. Kaplowitz, and Richard Wasserman. Navigating the recent articles on girls' puberty in *Pediatrics:* what do we know and where do we go from here? Online version: http://www. Pediatrics.org/cgi/content/full/113/4/911

Olga Karapanou and Anastasios Papdimitriou (2010) Determinants of menarche *Reproductive Biology an Endocrinology* 8, 115-123

M.E. McPherson and L. Korfine (2004) Menstruation across time: menarche, menstrual attitudes, experiences, and behaviors *Women's Health*

Issues **14(6):**193-200

Juan Roa and Manuel Tena-Sempere (2010) Energy balance and puberty onset: emerging role of central mTOR signaling *Trends in Endocrinology and Metabolism* 21, 518-528

Cheryl. L. Sisk and Douglas L. Foster (2004) The neural basis of puberty and adolescence. *Nature Neuroscience* **7(10),** 1040-1047

Puberty disorders

Lindsey A. Loomba-Albrecht and Dennis M. Styne (2012) The physiology of puberty and its disorders *Pediatric Annals* 41(4), 1-11

C. Traggiai and R. Stanhope (2003) Disorders of pubertal development. B*est Practice & Research Clinical Obstetrics & Gynecology.* **17,** 41-56

Chapter 5

(1) Title of video (1996) Elizabeth Sher, I.V. Studios, Berkeley

(2) William Shakespeare, *Hamlet,* Act 3, Scene 4)

(3) F. Borner (1887) *The menopause: Cyclopedia of Obstetrics and Gynecology Vol II,* William & Wood: New York

(4) C. Thompson (1971) *On women* New American Library: New York

(5) M. Anderson (1987) *The menopause* Faber & Faber: London

(6) W. Cooper (1987) *No change A biological revolution for women* Arrow Books: London

(7) R. A. Wilson and T. A. Wilson (1963) The fate of the nontreated postmenopausal woman. *Journal of the American Geriatrics Society* 11, 347-6

(8) R. Wilson and T. A. Wilson (1972) The basic philosophy of estrogen maintenance *Journal of the American Geriatrics Society* 20, 521-23

(9) Simone de Beauvoir (1953) *The Second Sex* Translator and editor, H. M. Parshley Alfred A. Knopf: New York

(10) Germaine Greer (1982) *The change: Women, aging and the menopause* Alfred A. Knopf: New York.

(11) Carol M. Mangione, Chair, NIH panel on menopause

(12) Sandra Tsing Loh (2011) The bitch is back. Are menopausal woman mad, bad, or dangerous? Yes, but they are just returning to normal *The Atlantic,* October

(13) Daryl P. Shanley and Thomas B.L. Kirkwood Evolution of the human menopause BioEssays 23(3), 282-287 (2001)

The peri-menopause

Peter T. Ellison (2001) *On Fertile Ground* Harvard University Press: Cambridge

C. Kalb. (1997, May 5). How old is too old? Newsweek, p. 64

March of Dimes (2002) Pregnancy after 35: Quick reference and fact sheet. White Plains, NY: March of Dimes (also accessible from www.modimes.org/professionals/681_1155.asp

M. Neumann (2003) Arc thcse women at high risk? AWHONN Lifelines 7(6), 423-430

R.J. Paulson, M.H. Thornton, M.M. Francis, & H. S. Salvador (1997) Successful pregnancy in a 63-yer-old woman *Fertility and Sterility* 67(5), 949-951

Kendall Powell (2004) Age is no barrier *Nature* **432**, 40-42

Johan Smitz and Rita Cortvrindt (2004) First childbirth from transplanted cryopreserved ovarian tissue brings hope for cancer survivors *The Lancet* **364,** 1379-1380

P. Viau, C. Padula & B. Eddy (2002) An exploration of health concerns and health promotion behaviors in pregnant women over age 35 *The American Journal of Maternal Child Nursing* 27(6), 328-334

The menopause

Daniel Delanoë et al (2012) Class, gender and culture in the experience of menopause A comparative survey in Tunisia and France *Social Science and Medicine* 75, 401-409

Filipa Pementa et al (2012) Menopause symptoms' predictors: the influence of life style, health – and menopause-related and sociodemographic characteristics *Journal of Women & Aging* 24(2), 140-151

Karen Roush (2012) Managing menopausal symptoms *American Journal of Nursing* 112(6), 28-35

Post-menopausal hormone therapy

Deborah Grady (2003) Postmenopausal hormones- therapy for symptoms only *New England Journal of Medicine* **348(19),** 1835-1837

John Studd (2010) Ten reasons to be happy about hormone replacement therapy: a guide for patients *Menopause International* 16(1) 44-46

Helen Roberts (2012) Hormone therapy for menopausal symptoms *British Medical Journal* 344, 1-2

The 2012 Hormone Therapy Position Statement of The North American Menopause Society *Menopause* 19(3), 257-271

Harvard Women's Health Watch (2011) Hormone therapy: the next chapter 18(7), 1-3

Evolution of menopause

Colin A. Finn (2001) Reproductive aging and menopause *International Journal of Developmental Biology* 45, 61-67

Kristen Hawkes (2004) The grandmother effect *Nature* **428,** 128-129

Lawrence M.A. Shaw and Sebastian L.J. Shaw (2009) Menopause, evolution and changing cultures *Menopause International* 15, 175-179

John Franklin Donaldson (1994) How did human menopause arise? *Menopause* 1(4), 211-221

Ricki Pillycove and James A. Simon (2011) The evolutionary origin and significance of menopause *Menopause* 18(3), 336-342

The Male

(14) Jonathan Swift *Miscellanies* (1711-1726)

(15) Martha Weinman Lear (1973) *Is there a male menopause?* New York Times, January 28

(16) David J. Handelsman and Peter Y. Liu Andropause: invention,

prevention, rejuvenation *Trends in Endocrinology and Metabolism* **16(2)**, 39-45 (2005)

Male reproductive health

Richard G. Bribiescas (2010) An evolutionary and life history perspective on human male reproductive senescence *Annals of the New York Academy of Sciences* 1204, 54-64

Harvard Men's Health Watch (February (2011) Testosterone replacement – A cautionary tale, 3-5

Ronald Swerdloff and Christina Wang (2011) Testosterone treatment of older men – why are controversies created *Journal Clinical Endocrinological Metabolism* 96(1), 62-65

Chapter 6

Fertilization, Implantation

(1) Brenda Clews. Brendaclews.blogspot.com/2005/10/one-hundred-millionsperm-day.html

(2) C.L.R. Barratt and J. Kirkman-Brown (2006) Man-made versus female-made environment – will the real capacitation stand up? *Human Reproduction Update* 12(1),1-2

(3) Charles E. Boklage (2006) Embryogenesis of chimeras, twins and anterior midline asymmetries Human Reproduction 21(3), 579-591

(4) S.S.C. Yen. (1994) The placenta as a third Brain *Journal of Reproductive Medicine* 39(4), 277-280

R. O'Rahilly and F. Müller (1996) *Human Embryology and Teratology.* 2nd edition Wiley-Liss, Inc., New York, NY

William V. Holet and Alireza Fazeli (2010) The oviduct as a complex mediator of mammalian sperm function and selection *Molecular Reproduction and Development* 77, 934-943

J. Michael Bedford (2008) Puzzles of mammalian fertilization - and beyond *International Journal of Developmental Biology* 52, 415-426

Jackson C. Kirkman-Brown and David J. Smith (2011) Sperm motility: is viscosity fundamental to progress *Molecular Human Reproduction* 17(8),

539-544

T. Fazleabas and J. J. Kim (2003) What makes an embryo stick? *Science* 299, 355-6

Chapter 7

Parturition

B. A. Gray (2006) A ticking uterus AHWONN Lifelines 10 (5), 382-389

Lactation

(1) Cited in K. Schwarz (1997) Missing the breast. In *The Body in Parts,* edit D. Hillman & C. Mazzio. Routledge: New York and London Taken from *The ciuile Conuersation of mr. Stephen Guazzo, written first in Italian, divided into foure bookes, the first three translated our of French* by G. Pettie (London: Thomas East, 1586), 13-143v.

(2) Cited in Diane Johnson (2012) Mother's Beware! *The New York Review of Books,* June 21, p.23-25

Anne Katz (2006) Breastfeeding How some things have stayed the same *AHONN Lifelines* 10(3), 203-204

Lisa Helen Amir (2006) Breastfeeding Managing 'supply' difficulties *Australian Family Physician* 359(8), 686-690

Collaborative Group on Hormonal Factors in Breast Cancer. Breast cancer and breast feeding: collaborative reanalysis of individual data from 47 epidemiological studies in 30 countries, including 50302 women with breast cancer and 96974 women without the disease (2002) *Lancet* 360, 187-195.

Jessica M. Faupe-Badger et al (2013) Postpartum remodeling, Lactation, and Breast Cancer Risk: Summary of National Cancer Institute-Sponsored Workshop *Journal of the National Cancer Institute* **105,** 166-174.

Chapter 8

(1) David Barker (2007) Cited in Stephen S. Hall *Small and Thin, The New Yorker,* November 19

(2) Keith M. Godfrey, Peter D. Gluckman and Mark A. Hanson (2010) Developmental origins of metabolic disease: life course and

intergenerational perspectives *Trends in Endocrinology and Metabolism* 21(4), 199-205

P. D. Gluckman and M. A. Hanson (2004) *Living with the past: evolution, development, and patterns of disease Science* 305, 1733 – 1736

P. D. Gluckman and M. A. Hanson (2006) *The consequences of being born small – an adaptive perspective. Hormone Research* 65 (suppl 3), 5 – 14

Keith M. Godfrey, Peter D. Gluckman and Mark A. Hanson (2010) Developmental origins of metabolic disease: life course and intergenerational perspectives *Trends in Endocrinology and Metabolism* 21(4), 199-205

C. Lau and J. M. Rogers (2004) Embryonic and fetal programming of physiological disorders of adulthood *Birth Defects Research* (Part C) 72, 300-312

Chapter 9

(1) Meg Campbell, New Zealand poet, 1937-2007

(2) J. Paget. 1882. Lancet **2,** 1017, cited in K. L. Moore and T. V. N. Persaud. 1993. *The Developing Human,* fifth edition, chapter 8. W. B. Saunders Co.: Philadelphia, PA

(3) J. Warkany (1971) *Congenital malformations. Notes and Comments.* Year Book Medical Publishers, Inc., p. 19

(4) Kári Stefansson, cited in Ewen Callaway, Fathers bequeath more mutations as they age, Nature 488, p439

(5) R. Forman, S. Gilmour-White, N. Forman. 1996. *Drug-induced infertility and sexual dysfunction.* Cambridge University Press, p. 106

(6) Casper, M. (1998) *The making of the unborn patient.* New Brunswick: Rutgers University Press

(7) Clare Williams et al (2005) *Women as moral pioneers? Experiences of first trimester antenatal screening Social Science & Medicine* 61, 1983–1992

Fetal Loss and Birth Defects

R. O'Rahilly and F. Müller (1996) *Human Embryology and Teratology*. 2nd edition. Wiley-Liss, Inc., New York, NY.

K. L. Moore and T.V. N. Persaud (1993) *The Developing Human* W. B. Saunders Company, Philadelphia, PA

Teresa Chiang et al (2012) Meiotic origins of maternal age-related aneuploidy *Biology of reproduction* 86(1):3, 1-7

E. Fragouli et al (2011) Chromosome abnormalities in human acolytes *Cytogenetics and Genomic Research* 133, 107-118

E. B. Hook, P.K. Cross, and D. M. Schreiemachers. (1983) Chromosome abnormality rates at amniocentesis and in live-born infants *Journal of the American Medical Association* **249,** 2034-2040

S. M. Conner and M. A. Ferguson-Smith (1987) *Essential Medical Genetics,* 2nd edition, Blackwell Scientific Publications: Oxford, UK

E. C. Gadow, L. Otaño, and S. E. Lippold (1996) Congenital malformations *Current Opinion in Obstetrics and Gynecology* **8(6),** 412-416

W. A. Woodal and B. N. Ames (1997) Nutritional prevention of DNA damage to sperm and consequent risk reduction in birth defects and cancer in offspring In *Preventive Nutrition: The Comprehensive Guide for Health Professionals,* A. Bendich and R. J. Deckelbaum, Eds. Humana Press: Totowa, NJ

James F. Crow (2003) There's something curious about paternal-age effects *Science* 301, 606-608

Abhi Bhandari et al (2011) Risks to offspring associated with advanced paternal age Journal of *Andrology* 32(2), 121-122

James F. Crow (2006) Age and sex effects on human mutations rates: an old problem with new complexities *Journal of Radiation Research* 47(Suppl B), 75-82

Environmental Teratogens

J. B. Bishop, K. L. Witt, R. A. Sloane (1997) Genetic toxicities of human teratogens *Mutation Research* **396,** 9-43

R. J. Golden et al (1998) Environmental endocrine modulators and human health: an assessment of the biological evidence. *Critical Reviews in Toxicology* **28(2),** 109-227

C. Ikonomidou *et al* (2000) Ethanol-induced apoptotic neurodegeneration and fetal alcohol syndrome. *Science* **287,** 1056 -1060

R. Loebstein and G. Koren (1997) Pregnancy outcome and neurodevelopment of children exposed in utero to psychoactive drugs: the Mother risk experience. *Journal of Psychiatry and Neuroscience* **22(3),** 192-196

T. D. MacKenzie, C. E. Bartecchi, and R. W. Schrier (1994) The human costs of tobacco use *New England Journal of Medicine* **330,** 975-980

A. J. Nahmias and A. P. Kourtis (1997) The great balancing acts. The pregnant woman, placenta, fetus, and infectious agents *Clinics in Perinatology* **24(2),** 497-521

T. H. Shepard (1995) *Catalog of Teratogenic Agents* John Hopkins University Press: Baltimore, MD

Alison K. Shea and Meir Steiner (2008) Cigarette smoking during pregnancy *Nicotine and Tobacco research* 10(2), 267-278

Faye Calhoun and Kenneth Warren (2007) Fetal alcohol syndrome: historical perspective *Neuroscience and Biobehavioral Reviews* 31, 168-171

Prenatal Screening and Diagnosis

Jacky Nizard (2010) Amniocentiesis: technique and education Current Opinion in Obstetris and Gynecolgoy 22, 152-154

Mary E. Norton (2008) Genetic screening and counseling *Current Opinion in Obstetrics and Gynecology* 20:157–163

R. Rapp (1999). *Testing women, testing the fetus.* Routledge: London

L. Wilton *et al* (2009) The causes and misdiagnosis and adverse outcomes in PGD *Human Reproduction* 14(5), 1221-1228

Joyce C. Harper and Sioban B. Sengupta (2011) Preimplantation genetic diagnosis: state of the art 2011 *Human Genetics* 131, 175-186

Chapter 10

(1) Sheldon J. Segal (2003) *Under the Banyan Tree* Oxford University Press: Oxford, p. 208

(2) Angus McLaren (1979) Contraception and its discontents: Sigmund Freud and Birth Control. *Journal of Social History* **12,** 513-529 (summer)

(3) Sarah Blaffer Hrdy (1999) *Mother Nature: Maternal Instincts and How They Shape the Human Species*

(4) Cited in Carl Djerassi (2001) *This Man's Pill. Reflections on the 50th Birthday of the Pill* Oxford University Press: Oxford, p, 18

(5) Alexander Sanger (2004) *Beyond Choice Reproductive freedom in the 21st century* Public Affairs: New York

Contraception

Bernard Asbell (1995) The Pill: *A Biography of the Drug that Changed the World* Random House: New York

Carl Djerassi (2005) No political will to seek innovative contraception *Nature* **433,** 683-685.

Angus McLaren (1980) *A History of Contraception: From Antiquity to the Present Day* Basil Blackwell: London

J. Trussel (2004) in R.A. Hatcher et al Contraceptive Technology, 18th ed. Ardent Media: New York

Lara V. Marks (2001) *Sexual Chemistry A History of the Contraceptive* Pill (Yale University Press: New Haven

Diana Mansour et al (2010) Efficacy of contraceptive methods: a review of the literature *The European Journal of Contraception and Reproductive Health* 15, 4-16

Sabitha Jayaraman and Melanie Mann (2012) Male and female sterilization *Obstetrics, Gynecology and Reproductive Medicine* 22(4), 85-92

E. Nieschlag (2010) Male hormonal contraception *In Fertility Control* (U.-F. Habenicht and R. J. Aitken, eds), Handbook of Experimental Pharmacology 198, Springer-Verlag: Berlin.

N. Hani et al (2011) Male hormonal contraception: potential risks and benefits *Reviews of Endocrinological and Metabolic Disorders,* published online May 2011

Abortion

A.M. Autry et al (2002) A comparison of medical abortion and dilation and evacuation for second-trimester abortion *American Journal of Obstetrics & Gynecology* **187(2)**, 393-397

R. de Heus et al (2004) Medical management for termination of second and third trimester pregnancies: a comparison of strategies *European Journal of Obstetrics & Gynecology and Reproductive Biology* **116,** 16-21

R. Dworkin (1993) Life's *Dominion An Argument about Abortion, Euthanasia, and Individual Freedom* Alfred A. Knopf: New York

M. F. Greene and J. L Ecker (2004) Abortion, Health, and the Law *New England Journal of Medicine* **350(2),** 184 –186

E. Kandel and J. Merrick (2003) Late Termination of Pregnancy Professional Dilemmas *The Scientific World Journal* **3,** 903-912

Daniel C. Maguire (2001) *Sacred Choice: The Right to Contraception and Abortion in Ten World Religions* Fortress Press: Minneapolis

Norma McCorvey with Andy Meister (1994) *I am Roe: My Life, Roe v. Wade, and Freedom of Choice.* HarperCollins: New York

A.Rahman, L. Katzive, and S. K. Henshaw (1998) A global review of laws on induced abortion, 1985-1997 *International Family Planning Perspective* 24(2), 56-64

Gilda Sedgh et al (2012) Induced abortion: incidence and trends worldwide from 1995-2008 *Lancet* 379, 625-632

Iqbal Shah and Elisabeth Ahman (2010) Unsafe abortion in 2008: global and regional levels and trends *Reproductive Health Matters* 18(36), 90-101

Chapter 11

(1) W. Shakespeare, *King John, III, iv, 93*

(2) Stephanie A. Beall and Alan DeCherney (2012) History and challenges surrounding ovarian stimulation in the treatment of infertility *Fertility and Sterility* 97(4), 795-801.

(3) Claire Rayner (1977). The meaning of sex: a view from the agony column *Journal of Medical Ethics* 3, 157-159.

(4) Belle Boggs (May, 2012) The art of waiting *Harpers Magazine,* p15

(5) Carrie Friese, Gay Becker, and Robert D. Nachtigall (2006) Rethinking the biological clock: eleventh-hour moms, miracle moms, and meanings of age-related infertility *Social Sciences and Medicine* 63, 1550-1560.

(6) Aser Garcia Rada (2012) Spanish women becomes pregnant through ovarian tissue transplantation *British Medical Journal* 344: d835

(7) Bethanne Power and Gwendolyn P. Wuinn (2012) Fertility prevention in cancer patients: ethical considerations *Advances in Experimental Medicine and Biology* 732, 187-197

(8) Kendall Powell (2012) Egg-making stem cells found in adult ovaries *Nature* 483, 16-16

(9) Leanne M. Redman and Anne B. Loucks (2006) Menstrual disorder in athletes *Sports Medicine* 36(9), 747-755

Female and Male Infertiltiy

Herman Tournaye (2012) Male factor infertility and ART *Asian Journal of Andrology* 14, 103-108

John W. MacDonald et al (2011) Age and fertility: can women wait until early 30s to try for first baby *Journal of Biosocial Science* 43, 683-700

Juan Balasch and Eduard Gratacos (2012) Delayed child bearing: effects on fertility and the outcome of pregnancy *Current Opinion in Obstetrics and Gynecology* 24, 187-193.

Sandros C. Esteves *et al* (2012) what every gynecologist should know about male infertility: an update *Archives Gynecological Obstetrics,* published online 6 March 2012.

Ozgur Oktem and Kutluk Oktay (2009) Current knowledge in the renewal capability of germ cells in the adult ovary *Birth Defects Research* (Part C) 87, 90-95

Infertility and lifestyle

Anne B. Loucks, B. Kiens and H.H. Wright (2011) Energy availability in athletes *Journal of Sports Science, suppl* 1, S7 – S15

ARTs

Stephanie A. Beall and Alan DeCherney (2012) History and challenges surrounding ovarian stimulation in the treatment of infertility *Fertility and Sterility* 97(4), 795-801.

Shilpi Pandey *et al* (2012) Perinatal outcomes in singleton pregnancies resulting from IVF/ICSI: a systematic review and meta-analysis *Human Reproduction Update* Advance Access published May 19, 2012

Michael J. Davies et al (2012 Reproductive technologies and the risk of birth defects *New England Journal of Medicine* 366, 1803-13

Andre van Steirteghem (2012) Celebrating ICSI's twentieth anniversary and the birth of more than 2.5 million children – the 'how, why, when, and where' *Human Reproduction* 27(1), 1-2.

APPENDIX 1

Appendix 1	*Genes, Sex Chromosomes, and Mutations*
Life as a Genetic Lottery	
What do genes do?	
How many human genes?	
Chromosomes	
Sex chromosomes – the odd couple	
The **X** – robust, healthy, smart, but complicated	
The **Y** – a genetic wreck?	
Why are the **X** and **Y** so different?	
Does the Y have a future?	
Mutations – "the suffering gene"	
Experiments of nature	
What causes mutations?	
We have met the enemy and he is us	
The mutation load	

What do genes do?

They are in you and in me; they created us, body and mind; and their preservation is the ultimate rationale for our existence. They have come a long way, those replicators. Now they go by the name of genes, and we are their survival machines. (1)

Genes are in fashion, not only as objects of serious study in many areas of biology and medicine, but also in the attention they receive in the popular media. Relating genes to human disease is a growth industry, and scientific journals are full of articles describing new correlations between genes and the physical and mental afflictions that take their toll on us, and many of these articles make their way into the popular media, often with a big splash of publicity. Reading many of these stories may give us a sense that we really understand genes. We all probably have an intuitive understanding of genes.

Genes, we understand, in some way or other determine traits, conditions, or even disorders that are passed down from one generation to another. This intuition, although largely correct, is incomplete, and doesn't really help us understand what genes do. A useful way to think about genes is as *units of stored information and as units of function*. When we think about it, all living organisms exist in a dual form – in the here and now, as an active living and breathing creature, and also as a carrier of information potentially able to make copies of itself that will live on after it dies. A dog, for example, is a dog because it was constructed from the blueprint for making a dog, and it can transmit that blueprint to its progeny so that they can transmit it to their progeny, and so on. As units of stored information genes form the basis for the blueprint, in that they embody the set of instructions for making a dog, a cat, or a human being.

As a unit of stored information a gene is defined by a sequence of molecules known as *nucleotides* that come in four forms abbreviated as A, T, C, and G. The nucleotides are chemically bonded to each other in sequence forming another molecule known as DNA. The information the gene carries is in the sequence of these four nucleotides much as the 0s and 1s in computer code defines the information the code carries. The average gene is about 1000 nucleotides long, but some are much shorter and others much longer.

A gene is a unit of function because its nucleotide sequence encodes a protein. Proteins the molecules in a cell that carry out all the functions that are required to keep the cells, tissues, and organs of the individual alive and give shape to our body. In our body, for example, the cells of the heart carry out the heart function; kidney cells are responsible for kidney function, etc. The workhorses in each cell type are proteins. Consider one protein that almost everyone has heard about, *insulin*. Insulin functions to help cells in our body to metabolize sugars in order to get the energy we need to stay alive. The insulin gene specifies the protein insulin. Consider another example, the protein, *hemoglobin*, found in red blood cells, and critically important because it carries oxygen to all of the tissues in our body. The general rule then is that one or more genes carry the instructions to make a given protein.

Living organisms, from those that we think of as primitive to those that are at the top of the evolutionary ladder, are amazingly complex. How many genes are required to specify each? The bacterium *Escherichia coli* a bug that normally lives in our colon is specified by 5000 genes. *E. coli* cells are not visible to the naked eye, and it would take over 5000 *E. coli* cells end-to-end to equal an inch. An *E. coli* cell has a fairly simple structure compared to any human cell. Humans, by any measure, are clearly more complex than the simple bacterium. Accordingly, we assumed that hundreds of thousands of genes, maybe even millions of genes, would be required to specify a human being. Unexpectedly, a few years ago we learned that probably no more than 25,000 genes are needed to specify a human being. It is difficult to imagine how only 25,000 genes generate a creature with all the complexity of a human being. Even more surprisingly, relatively crude estimates of the number of proteins indicated a figure much greater than 25,000. For example, estimates of the number of proteins produced in the brain ran at about 70,000. Since genes specify proteins, how could there be more proteins than genes?

It turns out that genes are pretty smart, and they have figured a way out of this dilemma. Think of a gene as a strip of magnetic tape carrying a piece of music. Now imagine that you cut up the tape into several segments and then splice the pieces in different orders. Each new splice is a variant of the original, that is, the splices represent a set of variations of the original piece of music. You can see that in principle dozens of variations can be generated quite simply. Genes do something like this – they generate splice variants by combining different pieces of the gene in different ways. Each splice variant produces a different protein. It is easy to see that the original 25,000 genes could easily generate 250,000 or more proteins. Clearly, then 25,000 genes have the capability of generating the complexity of a human being.

Simply counting genes, however, doesn't tell us why humans are different from even our nearest primate cousins. We share something like 99% of the DNA with the chimpanzee, but we are radically different from them. What accounts for that difference? Is there a set of genes that set us apart from all other primates? Somewhere along the way from our primate cousins to us, genetic changes took place. Does this mean that new genes appeared? Or, possibly new combinations of already existing genes that resulted in new functions? If there is anything like the quest for the Holy Grail in human genetics it is this. In the words of a pre-eminent human geneticist, Svante Paabo, *"What one dreams about is defining the genetic changes that we all share today, but that made modern humans so special." (2).*

Chromosomes

Genes do not exist as isolated entities but are joined together in structures known as chromosomes. One way to think about genes and chromosomes is as beads on a string – the beads are the genes, and the beads and string is the chromosome. The 25,000 or so genes that specify the human being are distributed among 22 chromosomes known as *autosomes*, and two *sex chromosomes*. The autosomes are the same in both females and males, and are numbered from 1 to 22, with number 1 being the longest. In almost every cell of the body the autosomes exist as members of a pair, that is, there are two chromosomes number 1, two number 2, and so on. Each autosome carries a different set of genes, and the number of genes per autosome differs from one chromosome to another. For example, chromosome 1 carries about 2900 genes, while chromosome 22 carries about 300 genes.

The human sex chromosomes, denoted as *X* and *Y*, were discovered in 1959, and we recognized that females have two *X* chromosomes, while males have one *X* and one *Y* chromosome. The X and Y were called sex chromosomes because they seemed to be involved in determining sex. This *XX/XY* sex chromosome system is not unique to humans, but is found in all mammals as well.

We now know that the *Y* is the principal determinant of sex – the presence of the *Y* leads to a male, while the absence of the *Y* leads to a female. In fact, only one gene on the *Y* is required to make a male. This gene, called **SRY**, discovered in 1990, is referred to as the *testis-determining gene* because as we will see in the following chapter, **SRY** acts as the trigger that stimulates the formation of the testis and the sexual anatomy of the male.

Every somatic cell (cells of body tissues, such as the heart, liver, bone, muscle, stomach) has a total of 46 chromosomes, 22 pairs of the autosomes, plus a pair of *X* chromosomes if we are female, or an *X* and *Y* if we are male. Each gene on the autosomes is present in two copies. Genes on the *X* are present in two copies in females, but only one copy in males. Genes on the *Y* are present only in the male.

Eggs and sperm are the exception to the rule of 46 chromosomes. These two cell types have 23 chromosomes – eggs have 22 autosomes, one copy of chromosome 1, one of chromosome 2, and so on, and one *X*. Sperm come in two types, those that have 22 autosomes and a *Y*, and those that have 22 autosomes and an *X*. An *X*-bearing sperm fertilizing an egg gives rise to a female, while a *Y*-bearing sperm fertilizing an egg gives rise to a male. These two types of sperm are produced in equal numbers, and appear to have equal fertilizing ability, thus resulting on the average in a 1:1 ratio of female to male conceptions.

We all start out from the fusion of an egg with a sperm – 23 + 23 = 46 chromosomes. The egg contributes one member of each autosomal pair, and the sperm contributes the other member. The fertilized egg initiates the cell divisions that will eventually give rise to all our tissues. These divisions conserve the chromosome number, ensuring that each somatic cell has 46 chromosomes. Another special type of division takes place only in the ovaries and testes, reduces the chromosome number from 46 to 23, but it does so in a way that the egg or sperm receive one copy of each chromosome. Hence, we can think of a chromosome cycle – 23 to 46 to 23 – and on and on. The crucial importance of cell divisions that produce the egg or the sperm will be made much clearer in Chapters 10 and 11 when we consider the terrible consequences of errors in these divisions.

The sex chromosomes – the odd couple

Alas, genetically speaking, if you've met one man, you've met them all. We are I hate to say it, predictable. You can't say that about women. Men and women are farther apart than we ever knew. It's not Mars or Venus. It's Mars or Venus, Pluto, Jupiter and who knows what other planets. (3)

The *X* and *Y*-chromosomes form an odd couple - they stand out because they are so different from each other. The *X* is one of the larger chromosomes in the human set, while the *Y* is the smallest. In addition, the *Y* chromosome is the only one that does not have a partner. The *X* chromosome has a partner in females, but the *Y* is always alone. At first sight we may accept this situation as "just the way things are". But in life there is always a reason for the way things are. And for the *X* and *Y*, the way they are turns out to be a really interesting story. We don't know how the story will end, but some excellent genetic detective work has given us a picture of their evolutionary past. Before we get into that let's look more closely at the differences between the *X* and the *Y*.

The X – robust, healthy, smart, but complicated

Current estimates suggest that the *X* carries about 1200 genes, which is about 4% of the total number of human genes. The *X*-linked gene catalog, that is, the genes that have been identified on the *X* to date, lists around 400. All of these genes are very important genes, that is, they control many critical cellular, tissue, and organ functions. We know that this is the case because mutations in them lead to serious disorders. A mutation is a change in the nucleotide sequence defining a gene. More often than not, this change results in a non-functional or poorly functioning protein. (I will discuss mutations in more detail below) The function of the remaining majority of *X*-linked genes is still unknown.

The spectrum of known genes on the *X* is also unusual. For example, the *X* is enriched for genes associated with brain function/cognitive abilities, skeletal muscle function, and reproduction. Consider the following: intellectual disability (ID) disorders in humans currently are associated with mutations in about 500 genes, 400 of which are distributed among the 22 autosomes, while 100 genes are carried by the *X* itself. Hence, while the *X* carries about 4% of the total number of genes, it carries about 20 % of the known mental disability/mental retardation genes, much more than you would expect by chance distribution of this set of genes throughout the chromosomes.

These new observations help to explain an observation made in the 1890 U. S. census - that more boys than girls were mentally disabled, a statistic that still holds true. Why should this be so? In females, a defective brain gene on one *X* chromosome can be 'covered' by the normal gene on the other *X*. In males, however, a defective brain gene on the *X* cannot be covered and will manifest its effects immediately.

The *X* also carries a disproportionate share of genes involved in skeletal muscle function, over twice as many compared to the autosomes. Genes involved in reproduction, such as ovarian and interestingly also testicular function, are also over represented on the *X* compared to the autosomes. Finally, the *X* carries genes associated with the development of tumors or cancers.

We don't yet understand fully why the *X* carries this unusual array of genes. Is it just chance, another one of many imponderable mysteries?

Maybe not. One intriguing hypothesis proposes that a process known as *sexual selection* can account for the preponderance of brain function genes on the *X*. The idea goes as follows. Very early in our history (tens of thousands of years ago), females developed a preference for intelligent mates, because having a smart mate aided survival. Having brain genes on the *X* would mean that new variants of genes that increased cognitive abilities would be immediately apparent in males, and females would also be able to choose the smartest mates. *"If higher cognitive abilities were a critical step in our own evolution, it makes sense that you might find those functions on the X chromosome" (4),* commented H. Willard, a leading expert on the *X* and *Y* chromosome. This selection process accelerates the increase in cognitive function, much as a snowball gets bigger as it rolls down the mountain, and over relatively few human generations the *X* accumulated a disproportionate share of brain function genes. Of course, both males and females contribute because it takes smart females to recognize smart males.

This process has a significant down side, however. Variants of genes that result in mental disability would also appear, and of course, they would be seen predominantly in males. Hence, one of the interesting predictions of the sexual selection hypothesis is that males would be over-represented in the extreme ends of the brain function spectrum – from high intelligence to mental disability. This is clearly the case for mental disability (which is what the statistical tables tell us), and it may true also for the very high range of intelligence.

Another intriguing mystery of the X

The *X* chromosome also has a complicated life. In every cell in the female one of the two *X* chromosomes undergoes a process known as *X* chromosome inactivation. In its original version, proposed in 1960, this was a mechanism that inactivates one of the *X* chromosomes completely in each cell of a female. The rationale for the inactivation – meaning silencing the genes on the inactive *X* - was that it was a way of equalizing the dosage of *X* genes in females and males. In a functional sense then, in each cell of a female and male there is only one set of *X* genes working.

The silencing of one of the *X* chromosomes in a female embryo occurs very early in gestation, perhaps 5 -7 days after fertilization. The inactivation process is random in the sense that when it occurs in about half of the cells of the embryo, the paternally-derived *X* is inactivated, and in the remaining half, the maternally-derived *X* is inactivated. Although originally it was thought that all of the genes on the inactive *X* were silenced, we have learned that around 15% of the genes on the *X* (200 to 300) are not silenced. Even more intriguing is that the spectrum of genes that escape silencing varies from one woman to another. From the author of this recent study: *"We now know that women have the full 46 chromosomes that they're getting work from and the 46th is a second X that is working at levels greater than we knew." (5)* We still do not understand the full significance of this intriguing finding.

The Y – a genetic wasteland

The *Y* chromosome appears to be the *X* chromosome's poor cousin. In the words of a prominent human geneticist – *"the Y married up, and the X married down". (5)* The *Y* is much shorter than the *X*, and also the shortest of all human chromosomes. The disparity in size between the *X* and the *Y*, as well as the paltry gene content of the *Y* has been of abiding interest to several generations of human geneticists. One of them puts it in very melodramatic terms:

Few research subjects in human genetics are as intriguing and polarizing as the Y chromosome. Like any good novel, the history of the Y is riddled with suspense, drama and the occasional resurrection. Indeed, the genetic vitality and evolutionary fate of this chromosome have long been a source of intense debate in the literature. (6)

Compared to the *X*, the *Y* has very few genes, perhaps no more than 50 according to current estimates. Given its length it could in principle harbor some 500 genes. In fact, the *Y* carried around 1000 genes in the past, but most of them have been discarded, and the remaining ones appear to be non-functional. Because of its paltry genetic content, the *Y* has been referred to, somewhat facetiously perhaps, as a "genetic wasteland".

The *Y*, with two exceptions, does not appear to carry any other genes of significant importance. First, the *Y* carries the gene **SRY**, which is required to develop an embryo into a male (we will examine this in more detail in Topic 4), and second, several genes required for sperm formation, that is, for male fertility. One human geneticist has commented humorously: *"We poor men only have 45 chromosomes to do our work with because our 46th is the pathetic Y that has only a few genes which operate below the* *waist and above the knees." (4)* Hence, in comparison to the X, the Y appears as a faltering, dilapidated chromosome.

Why are the X and Y so different?

According to evolutionary geneticists, the chromosomes that were the precursors to the current X and Y were members of a pair, that is, they carried the same complement of genes. The destiny of the Y chromosome was probably sealed at its birth, some 300 million years ago. This is about the time when our mammalian ancestor first separated from an as yet unknown reptilian species. Reptiles do not have sex chromosomes, yet they have no problem in producing males or females. The genes required to form a female or male are carried by every individual. Some type of switch is needed to form one sex over the other. In most reptiles today the switch is temperature – at a low ambient temperature males may form, while at higher temperatures a female will form.

Mammals differ in that they have an *XX/XY* sex determining system. The most primitive mammals are the monotremes, consisting of two species – the platypus and echidnae - egg-laying mammals found today only in Australia. Then, about 170 million years ago, the marsupials, such as the kangaroos, wallabies, and opossums separated from the monotreme line, and finally, about 80 – 100 million years ago, the placental mammals to which we belong separated from the marsupial line.

By comparing the genes on the X and Y-chromosomes from monotremes, marsupials, and placental mammals, we have come to understand that the X and Y evolved from a pair of autosomes present in our reptilian ancestor. The critical event was a mutation in a gene that converted it to a male-determining gene irrespective of temperature. The autosome that acquired the male-determining gene (we don't know which gene it was originally, but in marsupials and placental mammals this gene is *SRY*), started on its path to become the Y that we know today. The acquisition of the male-determining gene initiated the isolation of the proto-Y from it partner, now the proto-X, and according to human geneticists, this event is responsible for a process that has led to the continual loss and degradation of genes from the original Y. The estimate is that the Y has lost about 1000 genes in 300 million years. If the rate of loss of Y genes remains as in the past, the Y is predicted to become extinct in 5 – 10 million years. The Y chromosome may be well on its way to disappearing. To paraphrase Andy

Warhol, the *Y* has had its 15 minutes of fame, and is now ready to leave the scene.

Does the Y have a future?

Five to ten million years is a long time. Obviously, we don't have to lose any sleep over this. We don't even know if the human species is going to exist five million years from now. Still, the question of whether the human Y will be lost is of great interest to human geneticists. Not everyone agrees that the demise of the *Y* is in the cards. In fact, a scientific debate to consider the question of the *Y*'s future was held at the 18th International Chromosome Conference in August 31, 2011.

The arguments for the *Y*'s demise, presented by Jennifer Marshal Graves, include the following: the *Y*'s long history of gene loss, practically nothing is left of the original *Y*, and the few added parts are degrading rapidly, and perhaps more significantly, that the counterpart of the human *SRY* gene, the *sry* gene in certain rodent-like burrowing animals known as mole voles found in Eastern Europe has been lost, and that the *Y* has disappeared in at least two species of Japanese spiny rats.

The counter argument was presented by Jennifer Hughes, and runs something like this: the *Y* has not yet disappeared even after many millions of years, the *Y* chromosome has managed to retain many important genes over the long course of primate evolution, the human *Y* has not lost any genes since the human – chimpanzee split that took place 6 million years ago, and that the *Y* has added 8 different genes since that split. From the discussion it seems clear that most of the genes that remain on the *Y* are necessary for determining maleness and sperm formation and probably other as yet unknown functions. They are not likely to disappear.

The possibility that the *Y* may be lost elicited an interesting discussion. One important lesson from the mole voles and country rats is that sex determination is a dynamic, rather than a static process. Nothing is forever. There is nothing sacrosanct about the *SRY* gene. Clearly some other gene has taken over the role of *SRY* in mole voles and country rats, but the identity of that new male-determining gene is not yet known. In fact, *SRY* was not the original male determining gene – monotremes do not have *SRY*. *SRY* first appeared in marsupials, so that it has been around only a relatively short time.

The other lesson is that if the *Y* can be lost in these species, it can in principle be lost in any species. In a population as large as the human such a possibility cannot be discounted. What will happen if the *Y* is lost in humans? We don't really know of course, but we can speculate. One possibility is that other genes, either from the *X* or from the autosomes, can be recruited to take over the *SRY* function. But there may be a price to pay if that occurs. As in the mole voles, the *Y* would not be lost in all humans, but only in some. Individuals from these two groups would no longer be able to mate successfully because they would have two different sex determining systems. The human species would begin to separate into two non-interbreeding species, and over time would probably become quite different from each other. Something like this may already be taking place in the mole voles.

Is this science fiction? Life and living organism are full of surprises, and reality always trumps our limited knowledge. We are not the authors of the drama in which we think we are the protagonists.

Who won? What was the consensus of the delegates at the conference? A vote was taken on the question – is the *Y* disappearing or not? The following is how the commentator reports the result:

The esteemed scientific community present was split precisely and evenly, and the contest declared an honourable draw. Interestingly however, in an audience comprising a 50:50 sex ratio, two further votes were taken. The same question, but first for males only, then second for females only. A 2:1 ratio rejecting the notion the Y is disappearing in the first vote and a 2:1 ratio accepting the hypothesis in the second, is perhaps a reminder of the need for objectivity when making our scientific evaluations. (7)

Mutations – "the suffering gene" (8)

Experiments of nature – the bad and the good

Mutations were popular in the comic books from 1940s and 1950s. The typical story line was that someone exposed to radiation was transformed into a "mutant" with extraordinary powers, often to be used for evil purposes. Radiation was in the public consciousness then, probably because of atomic and hydrogen bomb tests being carried out by the U. S. and Soviet Union. Radiation was feared because of its mysterious power to create mutations. Since we didn't really know what mutations were, they remained mysterious, sinister, and malevolent. There was one exception, however, and that was Spider Man, who obtained his near miraculous powers by being stung by a radioactive spider. Spider Man was an example a good mutant.

Despite the fanciful nature of many of the comic book stories, they did get one thing right – that was the notion that the mutation became an integral part of the person, and in some fundamental way changed the person's nature. Today, we know that mutations become part of the genetic makeup of a person, and quite often produce a significant change in the person, in most cases for the worse. Let's look closely at what we mean by that.

Mutations produce what biologists sometimes call "experiments of nature". Let's consider just two examples. First, the *hemophilias*, disorders characterized by failure of the blood to clot. A consequence of this failure is that even small cuts or abrasions can lead to uncontrolled, perhaps even life-threatening bleeding. Hematologists (specialists in the blood disorders) tell us that around ten proteins, each a product of a distinct gene, are involved in the clotting reaction. Inability of any one of the proteins to function properly leads to a clotting failure.

A second example is *cystic fibrosis*, a disease characterized by the accumulation of thick mucus in the lungs. The consequences can be deadly if the mucus interferes significantly with lung action, leading essentially to the patient choking to death. Cystic fibrosis arises from the failure of a protein, referred to as a *chloride transporter*, whose normal function is to permit water and other small molecules to pass in and out of cells. Failure of transporter function is what leads to the mucus accumulation inside cells.

The defective clotting proteins that result in hemophilia and the defective transporter protein that produces cystic fibrosis are the products of "defective" or mutant genes, that is, genes that are different than the normal ones. A *mutation* in a gene is a change in the nucleotide sequence that defines that gene. This often results in a defective protein, which in turn leads to a "genetic disorder", such as hemophilia and cystic fibrosis.

Currently, the human genetic catalog has over 10,000 entries, that is, these are genes that have been identified because a genetic change in the gene has in one way or another manifested itself. A very large fraction of these 10,000 entries represents a genetic disorder. For example, over 200 genetic disorders are known to be due to mutations in genes on the X chromosome. Two of the ten or so hemophilias are due to mutations in genes on the *X* chromosome.

We need to keep in mind that the way we refer to these genes, the hemophilia genes, or the cystic fibrosis gene, can be misleading because it implies that the normal function of these genes is to produce a disease. That is not the case, of course, but it has become a short hand way of referring to the gene.

Many of the 10,000 gene mutations that we know about have harmful effects. Other mutations may have a relatively minor effect, and they won't be listed in our genetic disorder catalog precisely because they don't leave a clear trail that we can recognize. We can think of these as having a low profile - producing effects that we don't recognize immediately or easily. Some of these may lead, for example, to less resistance to disease, decrease in longevity, predisposition to long-term debilitating disorders, or a variety of conditions that compromise our health or well being in minor ways. In fact, it would not be surprising if many of the low grade physical and mental afflictions that we suffer from are due to the cumulative effect of such low-profile mutations. We know relatively little about these types of genes.

Then there are other changes in genes that geneticists call "polymorphisms" (meaning many forms) rather than mutations. This term is useful because we generally use the term mutation as a deviation from the normal, that is, abnormal. However, there are many traits for which we don't know what the normal is because a normal doesn't really exist. Consider, for example, red hair. Red hair, relatively rare in most populations around the world, occurs with a much higher frequency among northern Europeans, especially the Irish and Scottish. We have learned recently, for example, that red hair arises from three different genetic changes in the melanocortin receptor 1 gene, which encodes a protein in the melanocytes, the cells in our skin that produce the pigments that determine the color and hue of our skin. We certainly don't consider red hair abnormal, in the sense that hemophilia is abnormal. In the same way, then, polymorphic genes, genes that can have many variants, are responsible for the diversity in height, hair color, head and facial structure, body proportions, beauty, skin color, dexterity, athletic ability, musical talent, etc. In fact, most of the variability that we see in the humans around us may be due to the widespread distribution of these polymorphic genetic variants

Finally, you might ask: *are there any good mutations?* Well, we don't expect too many of these. The reason is fairly simple. Think of the gene as a finely tuned engine. Almost any change that you could make to the engine would be expected to reduce engine performance. Nevertheless, infrequently a mutation may turn out to have a beneficial effect, because the mutation appears in a different environmental context.

Let's consider, for example, genes that determine skin color. Human beings evolved in the savannah of East Africa, a region of intense sunlight. Dark skin was essential for survival because it protected against the harmful effects of ultraviolet radiation from the sun. Mutations that resulted in a light skin would be harmful under those conditions. Albinos, persons who lack the pigments in the skin (due to mutations in genes that produce the skin pigments), are at great risk for developing deadly skin cancers in regions of intense sunlight, and even now have a poor survival rate.

However, when some of our ancestors began to spread from Africa into Europe and Asia, regions of much less intense sunlight, light skin no longer was a disadvantage. In fact, it had an advantage over dark skin. This is because ultraviolet radiation also stimulates the synthesis of vitamin D. Before the days of synthetic vitamin D, exposure to sunlight provided our main source of vitamin D. Light skin facilitates vitamin D synthesis. Vitamin D synthesis is greatly reduced in dark skin because it absorbs most of the ultraviolet radiation, especially in regions where sunlight is not very intense. Hence, in the higher latitudes dark skin became a disadvantage. Mutations that resulted in light skin had a beneficial effect in the regions of less intense sunlight.

Another recent interesting example is the **CCR5** gene that encodes a protein found on the surface of cells of the immune system. Mutations in the **CCR5** genes that result in resistance to infection by the HIV virus and so to AIDS were found originally in western Europeans. HIV infects cells of the immune system by first binding to the CCR5 protein. The **CCR5** variants produce an abnormal protein to which the virus can no longer bind, and this failure prevents infection by the virus. Human geneticists have found that CCR5 mutation in Europeans appeared around the time of the bubonic plaque epidemic in the 14th century that wiped out a large percentage of the population. The plague is caused by the bacterium *Yersenia pestis*, which gains entry by also binding to the CCR5 protein. Hence, geneticists, suspect that people who carried the mutation survived the plague. New variants of **CCR5** have been discovered in African populations, and their frequency in population that is being decimated by AIDS has been increasing because of the resistance they confer.

These examples illustrate an important point: the effect of mutations, positive or negative, often depends on the environmental context.

What causes mutations?

Most mutations arise spontaneously and randomly, that is, we don't do anything deliberately to produce them. These "accidents", for that is what they are, nevertheless have an implacable reality. Although chance events, they don't arise without cause. They are the consequences of agents and processes that in general we understand fairly well now. For our purposes it is useful to divide agents that produce mutations, known as *mutagens*, into two broad categories – external and internal.

External agents fall into two classes – radiation and environmental chemicals.

X-rays were the first type of radiation discovered and their ability to produce mutations was clearly recognized in the 1930s. Since then other types of radiation have been added to the radiation catalog. Examples include cosmic rays, that is, radiation that comes from outer space; radiation from the decay of radioactive elements in the soil; radiation fall-out from the atomic and hydrogen bomb explosions during the 1940s and 1950s; and radiation from consumer items such as television sets, radium-dial watches. Radiation from all of these different types of radiation and including X-rays from diagnostic exams is referred to as the background radiation.

The environmental chemicals that are known to produce mutations number in the thousands and include compounds such as pesticides, most industrial chemicals, many household chemicals, and even many cosmetics. Our exposure to these varies considerably from one person to another, depending on our job, and use of many common chemicals.

The internal mutagens, known as free radicals, are compounds produced during the normal metabolic activity of all cells in our body. We cannot escape or shield ourselves from free radicals. Since all cells in all living organisms suffer from free radical damage, they have developed different mechanisms to inactivate free radicals or to repair free radical damage. One of these mechanisms, for example, is to use antioxidant compounds, such as vitamin C, vitamin E, and beta-carotene to inactivate free radicals. These repair mechanisms are highly efficient, but unfortunately not 100%

effective, and the consequence is that unrepaired free radical lesions will result in mutations.

We have met the enemy and he is us

We have a reasonable idea now of the relative contribution of the three classes of mutagens to the number of mutations that are produced in the average person. Given the known mutagenic potential of the background radiation and the fact that we are continually bathed in it, many geneticists initially thought that radiation was the major contributor to the spontaneous mutation rate. However, it wasn't until about 15 years ago that it became clear that the background radiation dose that we receive is too low to contribute significantly to the total number of mutations that are generated spontaneously.

Similarly, environmental chemical exposures for most of us are also too low to be significant. There may be instances in which the exposures may be much higher, for example, job-related exposures for those who work with toxic chemicals, or farm workers exposed to high levels of pesticides. Moreover, since environmental chemicals of the type and variety that we are exposed to now have been present in our environment for a relatively short time, they have played a minor role in contributing to the historical mutation rate.

Free radical damage, it turns out, is the major contributor to the mutation rate. Think of what this means - most mutations are a consequence of normal cellular processes, processes that are necessary for normal tissue and organ function, in effect, processes that are absolutely necessary for us to be alive. This is a bitter pill to swallow, for it means that our own cells bear the seeds of our own demise. Are we not like Brutus in Shakespeare's *Julius Caesar*, when he tells his co-conspirator, Cassius **"The fault, my dear Cassius, is not in our stars, but in ourselves"**, or like Pogo, comic strip character from the 1950s: *"We have met the enemy and he is us"*?

The mutation load

The current estimates of the spontaneous mutation rate suggest that each one of us is born with 2 to 4 new harmful mutations. These are mutations that we inherit from our mother and/or our father, that is, they came in with the egg and/or sperm that joined to form us. They become part of our genetic makeup. Our parents also inherited mutations newly arisen in their parents, and of course, we inherit some of those as well.

Each one of us passes on to our children mutations that are generated in the eggs or sperm that we produce, and in addition, some that we inherit from our long line of ancestors. Hence, every generation keeps adding to the number of mutations – all living things accumulate mutations. Together these mutations constitute our mutation load, and it appears that this is a very heavy load. So heavy, in fact, that some geneticists have argued that such a heavy load of mutations should have driven us to extinction long ago. The paradox is that we have managed to survive as a species despite the very high mutation rate. Human geneticists suggest that sexual reproduction is responsible for eliminating many harmful mutations or mitigating their effects.

Life as a Genetic Lottery

We rightly marvel at the intricacy and complexity of the living world, the incredible diversity of species, and what we think of as the perfection of the human body. We also marvel at the beauty of the non-living natural world – the mountains, oceans, rivers, forests, etc. As children we learned that Mother Nature was the source of all this beauty. We often wax poetic about Mother Nature, the embodiment of age-old wisdom, the Earth Mother who is the source of nourishment, succor, and livelihood. But Mother Nature also has another side – cruel, ruthless, and arbitrary – witness the hurricanes, typhoons, earthquakes, and other natural catastrophes that continually befall us. She is indiscriminate and spares no one or anything.

We as living organisms don't appear to have any special status as far as Mother Nature's concerned. All living organisms face an acute dilemma - the very processes that are necessary for life are also responsible for generating mutations, most of which have a harmful effect. The saving grace is that a rare few mutations may have a beneficial effect. It is these rare gems that drive the engine of evolutionary change and diversification of life. Without a mechanism for generating mutations, life would not exist or evolve. The continuation of life depends on the infrequent occurrence of beneficial mutations. Hence, living organisms accept the consequences of harmful mutations – essentially the sacrifice and elimination of those who inherit the harmful mutations – because of the few mutations that will permit life to continue. Every time an egg and sperm meet involves the rolling of the dice. Some win, and others lose. We are the unwitting participants in a gigantic genetic lottery.

Citations and Readings

1. Richard Dawkins (1976) *The Selfish Gene* Oxford University: Oxford
2. Svante Pääbo (2008) Cited in Jane Gitschler Imagine: an interview with Svante Pääbo PLoS Genetics 4(3), 1-4
3. Huntington Willard, cited by Maureen Dowd, NY Times, March 20, 2005
4. Erika Check (2005) The X factor *Nature* **434**, 266-267
5. Huntington F. Willard (2003) Tales of the *Y* chromosome Nature **423**, 810-813
6. P. Navarro-Costa, Sex, rebellion and decadence: The scandalous evolutionary history of the human Y chromosome, *Biochim. Biophys.* Acta (2012) doi:10.1016/j.bbadis.2012.04.010
7. Darren K. Griffin (2012) Is the Y chromosome disappearing? – both sides of the argument *Chromosome Research* 20, 35-35

David Bainbridge (2003) *The X in Sex: How the Chromosome controls our Lives.* Harvard University Press: Cambridge

L. Carrel and Huntington R. Willard (2005) *X* inactivation profile reveals extensive variability in X-linked gene expression in females. *Nature* 434, 400-4

J.A.M. Graves (2006) Sex chromosome specialization and degeneration in mammals. Cell 124, 901-914

Skuse, D.H. (2005) *X*-linked genes and mental functioning. *Human Molecular Genetics* 14 (Spec No 1), R27–R32

Ge´cz, J., Shoubridge, C., and Corbett, M. (2009) The genetic landscape of intellectual disability arising from chromosome X. Trends Genet. 25, 308–316

Herbert A. Lubs, Roger E. Stevenson, and Charles E. Schwartz (2012) Fragile X and X-linked intellectual disability: four decades of discovery *The American Journal of Human Genetics* 90, 579-590

Chris Gunter (2005) She moves in mysterious ways *Nature* **434**, 279-280

Steve Jones (2003) Y: *The Descent of Man*. Houghton Mifflin: New York

J.F. Crow (1997) The high spontaneous mutation rate: Is it a health risk? *Proceedings of the National Academy of Sciences (USA)* 94(16), 8380-8386

A. Eyre-Walker and P. D. Keightley (1999) High genomic deleterious mutation rates in hominids *Nature* **397**, 344-347

APPENDIX 2

Hormonal integration of the reproductive system

What are hormones?

All tissues of the body communicate with each other through hormones. A good way to think about hormones is as chemical messengers that coordinate and integrate tissue and organ function. Dozens of hormones are known today and they come in several different chemical forms, ranging from very small to very large molecules. Some hormones are probably household names, especially in families whose members suffer from diseases associated with hormone defects. Consider *insulin*, for example, made in the pancreas and necessary for the metabolism of sugars in our diet. Insulin is secreted into the circulatory system and distributed to all the tissues of the body. Inability to metabolize sugars properly leads to the disease known as diabetes, a serious disorder that afflicts millions of people around the world. Type I diabetes, sometimes also called juvenile diabetes, results from the destruction of cells of the pancreas that make insulin. In Type II *diabetes*, typically seen in older individuals and associated also with being overweight, the tissues of the body become resistant to insulin. Hence, diabetes can arise from either the inability to make insulin or inability to respond to insulin. The response to insulin depends on the presence of the insulin "receptor", a protein on the surface of cells to which insulin binds and triggers the appropriate cellular response. Cells that make the insulin receptor will respond to insulin. In the same way, the response to any given hormone by a tissue depends on whether the cells of that tissue synthesize the receptor. The binding of a given hormone to its receptor sets off a series of reactions that define the function of that hormone. Hormone disorders can be due to failure to make the hormone or failure to respond to the hormone.

Sex steroid hormones – the workhorses

Sex and reproduction depends on many different hormones. One critically important class is the *sex steroid hormone family*. This family of hormones has three members – the *progestins*, the *androgens*, and the *estrogens*. Each family itself consists of different members. For our purposes here we will consider only the most important member of each family. The most important progestin is *progesterone*. Progesterone has generally been thought of as the hormone of pregnancy because pregnant women have very high levels of progesterone. Its two most important functions are to prepare the uterus for implantation, and then to maintain the stability of the uterus so that the embryo once implanted will develop and mature. In a non-pregnant woman the ovaries are the primary source of progesterone, and during pregnancy the placenta takes over progesterone production.

The estrogen family has three members, *estradiol*, *estriol*, and *estrone*. Estradiol is the main estrogen, and has many critical functions. We will generally refer to estradiol simply as estrogen unless we need to make a distinction between it and its sibs. Estrogen is absolutely necessary for ovulation and menstruation, for breast development, for sculpting the female body shape, distribution of fat, for maintaining bone density and skeletal maturation in both females and males. During the latter stages of pregnancy estrogens produced by the placenta are necessary for the ability of the uterus to initiate contractions that begin labor.

The androgen family has two important members, *testosterone* and *dihydrotestosterone* (DHT for short). Testosterone is necessary to produce sperm, stimulates muscle growth and strength, is responsible for sculpting the male body and facial hair in the male, and is necessary for maintaining the male sexual drive (libido). DHT is responsible for the development and maintenance of the external genitalia, pubic hair, and plays a role in the development of acne. We hear a lot about the sex steroid hormones. They often make the news in our popular media, quite often associated with disease or certain types of disorders – estrogens with breast, ovarian, and uterine cancer, and androgens with prostate cancer, with birth control pills or in hormone therapy for postmenopausal women or aging males.

The regulators of gonadal function

Important as the ovary and the testis are they do not function autonomously. Their activity is regulated by hormones from the pituitary and hypothalamus, two small tissues that lie at the base of the brain. Despite their small size, these two tissues are immensely important for many critically important functions of the body. For example, they control appetite, thirst, growth, stress, and our reproductive system.

The pituitary

The pituitary was often called the master gland because it secreted many hormones that are essential for life, for example, thryroid stimulating hormone (TSH) that regulates thyroid function, *growth hormone* (GH) that regulates growth and development, *prolactin* that stimulates milk production by the mammary gland, and *adrenalcorticotrophic hormone* (ACTH) that regulates carbohydrate metabolism and sodium/potassium balance in our blood. The pituitary also secretes the two hormones *follicle stimulating hormone* (FSH) and *luteinizing hormone* (LH) that are essential for reproductive function. In the female, FSH and LH act in concert to stimulate the ovary to produce the egg, and to produce the two hormones, *estrogen* and *progesterone*. In the male, FSH and LH stimulate the testis to produce sperm and to produce the hormone *testosterone.*

The GnRH pacemaker

The pituitary, it turns out, is not really the master gland, because its function is also not autonomous but determined by hormones that are secreted by the hypothalamus. In fact, a hypothalamic hormone regulates the secretion of every pituitary hormone. In the case of reproduction in both females and males the hypothalamic hormone, *gonadotropin-releasing hormone* (GnRH), drives the synthesis of LH and FSH by the pituitary. Its discovery and the realization that GnRH is secreted in pulses, typically about one pulse every 80 to 90 minutes, ranks as one of the most important discoveries in reproductive biology in the last 40 years. A good way to think about the pulsatile release of GnRH is that it functions as a pacemaker. In analogy with the heart pacemakers that control the beating of the heart, the GnRH pacemaker controls the production of the pituitary hormones, LH and FSH. These two hormones in turn keep the ovaries or the testes functioning properly. The GnRH pacemaker begins working even before we were born, probably as early as 9 weeks after fertilization. It then enters a period of quiescence from the middle to the end of gestation. Pacemaker activity is triggered again within a few days after birth, and this lasts for about six months, after which it again enters a quiescent stage that lasts through infancy and childhood. The reawakening the GnRH pacemaker marks the end of childhood and the beginning of puberty. As far as we know, it continues working until we die.

Reading

R. Piñon Jr (2002) Biology of Human ReproductionUniversity Science Books: Sausalito, CA.

Appendix 3

Appendix 3 Disorders of Sexual Development (DSD)

What are DSD?
Origins of DSD
Sex chromosome anomalies
Gonadal disorders
Defects in sex hormone action
Medical and ethical dilemmas

What are DSD?

Neither the formation of the egg or sperm, nor the ovary or testis, nor the formation of the genitalia is fail-safe. Errors in any of these processes give rise to conditions in which the sex chromosome constitution of the embryo, or the gonadal, or anatomic sex is atypical. These conditions are referred to as *disorders of sexual development* (DSD). Although most DSDs are congenital (meaning present at birth), a few may not be detected until later in childhood or at the time of puberty. The DSD incidence is low, occurring in about 2 - 5 out of every 10,000 live births.

The term DSD was proposed in 2006 following an international meeting organized by the European Society for Pediatric Endocrinology and the Lawson Wilkins Pediatric Endocrine Society (USA). The charge for the more than 50 geneticists, pediatricians, surgeons, endocrinologists, and psychologists was to reexamine the diagnosis, terminology, and management of these types of disorders in the light of advances in our understanding of their causes. It was also important to provide a terminology that reflects the underlying cause when available, that is understandable by patients and their families, and avoids terms that may be perceived as psychologically harmful by the patient or family. Disorders of Sexual Development replaces terms that have been previously used in the clinical literature, such as *intersex, sex reversal, true hermaphrodites, and pseudohermaphrodites*. The difficulty with these terms was that they were imprecise and had the unfortunate feature of attaching a rather ugly label to someone, rather than describing the disorder. The newly adopted terminology marks a significant improvement over the older one.

The approach to the management of disorders of sex development (DSD) has undergone major changes in recent years. The catalyst has been a revised nomenclature, new classification of the causes of DSD and a willingness for health professionals to work in a multi-disciplinary format. In a remarkably short length of time, these revolutionary changes are becoming accepted practice across a range of medical and scientific disciplines. (1, I. A. Hughes The quiet revolution)

Origins of DSD

DSDs, or disorders of sexual development, arise in many different ways. It helps in getting an overview of these causes by grouping them into three categories – first, sex chromosome anomalies, second, errors that affect the formation and development of either the ovary or testis, (we call these Gonadal disorders), and third, errors that perturb the development of the genitalia (we call these Genitalia disorders). Scientifically, it is from these cases that we have learned about the tremendous complexity of our sexual development. It's only by understanding why something doesn't work that we can begin to understand how it really works. We owe much to all the DSD individuals who have willingly agreed to be examined and analyzed in ways that would make most of us uncomfortable.

Let's take a brief look at this very complex situation. The terminology may appear intimidating, but remember that it is necessary to make appropriate distinctions between very complex disorder conditions.

Sex chromosome anomalies

Recall that under normal conditions an egg has one X chromosome and one copy of each of the other 22 autosomes. A sperm, on the other hand, carries an X or a Y chromosome, plus of course one copy of each of the other chromosomes. Infrequently, however, an egg will be produced that carries two X chromosomes, or no X chromosome at all (the other chromosomes will be present in their usual number). We will denote these as XX or 0 eggs. These cases arise from errors in partitioning the chromosomes in the meiotic divisions that produce the gametes. In the male, these errors give rise to four types of sperm – those that carry both an X and a Y (XY sperm), two Xs (XX sperm), two Ys (YY sperm) or no sex chromosome at all (0 sperm). Let's consider what happens when these unusual gametes fuse with normal gametes. We will ignore the fusion of two unusual gametes fuse because these will occur at extremely low numbers.

A normal *X* or *Y* sperm fusing with an *XX* egg will rise to a *XXX* embryo or and *XXY* embryo, while fusing with a *0* egg generates an *X0* or *Y0* embryo. An unusual sperm fusing with a normal *X* egg will generate four types of embryos *XXY, XXX, XYY*, and *X0*. Embryos that are missing an *X* are completely unviable. These four cases – *XXX, XXY, XYY* and *X0* – are the most commonly observed sex chromosome anomalies in humans.

XXY individuals have normal male genitalia, although the testes are generally smaller than in *XY* males. The extra *X* chromosome for unknown reasons interferes with sperm production, and hence, *XXY* males are infertile. *XXY* males are also characterized by a number of other somatic differences. These were collectively defined as Klinefelter's syndrome many years before the chromosomal nature of the condition was understood. The *XXY* condition occurs in about 1 in 1000 male births.

The *X0* condition, characterized by a number of distinct somatic features was also defined clinically as Turner's syndrome before its chromosomal basis was recognized. *X0* individuals are female in appearance, but their ovaries are completely lacking in follicles, and hence, they are irreversibly sterile. It occurs in about 1 in 2500 female births.

The *XXX* and *XYY* conditions do not have any distinctive features that clearly distinguish them from *XX* females or *XY* males. Fertility does not appear to be affected significantly in either case. *XXX* individuals are female in anatomy, and they occur in about 1 in a 1000 female births. *XYY* individuals are males in anatomy, and occur in about 1 in 800 births. For a few years in the 1970s there were suggestions that *XYY* males were more prone to violent, anti-social, criminal behavior. However, these notions have not been substantiated. Height in excess of six feet may be the only unique *XYY* feature. But note: most males over six feet tall are not *XYY*.

Gonadal disorders

There are three types: *XX testicular DSD*, *XY gonadal dysgenesis*, and *ovotesticular DSD*.

All three are characterized by a mismatch between the chromosomal sex *(XX or XY)* and gonadal sex (ovary or testis). For example, in *XY* gonadal dysgenesis testes fail to develop in *XY* embryos. Failure to form a testis in an *XY* embryo has tremendous consequences because in the absence of testicular hormones, the "default" pathway, that is, the female pathway for the internal and external genitalia will take over. Hence, the general visible characteristic of *XY* gonadal dysgenesis will be female-like external genitalia, although in many cases, the external genitalia may not be completely normal.

On the other hand, in **XX** testicular DSD ovaries fail to form in **XX** embryos, and testes will develop instead. In many cases, the testes are not fully formed. If enough testicular function is present, male-like genitalia will develop. In both of these types of DSD (the older term was sex reversal) the external genitalia are often said to be 'ambiguous' because they do not correspond to either normal female or male genitalia.

Much rarer is ovotesticular DSD, characterized by the presence of both ovarian and testicular tissue in the same individual whether the individual is *XX* or *XY*. The older term for this condition was true hermaphroditism, and was fashioned from a combination of Hermes (god of war) and Aphrodite (goddess of love), a being from Greek mythology that was both male and female. It seems likely that the image of such a being was probably based on real individuals having the features of both females and males.

The distribution of ovarian and testicular tissue varies from one individual to another – from an ovary on one side and a testis on the other side, or an ovotestis (a composite gonad consisting of both ovarian and testicular tissue) on one side and an ovary or testis on the other side, or a pair of ovotestes. The internal and external genitalia vary from individual to individual and their appearance depends on the strength of the testicular function, i.e., more male-like as testicular hormone secretions increase.

How do these unusual cases arise? *XY* gonadal dysgenesis is known to arise in different ways – from the loss of the *SRY* gene from the *Y* chromosome, or from mutations in the *SRY* gene or other genes required to form a testis. The catalog of testis-determining genes (TDGs) now contains about six or seven genes, and mutations in any one of them prevent a testis from forming. Unfortunately, we don't really understand what any of them, including *SRY* itself, actually do.

We know much less about the origin of *XX* testicular DSD. A few cases are known to arise from the accidental transfer of the *SRY* gene from the *Y* chromosome to the *X* chromosome during sperm production. In these rare instances, some sperm are produced with an *X* chromosome carrying the *SRY* gene. If such a sperm fertilizes an egg, presence of the *SRY* gene on one of the *X* chromosomes triggers testicular differentiation. However, the origin of most cases of remains unknown. Perplexingly, the study of this condition has not yielded any ovary-determining genes, in sharp contrast to the way in which the study of *XY* gonadal dysgenesis has identified several testis-determining genes. This failure is extremely intriguing. We don't yet know whether the failure to find ovary-determining genes is telling us something fundamentally important about the development of the ovary, compared to that of the testis.

The origin of ovotesticular DSD is even more mysterious. It seems likely that this condition arises from mutations in genes that regulate the decision whether to form an ovary or a testis. Possibly some mutations may result in a delay in *SRY* action, thereby permitting both ovary and testis to develop at the same time. It's clear that we are still a long way from understanding the origin of these complex disorders. But it is also true that we are slowly getting a glimpse of the intricate mechanisms by which the testis and ovary are formed.

Genitalia disorders

These types of disorders are more common than the ones described in the section above. They are grouped into two types – **XY** DSD and **XX** DSD. In *XY* DSD, testes are present, but normal male genitalia do not form. There are two explanations for this: first, mutations in genes that are necessary to synthesize testosterone, or in the gene that converts testosterone to DHT; second, a mutation in the gene that encodes the androgen receptor through which testosterone and DHY exert their action is defective. In both of these cases, the defect in androgen action (either because androgens are absent or because their action is prevented) leads to abnormal male genitalia, which can range from being completely female to ambiguous.

One of the more interesting examples of these conditions is *androgen insensitivity syndrome* (AIS). AIS individuals are XY and have internal, but undescended testes. At birth, they look completely female, and hence AIS is not usually diagnosed at birth because the infant appears to be a normal female. However, failure to menstruate in the adolescent will bring the individual to the attention of an endocrinologist, and eventual recognition of the AIS condition. At puberty AIS individuals develop breasts, a female body form, and are indistinguishable from a normal female. Internally, they lack a uterus and fallopian tubes, but they do have a vagina.

The AIS condition is due to a mutation in the androgen receptor gene. Hence, although AIS individuals have functional testes and produce normal levels of testosterone, the body tissues that would normally respond to testosterone fail to do so. The consequence is that the external genitalia are female. Estrogen levels are similar to those found in normal females, and hence, the body shape is also female.

In *XX* DSD ovaries are present, but the external genitalia are masculinized due to excess production of testosterone, which as we saw above drives the development of the external genitalia in the male form. The excess testosterone is due to a mutation that results an overly active adrenal gland that produces excess testosterone. Clinically this condition is known as congenital adrenal hyperplasia (CAH).

These sex hormone disorders provide vivid examples of the critical importance of the sex steroid hormones, estrogens and androgens, in shaping the female and male body form, respectively. Both hormones can shape the body differently irrespective of the genetic sex.

Medical and Ethical Dilemmas

Why perform irreversible surgeries that risk sensation, fertility, continence, comfort, and life without a medical reason? (2, Elizabeth Reis Divergence or Disorder, the politics of naming intersex)

Many important questions are raised when a baby with a disorder of sexual development is born, or as in the case of androgen insensitivity syndrome, when the diagnosis is made later in childhood or in adolescence. In the first case, what should be the determining factor in deciding the final or definitive sex of the infant - genetic sex, gonadal sex, or the sex of the external genitalia? The genetic sex cannot be altered. Gonadal sex cannot be altered either, but the gonads can be removed surgically.

The external genitalia are, relatively speaking, the easiest to modify, and hence, the general medical response has been to try to normalize the external genitalia to either the male or female form according to the degree to which type of genitalia predominates. Surgical reconstruction is possible, but is definitively easier to perform a female reconstruction than a male one. In other cases it may be possible to maintain a male form with testosterone supplementation. Each case will be different, and a final decision is made only after a complete anatomical, physiological and hormonal evaluation has been made.

Significantly, one factor has until quite recently been ignored – the infant's gender identity. The normal assumption has been that gender identity and anatomical sex go hand in hand. Pressure to choose a gender is strong, not only because birth certificates require it, but also because parents understandably are uncomfortable with an infant whose genitalia are ambiguous. Hence, reconstructive surgery has been recommended as soon as possible after the birth, and the child will be raised congruent with the anatomical sex.

Gender identity, however, does not always correspond with anatomical sex. A particularly poignant demonstration of this fact comes from a recent review of 94 cases of children born with ambiguous genitalia and who had undergone sexual reconstructive surgery. More than half of the genetic males who had been converted to anatomical females and raised as females reverted to males as soon as they were able to do so. These cases and recent research on differences in gene expression in very young mouse female and male embryos (before the formation of the gonads or the production of the sex steroid hormones) tells us convincingly that gender identity is independent of sex steroid hormones. We don't really know in humans when gender identity is established. Studies suggest that it takes place after birth, perhaps completed by age 4 – 5. One important consequence of this new understanding is the recommendation that sex reassignment surgery be delayed until the child's gender identity is clearly certain.

The case of androgen insensitivity syndrome (AIS) presents another type of dilemma. The AIS condition typically will be recognized in an adolescent, a person who has been brought up as a female. She will come to the attention of a clinician because she will fail to start menstruating at the time of puberty. Should she be told that she is genetically male? How will she interpret this information? What will this mean for her? What psychological consequences can such a revelation have for an adolescent? You might ask yourself the same questions. How much of the truth would I want to know? How much of the truth could I handle? These are fundamental questions for which unfortunately there are no universally applicable answers. How they are answered could have an enormous impact on the well being of the affected individual and family.

Despite the growing acceptance of the term DSD among clinicians and parents of DSD children, the word *disorder* in DSD has met objections from the Intersex Society of North America (ISNA), the most important activist organization of DSD adults. Disorder implies a serious abnormality, something to be corrected. The ISNA argues that the disability rights movement has shown us that something that is atypical is not necessarily abnormal. While there may be DSD cases in which surgical intervention is necessary to save a life or to ensure proper voiding, not all atypical cases of sexual anatomy necessarily require hormonal therapy or surgical correction. The genital surgery that attempts to normalize sexual anatomy is often ineffective, and does not 'cure' the presumptive disorder. In fact, as suggested from a number of studies, the correction may do more harm than good. It is for reasons such as these that the word disorder in DSD be replaced by the word *divergence*, one more step in an effort to destigmatize these types of conditions. We will have to wait to see if the new term will be accepted.

GLOSSARY

abortifacient – agent that induces an abortion

acrosome – vesicle wrapped around the front end of a sperm cell containing factors that help the sperm penetrate the secondary oocyte.

acrosome reaction – fusion of the sperm head membrane with the outer acrosome membrane; necessary for fertilization.

adipose tissue – fat-storing tissue.

adrenarche – production of steroid sex hormones by adrenal glands at the onset of puberty.

agonist – a compound that binds to a hormone receptor and elicits a response similar to that of the naturally occurring hormone.

alendronate – a bisphosphonate; see bisphosphonates.

alveoli – milk-producing tissue in the mammary gland.

amenorrhea – lack of menstruation.

amnion – membrane that forms around developing embryo.

anabolic steroid – synthetic testosterone agonist often used to build muscle mass.

androgens – family of steroid sex hormones; testosterone and DHT, the most important members stimulate the male reproductive system development and maintenance, as well as secondary sex characteristics.

androgen insensitivity syndrome (AIS) – disorder caused by mutations in the gene encoding the androgen receptor protein; the consequence is the development of female external genitalia, breasts, and female body type in XY individual.

androgen replacement therapy – administration of testosterone or testosterone agonists to restore androgen-dependent tissues and erectile function in males who have suffered testicular damage or to restore muscle mass and tone and erectile function in older men.

anestrus – absence of an estrus period.

aneuploidy – condition in which the chromosome number is different than the normal.

anovulatory – lack of ovulation.

antioxidants – compounds that neutralize free radicals.

asexual reproduction – reproduction characterized by the division of the parent into two identical organisms.

aspermatogenic – unable to produce sperm.

assisted reproductive techniques (ARTs) – procedures developed to assist infertile couples to have children.

atresia – loss of oocytes and follicles beginning during gestation and continuing through menopause.

axillary – the underarm

autosome – a chromosome that does not determine sex; humans have 22 pairs of autosomes.

azoospermic – unable to produce spermatozoa.

bisphosphonates – nonsteroidal compounds used in the treatment of osteoporosis.

bone mineral density (BMD) – a measure of the mineral (mainly calcium) content of bone; bone with a low BMD fractures easily.

castration – see gonadectomy or orchidectomy.

chromosomal sex – determined by the sex chromosome contributions of each parent, with XX being female, and XY being male.

chromosomes – coiled, DNA-protein structures into which the genome is partitioned.

climacteric – the perimenopause.

clitoris – part of the external genitalia in the female derived from the genital tubercle.

coitus interruptus – in sexual intercourse, withdrawal before ejaculation.

combined oral contraceptives (COCs) – combinations of estrogens and progestins taken orally that suppress ovulation.

complete (central) precocious puberty – puberty due to the premature reactivation of the GnRH pulse generator.

conceptus – a very early stage embryo.

congenital – present at birth.

contraceptive – any agent that prevents fertilization.

corpus albicans – nonfunctional relic of the corpus luteum after corpus luteum involution.

corpus luteum – residual cells of the follicle after expulsion of the secondary oocyte; it secretes progesterone and estrogen.

cortical granule reaction – fusion of cortical granules with oocyte member immediately after fertilization to prevent polyspermy.

cryptorchidism – the failure of testis to descend from the abdomen to the scrotum.

depoprovera – synthetic progesterone analog often used in COCs.

dihydrotestosterone (DHT) – androgen derived from testosterone; required in the male for development of external genitalia.

dilation and evacuation – surgical abortion procedure relying on removal of the fetus by mechanical means.

dispermy – fertilization by two sperm simultaneously.

DNA – helical, double-stranded, nucleic acid molecule that contains the genetic material of the cell.

dominant follicle – the late tertiary stage follicle that is ovulated.

dopamine – amine hormone that regulates prolactin and GnRH release.

ectopic pregnancy – pregnancy resulting from implantation outside the uterine cavity.

embryo – an animal in the earliest stages of development in the uterus; in humans, from week 3 to week 8 of gestation.

embryo transfer – sequence in an assisted reproductive technique, transfer of the embryo generated in vitro into a receptive uterus for implantation.

endogenous – a product made within the body.

endometriosis – disorder characterized by the growth and development of endometrial tissue in regions outside the uterus.

endometrium – the outermost layer of the uterus whose periodic proliferation and destruction defines the menstrual cycle.

epididymis – a single, highly convoluted tubule that carries sperm from the rete testis to the vas deferens in the male reproductive system.

erectile dysfunction – inability to sustain an erection.

ERT (estrogen replacement therapy) – administration of estrogen or estrogen analogs to postmenopausal women to reduce the risk of coronary heart disease and osteoporosis.

estrogen insensitivity syndrome (EIS) – disorder due to a mutation in the gene encoding the estrogen receptor protein; only one case has been reported in humans, a male characterized by skeletal abnormalities and osteoporosis.

estrogens – a family of steroid sex hormones involved with control of the female reproductive cycle, breast development, and bone mineralization.

estrogen surge – peak in estrogen during the follicular phase that initiates the LH surge.

etiology – origin or cause of a disorder or disease.

exogenous – a product made outside the body.

external genitalia – the external structures of the reproductive systems; in the male, it includes the penis and scrotum, and in the female, it includes the clitoris and labia.

fallopian tube – see uterine tube.

fetal alcohol syndrome – developmental disorder due to exposure of the embryo and fetus to alcohol.

flagellum – whiplike organelle that provides the motive force for sperm movement.

follicle – functional unit of the ovary consisting of the primary oocyte and layers of granulosa and theca cells.

follicle-stimulating hormone (FSH) – hormone released from the anterior pituitary that stimulates the granulosa cells in females and the Sertoli cells in males.

follicular phase – phase of ovulatory cycle beginning with the onset of menses and during which the egg is prepared for ovulation.

free radicals – highly reactive metabolic compounds that generate the primary DNA lesions that may develop into mutations.

gametes – the haploid sperm or egg cells of sexually reproducing organisms.

gender identity disorder (GID) – disorder in which individuals of one anatomical sex feel that they are really of the opposite sex; also known as transsexualism.

gene – sequence of nucleotides that encode a polypeptide.

gene locus – the fixed and unique position of a gene along the length of a chromosome.

gene mutation – small-scale changes in DNA nucleotide sequence, such as nucleotide substitutions.

genital ridge – progenitor tissue that can develop into testes or ovaries during embryogenesis.

genotype – the genetic makeup of an organism.

germ cells or germ line – special subset of cells derived from the PGCs that have the ability to undergo meiosis.

GIFT – gamete intrafallopian transfer; an ART in which the oocyte obtained by ovarian stimulation and sperm are placed into the uterine tube to permit fertilization to take place in the uterine tube rather than in a culture dish.

GIFT – gamete intrafallopian transfer; an ART in which the oocyte obtained by ovarian stimulation and sperm are placed into the uterine tube to permit fertilization to take place in the uterine tube rather than in a culture dish.

gonad – gamete-producing organ; ovary in females and testis in males.

gonadal dysgenesis – failure of the gonads to develop.

gonadarche – development of the testis at the onset of puberty.

gonadectomy – surgical removal of the gonads.

gonadal sex – the presence of either of ovaries or testes.

gonadotropic hormones – hormones such as LH and FSH which are secreted by the pituitary gland and whose primary target are the gonads.

gonadotropin-releasing hormone (GnRH) – hormone produced by neurons in different regions of the hypothalamus; controls the synthesis of LH and FSH by the pituitary.

gonadotropin-releasing hormone (GnRH) pace maker – the set of neurons that coordinates and synchronizes their GnRH discharges in a periodic fashion (about one pulse per hour in humans).

Graafian follicle – the dominant follicle that has reached the final antral phase where the oocyte has moved to one pole of the follicle.

granulosa cells – the inner layer of cells surrounding the oocyte during follicular development.

gynecomastia – breast development in males causes by an increase an estrogen/androgen ratio.

haploid number (n) – the number of chromosomes in a gamete.

hormones – chemical messengers that allow the cells, tissues and organs of an individual to communicate with each other in order to coordinate and regulate activity.

HRT (hormone replacement therapy) – administration of a combination of estrogen and progestin to postmenopausal women to reduce the risk of coronary heart disease and osteoporosis.

human chorionic gonadotropin (hCG) – a hormone produced by the placenta that is essentially identical to LH and is one of the earliest markers of pregnancy.

human immunodeficiency virus (HIV) – pathogenic virus responsible for AIDS.

human menopausal gonadotropin (HMG) – mixture of LH and FSH found in the urine of postmenopausal women.

hypergonadotropic hypogonadism – disorder characterized by high levels of LH and FSH and lack of gonadal function.

hypogonadotropic hypogonadism – disorder characterized by low LH and FSH levels and failure of gonadal function.

hypogonadism – condition characterized by suppression of gonadal function.

hypospadia – failure of the urogenital sinus to develop properly in male embryos resulting in the external opening of the urethra being on the underside of the penis.

hypothalamus – a gland in the brain that secretes releasing factors, such as GnRH, that regulate pituitary secretions.

hysterotomy – surgical abortion method used in the third trimester, essentially equivalent to a cesarian section.

ICSI – intracytoplasmic sperm injection; an ARTs procedure in which sperm head is introduced mechanically into the oocyte.

idiopathic – a disorder or condition whose cause is unknown.

immunocontraception – fertility control formulations that rely on antibodies against a protein necessary for fertilization or implantation.

implantation – the process by which the newly formed embryo establishes contact with the uterus and initiates the development of the placenta.

imprinting – process in which certain genes are marked differentially in oogenesis and spermatogenesis.

incomplete precocious puberty – GnRH-independent precocious puberty.

indifferent gonad – the embryonic gonad from week 3 to week 6 of gestation when the sex of the gonad cannot be determined.

induced pathway – development of the internal and external genitalia in the male; dependent on fetal testicular hormones.

infecundity – inability to carry a pregnancy to term.

infertility – inability to conceive.

inner cell mass – progenitor tissue in blastocyst for embryo proper.

ionizing radiation – high energy, penetrating electromagnetic radiation such as X-rays.

instillation – abortion methods used in the second trimester that involve injecting toxic compounds into the amniotic sac.

intrauterine device (IUD) – plastic or copper coil placed in the uterus to function as a contraceptive device.

in utero – while still in the uterus

in vitro – in a test tube; in an artificial environment.

in vivo – within the living body

IUGR – intrauterine growth retardation; alterations in embryonic or fetal development resulting in slow or abnormal growth.

labor – process of giving birth

lactational amenorrhea – amenorrhea due to breast feeding.

lactiferous ducts – breast epithelial tissue involved in the synthesis or transport of milk.

leptin – hormone produced by adipose tissue; may signal the energy status in the individual.

Leydig cells – the androgen-producing cells in the testes.

LH surge – the rapid increase in LH that occurs 36 hours before ovulation and that is essential for the egg to be ovulated.

libido – the sexual drive or urge.

luteal phase – the second part of the ovulatory cycle in which the site of implantation for the fertilized egg is prepared.

luteal suppression – condition resulting from defects in corpus luteum function.

luteinizing hormone (LH) – hormone secreted by the pituitary gland that stimulates the Leydig cells in males and theca cells in females.

luteolysis – the involution and decay of the corpus luteum.

male factor infertility – infertility due to inability to produce sperm.

meiosis – a two-stage type of cell division in sexually reproducing organisms that results in gametes with half the chromosome number of the original cell.

menarche – the first menstruation.

menopause – the last menstrual period in a woman's life.

menses – see menstruation.

menstruation – periodic shedding of the endometrial tissue and blood from the uterus through the cervix and vagina.

mifepristone – also known as RU-486, antagonist at the progesterone receptor.

mitosis – cell division that preserves chromosome number.

monestrus – having only one estrus period per year.

monogenic – condition caused by only one gene.

monosexual – refers to organisms in which male and female gametes are produced by the same individual.

monosomy – chromosome condition defined as 2n-1.

mutagen – agent responsible for producing mutations in DNA.

mutation rate – the number of mutations produced in DNA per generation.

neonatal – pertaining to the first 4 weeks after birth.

neonatal testosterone surge – large increase in testosterone release in males right after birth.

neural tube defects – developmental defects affecting the spinal cord and brain.

nonionizing radiation – low energy electromagnetic radiation, such ultraviolet radiation.

oligospermia – low sperm count.

oocyte – cell type in the first meiotic (primary oocyte) and second meiotic (secondary oocyte) divisions of oogenesis. The secondary oocyte is ovulated and is also the cell that participates in fertilization.

oogenesis – the development of ova from primordial germ cells by meiosis.

oogonia – cells that are formed from the primordial germ cells (PGCs) and that then differentiate into primary oocytes.

orchidectomy – surgical removal of the testes.

osteoporosis – condition characterized by loss of calcium from **bone.**
ovaries – the female gonads which lie in the abdominal cavity and produce ova and reproductive hormones.

oviduct – see uterine tube.

ovulation – the expulsion of the secondary oocyte from the ovary midway through the ovulatory cycle; oocyte fimbrae of the uterine tube.

oxytocin – hormone produced by the posterior pituitary which stimulates uterine contractions during labor and milk letdown by the mammary glands.

parthenogenesis – development of the egg without a sperm contribution.

parturition – events that lead to birth.

pathogen – a disease-producing organism.

PCOS – see polycystic ovarian syndrome.

pelvic inflammatory disease (PID) – infections of the uterus and uterine tubes that often lead to severe complications such as infertility and ectopic implantations.

perimenopause – the period, a few years in length, prior to and just after the last menstrual period in a woman's life.

perinatal – pertaining to or occurring in the period shortly before and after birth.

pituitary – gland found at the base of the hypothalamus in the brain; it secretes hormones such as LH and FSH that stimulate the gonads.

phenotype – the physical and physiological traits of an organism.

phenotypic sex – the presence of either female or male internal and external genitalia.

physical stress – stress induced by intense exercise or physical activity.

placenta – a structure formed from extraembryonic tissues during pregnancy for nourishing the fetus.

PMDD – premenstrual dysphoric disorder; most severe form of premenstrual syndrome.

PMS – disorder of differing degrees of severity in which physiological and behavioral symptoms are manifested repeatedly a few days before the onset of menstruation.

polar body – nonfunctional product of meiosis in oogenesis.

polycystic ovarian syndrome (PCOS) –anovulatory disorder characterized by the accumulation of Graafian stage follicles in the ovary.

polygenic – trait determined by more than one gene.

polyspermy – fertilization by more than one sperm.

postcoital pill – a form of emergency contraception taken after coitus to prevent implantation.

preeclampsia – premature expulsion of the placenta.

preimplantation embryo – in humans, the embryo during the first 5 – 7 days after fertilization, during which it travels from the fertilization site to the uterus.

prevalence – the number of persons with a disease at a specified point in time.

primary oocyte – germ cell in oogenesis which undergoes the first meiotic division.

primary spermatocyte – germ cell in spermatogenesis which undergoes the first meiotic division.

primordial follicle – the smallest and simplest follicle consisting of the oocyte and a single layer of granulosa cells.

primordial germ cells (PGCs) – the precursors of the germ line that eventually develop into ova or spermatozoa.

progestins – steroid hormones that bind to the progesterone receptor.

prolactin (PRL) – a hormone produced by the anterior pituitary that stimulates the growth and development of the mammary glands and maintains lactation; also called somatomammotropin.

proliferative phase – the first phase of the menstrual cycle, which corresponds to the follicular phase of the ovulatory cycle.

psychogenic amenorrhea – amenorrhea due to emotional trauma.

psychogenic stress – stress due to emotional trauma or anxiety.

puberty – the onset of endocrinological changes that allow for reproductive capability.

receptor – protein that mediates all hormone action.

recruitment stage – the second stage in the formation of the dominant follicle.

reductional division – first division of meiosis that reduces the chromosome number to half.

regeneration – the first stage in spermiogenesis in which spermatogonial stem cells are continually replenished.

risk factor – any characteristic (environmental, behavioral, heritable) whose presence is associated with an increased probability of infection or disease development.

secondary oocyte – product of the first meiotic division in oogensis; released at ovulation.

secondary spermatocyte – product of the first meiotic division in spermatogenesis.

secondary sex characteristics – characteristics that develop during the endocrinological changes that occur during puberty, including the appearance of pubic and facial hair and enlargement of the external genitalia in males, and pubic hair, breasts, and changes in body form in females.

secretory phase – the second phase of the menstrual cycle, which corresponds to the luteal phase of the ovulatory cycle.

seminal fluid – produced by the prostate, seminal vesicles, and the bulbourethral gland in order to nourish the sperm.

seminal vesicles – component of the male internal genitalia; contribute secretions to the seminal fluid.

seminiferous tubules – the inner compartment of the testis that contain Sertoli and germ cells.

serotonin – amine hormone with many functions.

Sertoli cells – cells in the testes that regulate and direct all stages of spermatogenesis.

sex chromosomes – the chromosome pair that determine the sex of an individual; a female carries two X chromosomes and a male carries one X and one Y chromosome.

sex determination – conversion of the indifferent gonad into a definitive testis or ovary.

sex reversal – occurs when the chromosomal sex and gonadal sex are discordant.

sex-linked genes – genes located on a sex chromosome.

sexual differentiation – development of the internal and external genitalia.

sexual reproduction – reproduction in which the gametes from two parents fuse to form progeny with unique gene combinations.

somatic cell – any cell in a multicellular organism except the sperm or egg.

spermatogenesis – the continually renewable process of spermatozoa production. The three major stages are regeneration, meiosis, and spermiogenesis.

spermatogonia – cells that are formed from the primordial germ cells (PGCs) and that then differentiate into primary spermatocytes.

spermatozoon – male gamete.

spermicides – agents that kill sperm.

spermiogenesis – the last stage of spermatogenesis in which the acrosome and flagella are formed.

SRY gene – gene located on the Y-chromosome necessary for the conversion of the indifferent gonad into a testis.

SSRIs – selective serotonin reuptake inhibitors; compounds that have been found useful in the treatment of depression and PMDD.

steroid sex hormones – hormones synthesized from cholesterol that include the progestin, androgen, and estrogen families.

subdermal implants – progestin-only contraceptives implanted into the axillary region; provide protection for 3 to 5 years.

teratogen – agent that can produce developmental abnormalities during embryogenesis.

teratology – study of developmental disorders.

testis – the male gonad in which hormones and sperm are produced.

testosterone – the most abundant androgen in males.

tetraploid – cells containing four complete sets of chromosomes.

theca cells – the outer layer of cells surrounding the oocyte during follicular development.

thelarche – initiation of breast development in puberty.

transmission (horizontal) – the spread of an infectious agent from one individual to another, usually through contact with body fluids.

triploid – cells containing three complete sets of chromosomes.

trisomy – chromosome condition defined as 2n+1.

tubal ligation – sterilization involving the ligation or clamping of the uterine tubes.

tubal pregnancy – implantation in the uterine tube.

urogenital folds – progenitor tissue for labia or scrotum.

urogenital sinus – progenitor tissue for vagina or urethra in males.

uterine tube – part of the genital tract in the female extending from the uterus; transports sperm and zygote; also known as the oviduct or fallopian tube.

uterus – the female reproductive organ in which the embryo implants and develops.

urethra – the duct that carries the urine from the bladder to the exterior of the body.

vacuum respiration – surgical abortion procedure for removing a very early stage embryo by suction.

vagina – a thin-walled chamber extending from the uterus to the exterior of the body; it is the repository for sperm and the birth canal during labor.

vas deferens – the tube that carries sperm in the male reproductive system connecting the epididymis to the urethra; also known as the ductus deferens.

vasectomy – sterilization involving ligation and excisions of the vas deferens.

virus – submicroscopic infectious agent characterized by a lack of independent metabolism; dependent for replication and transmission on host cells.

X-linked gene – gene located on the X-chromosome.

Y-linked gene – gene located on the Y-chromosome.

ZIFT – zygote intrafallopian transfer; ART in which the zygote formed in vitro is transferred into the uterine tube before cleavage divisions begin.

zona pellucida – the glycoprotein layer between the oocyte and the inner granulosa cell layer.

zygote – the fertilized egg.

www.ingramcontent.com/pod-product-compliance
Lightning Source LLC
Chambersburg PA
CBHW062116020426
42335CB00013B/994